CW00689032

Praise for *The Promise of a Sacred Teaching of Other Power*

This book is a major contributor to the growin̲
non-Japanese audience. The author has profoundly entered the Pure Land imaginative world with his own bold sense of existential authenticity. Writing against the modern trend towards the ultra-secularization of Buddhism, he tackles themes of existential boundedness, the Pure Land mythos, and Shinran's particularity. He makes use of a large swath of the literature on Shin Buddhism in English and refers to dozens of major literary, artistic, and philosophical figures from the West, producing a discourse illuminated by many global traditions. The author has a tremendous sense of the profundity of Shinran's mythical, imaginative language, and applies a heightened level of hermeneutical strategies to his writing, offering one of the richest appreciations of Shinran to date. Along with its rich intellectualism, the book is an astonishing, highly poetic, magical, mystical, personal, emotional, and even confessional encounter with Shinran, which strikes a brilliantly fresh note. This book should become a foundational stepping stone into a new era of engagement in the English-language world with this seminal Japanese thinker. – **Galen Amstutz**, Adjunct Instructor, Institute of Buddhist Studies/Graduate Theological Union, Berkeley, USA

In this book, Nagapriya shares with us his journey into the heart of Shinran's teachings and the Pure Land traditions with which he is associated. He offers a unique and valuable introduction to the Japanese Pure Land master, Shinran, who is recognised as the founder of Jōdo Shinshū, Japan's largest Buddhist school. Drawing on western theologians and philosophers to elucidate Shinran's message for the western context, as well as exploring the historic roots of the tradition in India and China and their traditional representation in the lineage of Shinran's tradition, Nagapriya demonstrates the relationship between this tradition and Buddhism as a whole, finding links to both the Mahāyāna and Theravada. The result is a remarkable book that presents a clear overview of the core points in Shinran's teaching, well grounded in original sources and in the broader context of Pure Land Buddhism. This very readable book will particularly aid those new to Shinran's works in appreciating their spiritual depth, but it will be of interest to practitioners from all Buddhist schools, as it offers new perspectives on Buddhist fundamentals. – **Caroline Brazier** is a priest in the Jōdo Shinshū tradition and a psychotherapist. She is the author of seven books on Buddhism and therapy.

Shinran's teachings are the perfect antidote to our striving, self-power culture. Nagapriya is a reliable and personable guide as we journey into Shinran's world, examining his philosophy and applying it to our everyday lives. This book will wake you up to a new way of life, where everything is assured, and where we can relax into knowing that we are accepted just as we are. Comforting, poetically written, and full of inspiration. – **Satya Robyn**, author of *Coming Home: Refuge in Pureland Buddhism*

Not only does Nagapriya's book offer an intelligent and sympathetic exploration of the writings of Shinran and those authors from which he drew inspiration, but it also explores ways in which legend and mythic narrative complement historical narrative as vehicles of important truths. Drawing upon his academic training in philosophy and the history of religions, Nagapriya deftly weaves reflections of Western theologians and philosophers into his rich and colourful tapestry, the most dominant theme of which is accounts of ways in which he has been inspired and transformed by decades of contemplating the implications of Shinran's seemingly simple but actually nuanced commentaries, essays, and letters. A result of Nagapriya's rumination, this is a delightfully readable book that is sure to be of interest to practising Buddhists, as well as to those studying comparative religions and spirituality. – **Dh. Dayamati (Richard P. Hayes)** is a retired professor of Sanskrit and Indian Buddhist philosophy and author of *Land of No Buddha* and of numerous dry and tedious scholastic works. His non-academic website is: 'Inquiring Buddhist', dayamati.org.

Nagapriya's book accomplishes a rare feat, which is largely unprecedented in the English-language literature on Jōdo Shinshū. He explores the teachings of Shinran Shōnin through the larger context of Pure Land Buddhist thought in India, China, and Japan in a readable, accessible manner. Whereas sectarian scholarship narrowly focuses only on the figures selected and quoted by Shinran, this book explores the teachings and writings of Buddhist teachers outside of the Jōdo Shinshū historical lineage, who doubtlessly contributed to shape Japanese Pure Land Buddhism, and, by extension, Jōdo Shinshū, in crucial ways. This book also accomplishes an original reading from outside the Jōdo Shinshū tradition(s), while remaining faithful to the sectarian interpretations. By drawing on other Buddhist traditions and on Western thought, Nagapriya offers a view of Shinran that transcends sectarian boundaries, while showing a deep and thorough engagement with English-language Jōdo Shinshū materials. – **Enrique Galvan-Alvarez** is a Jōdo Shinshū priest from the Hongwanji-ha school and an Associate Professor at the Universidad Internacional de La Rioja.

This is a truly extraordinary book. It's about Shinran, the founder of the Jōdo Shinshū or True Pure Land School, but it's also a sustained and searching enquiry into the nature of the Dharma life, actually, the nature of any spiritual life. Western Buddhists, on the whole, find Shinran's very particular, even unique interpretation of the Dharma – absolute dependence on Other Power – startling, puzzling, and I have known some to question whether he was really a Buddhist. He definitely was, but in order to understand him, you need a guide, and Nagapriya is an excellent one. A practitioner of the Dharma for 30 years, he has read widely and thought deeply about Shinran's teaching, and in this book he generously shares his wisdom. He discusses the idea of 'reading as existential transformation' that can occur if we are willing to engage with a text. I *was* willing, and there were many times when I was so struck by an idea, a phrase, a truth, that I stopped reading, closed my eyes, and allowed it to reverberate through me. At those times I experienced faith, gratitude, and joy. Now I'm going to read it again. – **Ratnaguna**, author of *The Art of Reflection* and *Great Faith, Great Wisdom*

The Promise of a Sacred World

Shinran's Teaching of Other Power

Nagapriya

Foreword by Kenneth K. Tanaka

𝑤

Windhorse Publications
38 Newmarket Road
Cambridge CB5 8DT
info@windhorsepublications.com
windhorsepublications.com

Cover design by Katarzyna Manecka

Typesetting and layout by Tarajyoti
Printed by Bell & Bain Ltd, Glasgow

British Library Cataloguing in Publication Data:
A catalogue record for this book is available from the British Library.

ISBN 978-1-911407-90-4

Coleman Barks, quotation from *Feeling the Shoulder of the Lion: Poetry and Teaching Stories of Rumi*, versions by Coleman Barks. Copyright © 1991 by Coleman Barks. Reprinted by arrangement with The Permissions Company, LLC on behalf of Shambhala Publications Inc., Boulder, Colorado, shambhala.com.

Wendell Berry, quotation from 'Poetry and Marriage', in *Standing by Words*. Copyright © 2011 by Wendell Berry. Reprinted by permission of San Diego Catapult.

Quotes by Shinran in this book are reprinted from *The Collected Works of Shinran*, translated by the Jodo Shinshu Seiten English Translation and Editorial Committee, Jodo Shinshu Hongwanji-ha, Kyoto, 1997. Copyright © 1997 by the Jodo Shinshu Seiten English Translation and Editorial Committee. Reprinted by permission of the Jodo Shinshu Seiten English Translation and Editorial Committee.

Denise Levertov, 'Bearing the Light', in *Sands of the Well*. Copyright © 1996 by Denise Levertov. Reprinted by permission of New Directions Publishing Corp.

Rainer Maria Rilke, 'Buddha in Glory', translated and edited by Edward Snow, in *The Poetry of Rilke: Bilingual Edition*. Copyright translation 2009 by Edward Snow. Reprinted by permission of North Point Press, a division of Farrar, Straus and Giroux.

Miranda Shaw, 'Nature in Dōgen's Philosophy and Poetry', *The Journal of the International Association of Buddhist Studies*, Vol. 8, No. 2, 1985, pp.111-132, p.121. Copyright 1985 by Miranda Shaw. Reproduced with permission of *The Journal of the International Association of Buddhist Studies*.

Georg Trakl, 'Winter Evening', in Janae Sholtz, *The Invention of a People: Heidegger and Deleuze on Art and the Political*. Copyright 2015 by Janae Sholtz. Reproduced with permission of the Licensor through PLSclear.

All reasonable attempts have been made to contact the copyright holders of these works. The copyright holders are invited to contact us at info@windhorsepublications.com

Extracts from *The Land of Bliss: The Paradise of the Buddha of Measureless Light*, trans. Luis Gomez, University of Hawai'i Press, Honolulu, HI, 1996.

Extracts from *Hōnen's Senchakushū: Passages on the Selection of the Nembutsu in the Original Vow*, trans. English Translation Project, Kuroda Institute, University of Hawai'i Press, Honolulu, HI, 1998.

Gwendolyn MacEwen, 'Dark pines under water', in *Volume 1 (The Early Years)*, Exile Editions, Toronto 2001, p.156.

Extract from Burton Watson, *Saigyō: Poems of a Mountain Home*, Columbia University Press, New York 1991, p.81.

Dedication

For Ratnaguna and Dayamati
precious spiritual benefactors

Contents

About the Author

Nagapriya was born in the UK in 1969. While studying for a philosophy degree in Leeds, he began practising with the Triratna Buddhist Community and was ordained as a Dharmachari in 1992. He later studied for a master's in the history of religions at the University of Manchester. In 2013 he moved to Mexico and helped found the Centro Budista de Cuernavaca. He is also co-founder and director of Editorial Dharmamegha, a small publishing venture dedicated to sharing Buddhist teachings in the Spanish-speaking world. In addition, he works as part of a team training men from Latin America for ordination into the Triratna Buddhist Order. Since 2019 he has been a member of the College of Public Preceptors.

Some of Nagapriya's other books are: *Exploring Karma and Rebirth* (Windhorse Publications, 2004), *Visions of Mahayana Buddhism* (Windhorse Publications, 2009), and *Seeing Like a Buddha: The Four Noble Truths* (Triratna Inhouse Publications, 2020).

Author's Acknowledgements

Many kind benefactors have helped bring this book to life. First, my enduring gratitude goes to Ratnaguna for introducing me to Shinran's teachings. Second, without the advice and encouragement of Dayamati I would never have even begun this book. We studied Shinran's *Collected Works* together over a period of six months or so, and this was really the catalyst behind what you read here. Dayamati read various drafts and offered many invaluable insights. My thanks also go to Dr Graham Ward for introducing me to hermeneutic tools that have informed the approach taken here to Shinran's works. I am very grateful to Kenneth K. Tanaka who, despite his demanding schedule, kindly agreed to write the foreword. My heartfelt thanks also go to Hannah Atkinson, Dharmapriya, Dhivan, Saccanama, Satya Robyn, Dr Will Buckingham, and Dr Tim Stanley for their helpful comments and encouragement. Finally, Dr Enrique Galván gave much-needed reassurance and offered clarifications on many points of Shin doctrine.

Huge thanks to Windhorse Publications, and especially to Dhammamegha, for having confidence in this project and helping me to see it through to completion.

Publisher's Acknowledgements

Windhorse Publications wishes to gratefully acknowledge a grant from the Future Dharma Fund and the Triratna European Chairs' Assembly Fund towards the production of this book.

We also wish to acknowledge and thank the individual donors who gave to the book's production via our 'Sponsor-a-book' campaign.

Abbreviations

The following two works are frequently cited. References to them are given with the abbreviation and page numbers directly in the text:

CWS *The Collected Works of Shinran*, trans. Hongwanji International Center Translation Committee, 2 vols., Jodo Shinshu Hongwanji-ha, Kyoto 1997, vol.1.

Sen *Hōnen's Senchakushū: Passages on the Selection of the Nembutsu in the Original Vow*, trans. English Translation Project, Kuroda Institute, University of Hawai'i Press, Honolulu, HI, 1998.

Foreword

by Kenneth K. Tanaka

As a priest and an academic in the Jōdo Shinshū or Shin Buddhist tradition, I am honoured and pleased to recommend this impressive book by Nagapriya to the English-speaking world. What makes this book even more impressive is that the author is not, in the usual sense of the word, an 'insider' of the tradition. Nevertheless, he has, in my view, accurately presented Shinran doctrinally as a scholar but also spiritually as a seeker of the Dharma.

Unfortunately, Nagapriya is more of an exception since it is often the case that those outside the tradition fail to correctly understand Shinran. For example, a German scholar of Buddhism, Heinz Bechert, has remarked:

> Amida Buddhism has won a broad following through
> all of East Asia, primarily as a *folk religion*. [...] While Zen
> Buddhism [...] has preserved and continually renewed
> essential elements of the spirit of the old teachings and
> of the traditional meditative practices, Amidism is a
> 'Buddhism of faith. It takes the ideas of the Buddha and,
> in a way, *twists them into their opposite*. The most radical
> spokesman for this approach is Shinran-Shōnin.'[1]

Far from being 'primarily a folk religion' Shin Buddhism is rooted in Mahāyāna scriptures and commentaries, some in Sanskrit dating back to the second century CE. Their translated texts are included in the Chinese and Tibetan Buddhist canons, and were the objects of commentaries by eminent scholar monks.

Bechert further fails to see the commonality that Shin has with other branches of Buddhism. He voices what he perceives to be a deviation of what he calls 'Amidism' by contrasting it with Zen Buddhism. He thus presents the two traditions as being radically different. I, however, cannot disagree more with this understanding, which is why I was pleased to find Nagapriya correctly presenting Shinran's position as being very much in line with the views of Dōgen, the founder of Sōtō school of Zen. Nagapriya writes: 'Despite their apparent incommensurability, Shinran's approach to nembutsu reveals surprising overlaps with Dōgen's vision of zazen' (p.118). Nagapriya recognizes that, for both Shinran and Dōgen, practice is not a self-directed effort towards the goal of enlightenment. Instead, enlightenment is essentially already achieved, so their 'practice' is not a means to but an expression of enlightenment. Dōgen referred to this relationship between meditation and enlightenment as the '"oneness of practice and realization" (*shushō ittō*)' (p.119). Enlightenment is present in the very act of meditation. Regarding Shinran's understanding of the relationship between nembutsu (oral recitation of the name of Amida) and Amida's compassion, Nagapriya expresses it beautifully as follows:

> The nembutsu is no longer a means through which we come to identify ourselves with Amida's mind, or through which we accumulate merit, or even a means that facilitates our liberation. Rather, the nembutsu confirms and celebrates that we have, in a sense, always already attained liberation. The nembutsu irrupts as the mental, verbal, and even physical manifestation of Amida's compassionate working through us. (p.120)

Thus, Nagapriya does not make the same error as Bechert. He does not see Shinran to be the opposite of Dōgen, for he correctly sees the basic parallels in the two founders' understanding of the relationship between the nembutsu and enlightenment (for Shinran) and meditation and enlightenment (for Dōgen).

On another issue, Bechert considers the reliance on 'grace' as one more reason for regarding Shinran as deviating from the Buddhist tradition. He characterizes Shinran's position as one that 'maintains that we attain salvation purely and simply through the *grace* of

Amitābha'.[2] If Bechert has a problem with what he calls 'grace', he is either unaware of the prevalence of the teachings of grace throughout Mahāyāna Buddhism or choosing to ignore them.

Even a cursory look at Mahāyāna texts will yield findings of discussions on what can only be regarded as 'grace'. It is found in such terms as 'ultimate body' (*dharmakāya*), 'power of the Buddha' (*buddhānubhāva*), and 'sustaining power' (*adhiṣṭhāna*). These are clearly found in Mahāyāna sutras and commentaries, such as the *Prajñāpāramitā-sūtra* and *Avataṃsaka-sūtra*, Vasubandhu's *Commentary on the Sutra of Ten Bhūmi Stages*, and Bhāvaviveka's *Verses on the Heart of the Middle Way*. And none of these is considered a Pure Land text, but they constitute key doctrines within Mahāyāna thought.

The third and the last point has to do with shinjin, a form of enlightenment or satori. Bechert refers to Shinjin simply as 'faith'. However, as Nagapriya correctly points out, Shinjin does not only mean faith and notes the multivalent quality of shinjin. I concur and have suggested that we should not be limited to the primary rendering in English as 'faith' and 'entrusting'.

Shinjin, in my view, contains four main dimensions, which are (1) entrusting, (2) no doubt, (3) joy, and (4) realization. Among these, realization is a quality that is in keeping with Buddhism as a religion of awakening based on wisdom (*prajñā*) or realization. 'Realization' is supported in many places in Shinran's writings, for example:

> It is by entering the wisdom of Shinjin
> That we become persons who respond in gratitude to the
> Buddhas' benevolence.[3]

Shinran goes on to explain, 'the emergence of the mind of entrusting oneself to it is the *arising of wisdom*'. Based on this, we can assume that some degree of wisdom or realization arises in the aspirant's mind.

In the same vein, Nagapriya discusses at length the various ramifications of what shinjin meant for Shinran, and what it can mean for us in the contemporary world. He also points out, as noted earlier, that no one word can fully capture its meaning:

While the translations 'true entrusting', 'entrusting heart', or 'surety' offer some indications [as to shinjin's orientation], no single word or phrase can capture shinjin's many shades of meaning, several of which will be highlighted below. Translated more freely, shinjin might even be rendered as 'letting go' or 'letting *through*'. (p.125)

I very much applaud Nagapriya's insight into the nature of the most important element of Shinran's spirituality, and appreciate his effort to offer a new way of understanding shinjin. In particular, Nagapriya's suggestion of 'letting go' and 'letting through' as possible renderings for shinjin symbolizes for me the significance of his contribution. He not only accurately captures the heart of Shinran's spirituality and teachings, but conveys it in ways that are novel and easier to understand, which an 'insider' like me may overlook. Such is the quality and tenor of this book, which I believe will contribute enormously to the accurate presentation of Shinran's teaching of Other Power.

Kenneth K. Tanaka
Professor Emeritus, Musashino University, Tokyo
Past President, International Association of Shin Buddhist Studies
Author of *The Dawn of Chinese Pure Land Buddhist Doctrine*, SUNY Press, 1990.

The Primal Vow

本願

May I not gain possession of perfect awakening if, once I have
attained Buddhahood, any among the throng of living beings in
the ten regions of the universe should single-mindedly desire to
be reborn in my land with joy, with confidence, with gladness,
and if they should bring to mind this aspiration for even ten
moments of thought and yet not gain rebirth there.[1]

Chapter One

Introduction:
The Bandaged Place

Shinran (1173–1263) was born in Japan in the late twelfth century. He enjoyed a long life and by the time he died, at the age of almost ninety, Dante was just learning to read, Hildegard of Bingen was deep into old age, Marco Polo had just embarked on his travels along the Silk Route, and Columbus would not set sail for the New World for more than two centuries. Shinran lived in a medieval Japanese society that was very different from ours. Shoguns were on the warpath, natural disasters were commonplace and devastating, few people could read or write, and Buddhism was mostly within the ambit of the privileged rather than something that was accessible to the common people.

Shinran was an older contemporary of the scholastic theologian St Thomas Aquinas (1225–1274), who wrote his unfinished *Summa Theologiae* in the years immediately following Shinran's death. But Shinran left little that resembled the systematic religious writings that Aquinas was to bequeath to the Catholic Church. Instead, his revolutionary, religious sensibility leaked out through his works, all written in the latter decades of his life. Moreover, it was to take up to two centuries for his approach to the Dharma to really capture the Japanese imagination at the popular level. Shinran is now recognized as the 'founder' of – and certainly as the inspiration for – the largest denomination within Japanese Buddhism: the True Pure Land tradition (Jōdo Shinshū).

Judged through the cold gaze of secular history, Shinran might be dismissed as a failed medieval monk who doctored his sources. He insisted on a narrowly drawn, even sectarian, approach to Buddhist practice that strayed a long way from the path that early Buddhism trod. Perhaps even beyond the boundary of genuine Dharma. He seems naive in his exclusive reliance on Amida Buddha as a kind of 'saviour' and his insistence on the pre-eminence of scriptures that, we now know, were created hundreds of years after the death of the Buddha. Moreover, his absolute dependence on 'faith' seems to undermine one of the most basic truisms of Buddhism: that through our own efforts we can gain enlightenment. Given this, what existential value can his teachings possibly command in the world of today? What could this medieval Japanese, poring over textual commentaries written in classical Chinese, and making his careful ink marks on his hand-copied manuscripts, possibly have to say to me? To us? To now? Such questions have inspired what follows.

If we soften our gaze, we may see things rather differently. Shinran approaches us as a devout Buddhist, sophisticated yet humble, attentive to human frailty, especially his own. He invites a subtle reading of the existential condition that undoes the sovereignty of the egocentric will and opens out, instead, in wonder and reverence towards something that transcends it. Shinran evokes a milieu that fully encompasses us and in which we are always blessed by wisdom and compassion. It is a milieu that is sacramental, full of light, and saturated with meaningfulness. The Pure Land scriptures reveal themselves as the sacred word of the Buddha and offer a consoling, transformative message. This message points towards the super-abundance that is Amida's compassionate gift and urges us to say Amida's name, which calls forth unfathomable qualities and so consecrates our moment-to-moment existence. Shinran's religious vision promises a sacred world.

Through Shinran, the sacred context of my own life has been restored. New possibilities for what it means to be human have opened out. I don't have to rely exclusively on my ego-directed efforts to connect with the sacred dimension. What a relief. Despite my all-too-obvious limitations, and even because of them, there is an Other Power that is reaching out to me and drawing me towards liberation. Without this, my situation would be rather hopeless.

Rumi, who outlived Shinran by ten years, wrote: 'Don't turn your head. Keep looking at the bandaged place. That is where the light enters you.'[1] To look at the bandaged place means to be

The Promise of a Sacred World

humbly attentive to my own fragility. It also means to turn towards others and recognize that they are like me. We all experience suffering, we all experience loss and longing. As this awareness deepens, the motivation for an authentic relationship with life may burst through.

Shinran appears as one of sixteen historical teachers on the Triratna Tree of Refuge and Respect, a symbolic representation of lineage created in the 1990s by Urgyen Sangharakshita, the founder of the Triratna Buddhist Order to which I belong.[2] What is so special about Shinran that he warrants such reverence? While characterized by a critical ecumenism, the Triratna Buddhist Order has absorbed very little influence from Japanese Buddhism and even less from Shinran's particular orientation. Despite this, our teacher considered Shinran sufficiently important to incorporate him into a visualization practice that is concerned with evoking a sense of tradition and lineage. Why? This may have as much to do with the example he set as with the specific doctrines he proposed. Just like Sangharakshita, Shinran chose to step outside the established institutional tradition in which he trained, and came to consider himself neither monk nor layman. Again like Sangharakshita, Shinran was inspired to establish a pattern of practice that was relevant to his time and that could be followed by anyone, not just the privileged elite. Both were also translators seeking to make the Dharma accessible to their respective historical and cultural contexts.

The lines you underline change

Daitsū Tom Wright tells a wonderful story about a meeting with his Dharma teacher, Uchiyama Rōshi, a renowned Zen master of the twentieth century. He wanted to ask a question about a text called *Shōbōgenzō Zuimonki*, which is a series of notes compiled by a disciple of Dōgen.[3] As it happened, the Rōshi already had a copy of the book open on his desk. Daitsū couldn't help but notice how tatty the book was, and that it was also scarred with underlinings and crammed with margin notes. Joking, he suggested that it was perhaps time the Rōshi bought a new copy. Silently, Uchiyama Rōshi raised a finger and gestured in the direction of a bookshelf.

Looking around, Daitsū eventually fixed his eye on the indicated shelf and saw that there were no fewer than fourteen other copies of the same text, which were in the same condition; on closer inspection, each was equally decorated with many underlinings and margin notes. Thinking for a moment, Daitsū asked the Rōshi what changes when you read a book so many times. 'The lines you underline change', he replied.[4]

When we read a Dharma text for the first time, certain phrases or ideas may strike us as noteworthy. But if we read it again, what we consider to be significant often changes. What seemed pertinent on first reading may seem less so after several readings. Moreover, something that we may not have even noticed on our first few readings suddenly leaps out at us as being of vital importance. I have certainly found this reflection to be true when reading Shinran. I cannot claim to have read his works hundreds of times, as Uchiyama Rōshi must have read Dōgen's words, but each time I return to a text by Shinran I am different and so I read it differently. What calls my attention changes. Understanding is never finished – it only ever pauses. When we return to a text or teaching after an absence, our understanding is renewed and, in some sense, it begins again. But our starting point is always unique, informed by all the accumulated understandings and readings we have assimilated from the past. In a sense, we can never read the same text twice. This is because we are in a relationship of mutual responsiveness with the text, whereby we are *both* changed in the experience of reading. Of course the marks on the page don't change, but the sense that we make of those marks does. The world that the text opens up changes as we return to it from our always-new existential situation.

A record of sacred encounters

What are you getting yourself into by reading this book? Everything that you will find here must inevitably reveal the melange of interests and points of reference that inform my particular way of seeing the world: my itinerary of Dharma practice, my uncertainties, and my journeys towards the limits of my own understanding. At root, it is an invitation to engage with the meaning of the 'religious' or the 'sacred' within Buddhism.

Shinran, I believe, offers thrilling and profound insights into the possibility of a non-theistic religious life.

You will be offered bits of Buddhist history as well as of doctrine and practice. You will also be brought into relation with Shinran's writings and my stuttering attempts to interpret them. So far, none of this should be a surprise. But you will also find several philosophers and theologians making an appearance, and even the odd poet, as they may help to hint at things that can only be seen out of the corner of one's eye. The overall intention is to situate Shinran in relationship with both the Buddhist tradition and the existential condition.

What follows is a kind of record of my sacred encounters with Shinran: his life, his writings, his religious milieu, and his imagined lineage. Its purpose is to underline how engaging with eminent Buddhist texts is not just edifying but existentially transformative, and to invite you into similar encounters. It is organized into three parts, each of which has its own mood.

Part 1, 'Portal to the Infinite', might be framed as a series of meditations on existential boundedness and our longing for the unbounded. It evokes a personal encounter with Shinran as a situated human being, someone with whom we might drink tea, who is trying to imagine a meaningful lifeworld. It steers towards the horizon of the past not in order to recover facts, but as a spiritual exercise that has the power to remake us. It also documents how Shinran's life and teachings call to me, inspire me, and console me across the impossible distance that separates us.

Part 2, 'Cascade of Blessing', evokes the myth of Amida Buddha, the Pure Land, and the corresponding Mahāyāna scriptures. It introduces a set of hermeneutic tools in order to approach Amida as a sacred, transcendent reality that blesses us from beyond the known self. It details how Shinran applied a range of imaginative strategies in order to affirm his commitment to tradition while at the same time reshaping it. I position Shinran as a kind of Dharma intrapreneur who, while immersing himself within the living flow of Buddhist heritage, formulates profound innovations. Among other tools, I apply the metaphor of a palimpsest and the notion of imagined discipleship to give form to Shinran's way of making sense of his religious inheritance.

Part 3, 'Other Power', offers a series of readings of key concepts that Shinran draws on to disclose his liberative vision. This section pays careful attention to Shinran's writings in order to elucidate his central ideas. It explores Shinran's unique understanding of the meaning and purpose of calling to Amida Buddha or the nembutsu. It also opens out the central concept of shinjin or wholehearted entrusting, which is the heart of Shinran's religious universe, the concept of practice (or no-practice), and the related concept of jinen or naturalness. I approach these topics not as historical curiosities but as living options that have transformative force. They are concepts that *matter* for our existence. The book closes with a contemplation on the importance of the sacred and of the mythic world.

Looking at a bit of sky and trees

But according to what (or whose) authority am I writing about these topics? We are accustomed to believe that some people have an expert, privileged view of certain matters, and this is of course sometimes the case. At the same time, it is worth remembering that no one has a bird's eye view of anything. In his travel writings, *Mornings in Mexico*, D.H. Lawrence opens with the following observation:

> One says Mexico: one means, after all, one little town away South in the Republic: and in this little town, one rather crumbly adobe house built round two sides of a garden patio: and of this house, one spot on the deep, shady verandah facing inwards to the trees, where there are an onyx table and three rocking-chairs and one little wooden chair, a pot with carnations, and a person with a pen. We talk so grandly, in capital letters, about Morning in Mexico. All it amounts to is one little individual looking at a bit of sky and trees, then looking down at the page of his exercise book.[5]

Lawrence's reflection about his stay in Oaxaca underlines the inescapable *situatedness* from where we each look out upon the world as we try to engage with its mystery in order to make some sense of it – Shinran himself was no exception. At times we may be tempted to make grand claims about our relationship with the world and what we can understand of it, but, as Lawrence points out, the world that we see is a particularized one: 'one little individual looking at a bit of sky and trees, then looking down at the page of his exercise book'. One little individual shuffling words around with a word processor. This does not disqualify that perspective, since no other relation is possible, but rather serves as a warning to be careful of assuming too much about our own capacities.

I am reminded of the story of the frog and the well. A frog that lives by the sea arrives at a well and says: 'I come from a vast place where there is so much more water than in your little well.' 'How much more?' asks the well frog, 'Twice as much? Three times as much?' Given the vast mystery that is existence, our current horizons can seem so painfully limited. Lawrence goes on to say that when reading books that make grand claims about the future of the United States or the situation of Europe we should do well to visualize 'a thin or a fat person, in a chair or in bed, dictating to a bob-haired stenographer or making little marks on paper with a fountain pen'.[6]

Thus there can be no question of offering an exhaustive overview of Shinran's religious universe. Instead, this is a somewhat modest series of enquiries that aims to shed light on topics central to the theme of existential liberation. There is a certain degree of circling in what follows. A number of themes come up several times as I attempt to unpack them from different points of view and in relation to connected ideas. If this book does its work, it may at least inspire you to delve more deeply into Shinran's startling and profound religious vision in order to allow its transformative light, and so the light of Amida Buddha, to shine on you as I believe it shines on me. To put it another way, and to anticipate something of Shinran's religious perspective, you may come to see that this light *already* shines upon you as it does on everyone.

Part 1

Portal to the Infinite

But sometimes illumination comes to our rescue at the very moment when all seems lost; we have knocked at every door and they open on nothing until, at last, we stumble unconsciously against the only one through which we can enter the kingdom we have sought in vain a hundred years – and it opens. (Proust, *Time Regained*)[1]

Chapter Two

Betting on the Symbolic World

A lover doesn't figure the odds.

[...]
[...] he gives without cause
or calculation or limit.

A conventionally religious person
behaves a certain way
to achieve salvation.

A lover gambles everything, the self,
the circle around the zero!
He or she cuts and throws it all away.

This is beyond any religion.

[...] (Rumi, 'The Circle around the Zero')[1]

I first came across Shinran Shōnin (1173–1263) in the late 1990s. Picture me, if you will, living in a remote, semi-derelict farmhouse in North Wales, where a small team of us offered Buddhist study retreats. I had moved there to help my friend and mentor Ratnaguna to run the place. The circumstances weren't favourable as we had little money, the facilities were very basic (there was just one shower for up to seventeen people at a time), and study retreats were not so in demand. Nevertheless, we got by, at least for a few years.

I look back on my time in North Wales as one of the most difficult periods of my life (and there have been some tough ones), even as a time that broke me. Broke me irrevocably. Reflecting on it more than twenty years later, it is hard to say why – maybe the brooding sky, maybe the seclusion, or maybe it was just a necessary consequence of how I had been ordering my life until that time. Notwithstanding – or, better, *because* of – that, certain moments stand out as blessings. Among those was my first encounter with the teachings of Shinran. It was a moment that was reassuring and unsettling at the same time. On the one hand, it contradicted everything that I had learned so far about Buddhism. And yet, on the other, I immediately recognized it as true. Having trained in philosophy academically, I was alert to the problematic nature of truth claims. Yet, I can only repeat, when I was first exposed to Shinran's teachings I found them compelling and true in a way that I have rarely experienced. I *believed* them. I still do, even though I can neither fully understand them nor fully justify them, at least not rationally. But then can we say that we fully understand a painting or that we can 'justify' it? Can we ever say that we fully grasp a poem and can 'prove' it? Even to try to do so would be to reduce them, to explain them away somehow.

Ratnaguna had been reading around Shinran and the True Pure Land perspective for some time, and had led retreats on this theme.[2] I was curious to learn something about a Dharma teacher outside my usual range, so I asked Ratnaguna if he would study something with me. He kindly agreed, and we began to explore a relatively short text called the *Shōshinge* or *Hymn of True Faith*. I didn't know it at the time, but this forms the concluding part of the second chapter of Shinran's most esteemed work, known in Japanese as *Kyōgyōshinshō* (*The True Teaching, Practice, and Realisation of the Pure Land Way*, CWS, pp.69ff.).

When I opened the *Shōshinge* for the first time, I had been practising Buddhism fairly diligently for about ten years. I had already suffered my fair share of disappointments and humiliations. Aspirations had been thwarted, ambitions crushed. Far from feeling that I was smoothly proceeding towards perfect enlightenment, I felt increasingly burdened by my karmic conditioning, like a man trying to take off in a hot-air balloon but who can't undo the tethers or lift out the sandbags that are weighing him down. My spiritual ambitions were contaminated by my seemingly inescapable self-preoccupation. I was beginning to feel like a spiritual failure. No,

I *was* a spiritual failure. It was clear to me that I was not going to break free of my limiting patterns of thought and conduct in the way that I had previously envisaged, especially on the heady day of my ordination into the Triratna Buddhist Order in 1992. At that moment, I was entrusted with the Buddhist name Nagapriya ('beloved by the nāgas', or serpent deities) in the spirit of the bodhisattva ideal – that is to say, for the benefit of all beings. But now the idea of benefiting all beings through leading a heroic life in the Dharma already seemed a pipe dream, an arrogant delusion. How could I benefit anyone if I was so fettered by ill-will, self-hatred, dejection, and sporadic delusions of grandeur?

Shinran's response to this existential predicament came as a huge relief. I *am* a spiritual failure, he confirmed. But he was too. In fact, we all are. He writes, for instance:

> I am such that I do not know right and wrong
> And cannot distinguish false and true;
> I lack even small love and small compassion,
> And yet, for fame and profit, enjoy teaching others.
>   (*CWS*, p.429)

While at first glance this might not seem much of a consolation, according to Shinran, an honest assessment of our own limitedness is the beginning of a more sincere relationship to Dharma practice, to oneself, and to others. It is the catalyst for a *metanoia*, a 'change of mind' or conversion. Once we learn to recognize that our ego-directed effort is ultimately futile in the pursuit of spiritual liberation, we can begin to live in a way that more fully honours how things are. I felt as though I now had permission to put down an enormous burden that was crushing me. Shinran confirmed that my ego-directed efforts would only serve to enmesh me further in saṃsāra, like a coyote caught in a snare, every attempt to free myself just tightening the noose, and redoubling my suffering and hopelessness.

Based on his awakening to his own spiritual fraudulence, Shinran came to realize that he could never be the agent of his own liberation because his very aspiration to do so was tainted by his incorrigible greed, hatred, and delusion. There was no advancing, no smooth ascent; all such ideas are nothing more than ways to inflate the fragile ego, which reality must inevitably puncture. Such ideas, he came to realize, had nothing to do with what the Buddhist life is really about, since what is required is not the culmination of the egocentric vision but rather its *transcendence*. In other words, what is called for is the renunciation of the quixotic attempt by the ego to liberate itself, an attempt inherently doomed to fail. This misguided project is known in more technical terms as the 'self-power' (*jiriki*) approach to spiritual freedom.

Shinran came to place his confidence not in his self-power but rather in Other Power or *tariki*. Other Power turns out to be Amida or Amitābha (whose name means 'infinite light'), a cosmic Buddha whose legend is told in a group of texts known as the three Pure Land scriptures. Aeons ago, Amida made a series of vows, which they then fulfilled on the arduous path towards awakening (here and elsewhere, I use the gender-neutral pronoun to refer to Amida).[3] We will learn more about their mythic narrative later. According to Amida's vows, we are basically guaranteed awakening if we just invoke Amida's name sincerely. That's right; all we need do is call Amida's name sincerely through what came to be known as the nembutsu: *Namu Amida Butsu*.[4] Homage to Amida Buddha. That's all. It sounds too easy, doesn't it?

According to Shinran, this simple practice becomes the portal through which Amida's incalculable spiritual merits are entrusted to us. To put it another way, through the nembutsu, Amida's awakened mind is gifted to us so that it becomes ours. Our mind fuses with the awakened mind. This strikes at the heart of the tantalizing and puzzling message of True Pure Land Buddhism. It all seems so easy, and yet doubts persist. How do I know if this has happened or not? We can all recite the name, but how do we know if we have done it *sincerely*? Self-doubt, or lack of reliance on Other Power, drives us to keep striving, to persist in trying to make ourselves worthy through discipline and good works. Yet, says Shinran, this desperate effort just digs us deeper into our spiritual predicament since it is rooted in ego-clinging. So how do we come to trust in Amida's generosity and compassion? And what does that even mean? We will explore these questions in what follows.

Since my first encounter with Shinran's thought, I have drifted away and then circled back to it every few years or so. Each time, I have read more of his works and returned to others. And each time I have a similar response: there is something deeply *true* about what I am reading and yet, on the rational level, it seems no more credible than a fairy tale. Each time, I have been propelled into a condition that one theologian has called 'assailed certainty',[5] a confidence that constantly struggles with doubt but that is always called back again, that returns to itself.

Reading as existential transformation

Over the years, I have thought about formulating a response to Shinran, only to find myself incoherent, lacking in the communication tools to carry out the task. I became interested in the Reformation theologian Martin Luther as I began to see broad overlaps between his doctrine of faith alone (*fides sola*) and Shinran's teaching on Other Power.[6] I even considered writing my master's thesis on just this topic. I dropped that plan and instead fixed on a doctorate that proposed a programme of 'existential hermeneutics'. I wanted to explore how interpreting Shinran's works might function as a transformative process, even as a religious practice. This meant approaching his writings not as historical curiosities but rather as 'creative agents' that have the power to instigate existential awakening. Shinran's works constitute what I described as 'a living organism in constant process of formation'. If we are willing to cooperate, reading them can catalyze transformative insights. The relationship between texts and reader might then be framed in terms of a process of mutual transformation and therapeutic restoration.

The thesis also proposed to examine how the myth of Amida as Other Power and the utopian Pure Land might be interpreted in the context of post-traditional society, especially without recourse to theistic assumptions. Finally, while the project was to focus on a specific body of eminent texts, it would be located within the broader enterprise of interpreting any cultural artefacts that are historically, culturally, linguistically, and philosophically distanced. Rather than dismissed as barriers, these forms of hermeneutic distance could favour rich existential insights.

These were some heady aims. For various reasons, I never fulfilled this ambitious project but I don't regret it. My life went in a different direction, which brought me many unexpected blessings. Part of the reason why I abandoned it was the intuition that the academy was not the appropriate milieu in which to carry out such a sacred enquiry. Quite frankly, I was also daunted by the task, by the existential risk implied. Yet the basic premise, that is to say engaging with Shinran's teachings as a practice in existential hermeneutics, still holds good. I might also frame it now as a process of the iconization of sacred texts. Sacred texts offer a portal to the infinite. To borrow an image from the Spanish poet Miguel de Unamuno, they are 'a lever by which to immerse oneself in the infinite'.[7]

After all, why read Shinran at all? Of course to understand his ideas, perhaps to know something about the history of Buddhism and one of its more important figures, but more significantly to be *transformed*, even reconstituted, in the light of what has been revealed. As Pierre Hadot wrote, the purpose of dialogue is 'to let ourselves be changed, in our point of view, attitudes, and convictions. This means that we must dialogue with ourselves, hence do battle with ourselves.'[8]

To read a sacred text, then, is to engage in a process of existential dialogue from which we should not expect to emerge unscathed. We are required to give up a part of ourselves, even our entire conception of who we are and what our place is in the world. We may even be required to die. Maybe it all sounds a bit dramatic, but this is really the only way to understand anything in any meaningful way: to open ourselves to the claims that the text places upon us and to surrender to the transformation that this demands. As Paul Ricoeur puts it: 'To understand oneself in front of a text is [...] to let the work and its world enlarge the horizon of the understanding which I have of myself.'[9] This process can be both thrilling and scary all at once. To read a text is to enter a new world. Of course we must be willing to cooperate, and this underlines the importance of receptivity or 'good faith', as we might say. After all, what is the point of reading anything if we are not prepared to be enlarged by it, called into question by it, even turned upside down by it?

Distance and the recuperation of the sacred dimension

Shinran is historically, culturally, linguistically, and religiously distanced from us. His lifeworld is now lost in the sands of time and I suppose we can never retrieve it, not exactly. Yet he left a treasure trove of writings that we can pick through in order to come to an enlarged understanding of ourselves right now. We live at a time when the transcendent is, for many people, no more than an outdated superstition, where consciousness is flattened, where the highest value is the grasping, individual will. We live mostly in a deconsecrated world. Disenchantment with traditional theological visions of human existence has provoked reaction, even a radical atheism that sees religious perspectives not simply as wrong or naive but even as menaces to right-thinking people. Yet the flattened narratives that we now tell ourselves about who we are and what we are here for never satisfy. To enter into the myth of Amida is to immerse ourselves within an imaginative narrative, like living through a poem. It is to recognize that there is an additional dimension that transcends the self-preoccupied human will. It is to recognize that there is an infinite source of value, an indefatigable compassionate impulse that is eternally reaching out to bless us and fulfil itself through us. We can embrace this impulse or, rather, allow it to embrace us. We can be 'grasped never to be abandoned' by Amida's compassion, to use one of Shinran's refrains.

In contrast to Zen, Theravada, and Tibetan Buddhism, Pure Land has attracted limited attention outside East Asia.[10] It is worth reflecting on why this might be. While other schools establish Dharma centres that attract many converts outside traditional Buddhist contexts, Pure Land has mostly remained the preserve of diaspora communities, which generally have not reached out to their host societies. Yet there is nothing especially Japanese about its basic vision. Many converts to Buddhism are either consciously rejecting Christianity or else have never had a religious sensibility. They see in Buddhism tools that they can make use of in their process of personal growth, their search for well-being and peace of mind. They are looking not for redemption or salvation but for adjustment. Richard Payne has suggested that Shin Buddhism doesn't offer a 'compelling religious product'.[11] Its focus on a seemingly external locus of awakening (Amida Buddha and their Pure Land) 'precludes it from being easily commodified and marketed within the religio-therapeutic marketplace'.[12]

Shinran's vision is, in some ways, brutal. It is an assault on the notion of personal growth and self-development. It is an assault on human autonomy. It is an assault on the idea that I can redeem myself. Unlike Zen and Theravada, which emphasize personal effort and discipline as means to 'advance' on the spiritual path, the Shin perspective only becomes relevant to someone prepared to abandon this self-directed project. Better, it speaks to those who have no choice *but* to abandon this project because it has burned itself out. It requires us to surrender the ambition to redeem ourselves and to recognize that liberation occurs when ego-driven effort collapses. Liberation occurs as we open ourselves to a transcendent impulse: the transferred merits of Amida, whose infinite light of wisdom eternally shines upon us and all other beings.[13]

A trend in the Western assimilation of Buddhism has been to deconsecrate it.[14] Rather than framing it as a religion, a word that for many people is now irredeemably contaminated, Buddhism is exalted as a philosophy or even a way of life. It is seen as rational, empirical. It demands no metaphysical leap of faith. As part of this trend, Buddhist teachings and practices have been brought into alignment with evolution, with neuroscience, and with modern psychology. Buddhism has been greedily assimilated by the self-help genre and adorns the well-being spa. What could be more soothing than to go for a hot-stone massage and encounter a Buddha figure cradling a scented candle in his lap? A lot of what passes for Buddhism has been shorn of its traditional cosmology, its ritual language, and even its reverence and devotion. But the Buddha's range extends beyond personal growth, relaxation, and adjustment. The Buddhist vision entails a radical reorientation of oneself, which might be understood as a process of spiritual death and rebirth. Shinran's theology[15] is a welcome reminder of the calculating nature of the unenlightened mind; of how, rather than submit itself to the urgings of enlightenment, it instead coopts the transcendent into its self-serving intentions.

The orientation and language of Pure Land Buddhism is explicitly *religious*.[16] At its heart is shinjin (信心, 'wholehearted entrusting'). It relies upon a transcendent factor, a beneficent influence that is beyond our individual capacities and deserts, that is beyond our own karma. It reveals a cosmic drama in which all beings participate, and it trusts in an inexhaustible compassion that is the source of all enduring significance and value. Pure Land Buddhism opens up a multi-dimensional, infinite universe illuminated by the untrammelled play of Amida's compassionate light. Awakening is not earned, it is not even inherent, but rather *gifted*. Yet it is not gifted at a particular moment in time, like on our birthday, but eternally bestowed or even *always being* bestowed. It is through savouring this spectacular gift that we may come to experience the joy, gratitude, and indebtedness that is the condition of the 'truly settled'. Instead of practice being something we rely on to earn awakening, practice becomes a joyful affirmation of blessing and an offering for others, which may in turn help draw them towards their own liberation. Practice doesn't save us, it overflows as a surplus of humble reverence.

One aim of this book is to rehabilitate an explicitly religious way of thinking and talking about Buddhism. For many, such a rehabilitation no doubt seems unnecessary, since they feel that Buddhism has never ceased to speak religiously. For others, it may be precisely the lack of religious language within Buddhism that appeals. You may have turned away in disgust from all ideas of formalized religion, and so regard Buddhism as belonging to some different category. I would put it like this: religion gives voice to our ultimate concern. Shinran offers his vision of the religious life as a response to that ultimate concern. It addresses a deep longing and intuition within us. At the centre of it is a myth: that of Amida's progress towards complete enlightenment and their promise of rebirth in the Pure Land.

In this context, a myth is not a lie but rather a truth communicated in symbolic form. In the words of Rudolf Bultmann, 'myths give to the transcendent reality an immanent, this-worldly objectivity.

Myths give worldly objectivity to that which is unworldly.'[17] We might gloss the unworldly here as signifying that which goes beyond the reactive mind, that which is mysterious and unsayable. It is the dimension of our ultimate concern.

Myths are the language of the religious. In unfolding their meaning, and indeed the meaning of anything, we always begin with a prior relation to the subject matter and some kind of investment in its possible significance. Bultmann calls this the 'life-relation'.[18] Without this, he argues, it is impossible to make sense of anything. Our life-relation with the myth of Amida and his Pure Land must inevitably be far removed from Shinran's. Not only this, but our life-relation with Shinran's own writings is very different from that of his immediate followers and contemporaries. This does not disqualify us from engaging with these topics, but rather informs the questions that will come alive for us and so the answers that we call forth.

Shinran's religious vision underscores the inherent limitations of human capacity. He affirms that to be human is, in some sense, to be incorrigible. We human beings are irrevocably situated, contingent, and compromised. We are incapable of perfecting ourselves since to be human is to be embodied, inevitably lacking panoramic awareness, and always morally flawed because we are wedded to the egocentric will. While on first reading this might seem a dispiriting proposal, and even in conflict with the basic Buddhist commitment to our potential for enlightenment, it points to a deep existential truth. To be aware is to be particular and bounded, constrained by the requirements of individual flourishing and purposes.

At the same time, Shinran gestures towards a higher source of value and direction, one not under the sway of the egocentric despot that is our calculating will. Self-directed effort can only take us so far, he realized. When we reach its limits, we may let go into a different kind of orientation, one that allows a higher will to emerge through us. This higher will, or way of being, is personalized in the form of Amida Buddha. Amida is conceived in the first instance as a transcendent factor that works upon or through us but that never fully belongs to us. Better, it can never be appropriated by us. Nor can it in any way be manufactured or contrived. Amida is pure compassion reaching out to all beings through us. Amida's infinite light eternally shines upon all without exception.

The interpretive wager

In his approach to interpreting symbols and myths, Paul Ricoeur reflects on the hermeneutic situation by restating Anselm's famous maxim: I must believe in order to understand, but in order to believe I must understand. How to get out of this bind? Ricoeur proposes a kind of wager in order to move forward in our process of understanding.[19] We must wager that we will gain a deeper understanding of the matter at hand if we are prepared to follow the promptings of symbolic thought. More specifically, we must wager on the fact that Amida's myth has something significant to say to us about our existence and that, through engaging with it, through interpreting it – I would even say through entering into it – we will be recompensed with enlarged self-understanding. He points out that while we remain outside the world of the myth it can have no true value for us. We must give up on our neutrality and bet on the benefits that will result. While we remain outside the myth, as a spectator, it can never come alive for us as a world of living significance. We will never know what the ocean feels like until we plunge in. Understanding, he argues, begins not from a bird's eye view (which is impossible) but from a particular and restricted standpoint.

Having risked the wager, says Ricoeur, we then go about the process of verifying it through saturating the myth with intelligibility. Having bet on the significance of the symbolic world, that is having committed ourselves to the idea that it has something to say to us, our wager is restored to us in interpretive power, in the sense that we are able to make of the myth. This kind of interpretation entails a transformation in consciousness. Ricoeur asserts that 'Every symbol is finally a hierophany, a manifestation of the bond between humanity and the sacred.'[20] Through their interpretation, symbols and myths assume the gravity of existential agents, they become means by which we can bring alive our understanding of what it means to be human and what is truly valuable to us. Let's make that bet...

Chapter Three

Hell Is Decidedly My Abode

I know nothing at all of good or evil. For if I could know thoroughly, as Amida Tathāgata knows, that an act was good, then I would know good. If I could know thoroughly, as the Tathāgata knows, that an act was evil, then I would know evil. But with a foolish being full of blind passions, in this fleeting world – this burning house – all matters without exception are empty and false, totally without truth and sincerity. (*CWS*, p.679)

Imagining a saint

My first vision of what a saintly person might be like came from the film *Brother Sun, Sister Moon*,[1] an imaginative retelling of the life of St Francis of Assisi, which I saw when I was about twelve. Incidentally, St Francis (1181–1226) was an exact contemporary of Shinran. From memory, I picture Francis in some kind of religious rapture, stripping off his privileged clothes in the town square and proclaiming with joy his renunciation of the ordinary world and his entrance into a new life as a servant of God. He then proceeds to gather a community around himself and to restore an abandoned church, cheerfully labouring through freezing conditions to create a sanctuary fit for transcendental communion. Seemingly oblivious to the callings of the body, his gaze is fixed upwards as he contemplates the divine mystery. I have no idea if this portrayal of St Francis was remotely realistic, but it certainly planted a seed in me, the possibility of another kind of being, one that is born of this world but is not confined by it, who transcends it.

For some reason, saints always turn out rather corny in films, perhaps because what they exemplify is so difficult to show, or perhaps because we are unable to reconcile what is earthly with what is transcendent. In a fascinating essay on Gandhi, George Orwell argues that being a saint and being human are incompatible.[2] He asserts that sainthood is something that human beings should avoid, since the essence of humanity is that 'one is prepared in the end to be defeated and broken up by life, which is the inevitable price of fastening one's love upon other human individuals'.

Orwell goes on to comment:

> In this yogi-ridden age, it is too readily assumed that
> 'non-attachment' is not only better than a full acceptance
> of earthly life, but that the ordinary person only rejects it
> because it is too difficult: in other words, that the average
> human being is a failed saint.[3]

Orwell doubts this and suspects that the main motive for non-attachment is a desire to escape from the pain of living and especially from love, which is often hard work. Shinran might have had sympathy with Orwell, and would certainly have laughed at the idea of being considered a saint. Following his defenestration and exile, which involved being stripped of his Dharma name and official status, he was to rename himself 'Gutoku': ignorant, bald-pated one. Despite the fact that he was posthumously canonised as Shinran *Shōnin* (St Shinran), there is no doubt that he was 'defeated and broken up by life'. And more than once. In old age, for instance, he suffered the indignity of disowning one of his sons for propagating lies and undermining the sangha.

Shinran was keenly aware of his own fallibility, and this was to become a cornerstone of his theology. In *Tannishō*, for instance, he is recorded as saying:

> I have no idea whether the nembutsu is truly the seed for
> my being born in the Pure Land or whether it is the karmic
> act for which I must fall into hell. Should I have been
> deceived by Master Hōnen and, saying the nembutsu, were
> to fall into hell, even then I would have no regrets.
>   The reason is, if I could attain Buddhahood by
> endeavouring in other practices, but said the nembutsu

The Promise of a Sacred World

and so fell into hell, then I would feel regret at having been deceived. But I am incapable of any other practice, so hell is decidedly my abode whatever I do. (*CWS*, p.662)

Through these words, we may empathize with a fragile human being, not a saint. We get the sense of a sincere grappling with the mysteries of existence, the transcendent, human doubt, aspiration, and limit. At least in his own words, Shinran is as remote from the spiritual superhero as it is possible to be. His writings are characterized by humility, a keen sensibility of human contingency and erring, and an enduring awareness of his own existential lack. This apparent incompleteness is precisely what draws me towards him and consoles me in relation to my own religious stumblings. For me the idea of a perfect saint is a thing to be found only in fantasy, an archetype for sure, but nothing that a real human being could ever fully embody. Always the horizon. To bring Shinran alive in the imagination, as a *kalyāṇa mitra* or spiritual friend, facing the same basic challenges of human existence as I do, confronting the reality limits of his particular lifeworld, struggling to unravel his own destiny and purposes, to me this is not only inspiring but transformative.

Such a process of imagining could be termed *fiction*. But this is not to devalue it, quite the opposite. The historian de Certeau has proposed that 'Fiction is the repressed other of history.'[4] While history prides itself on presenting what is 'true', fiction can instead reveal to us what is *real* and, in this way, fill out the realm of the interior in order to engage with what one academic has called 'the practical past'.[5] The practical past

is made up of all those memories, illusions, bits of vagrant information, attitudes and values which the individual or the group summons up as best they can to justify, dignify, excuse, alibi or make a case for actions to be taken in the prosecution of a life project.[6]

Why might we want to recall the past? It is not just a disinterested curiosity but rather one that expresses an existential investment on our part, a search for a transformative space that may enable us to expand our range of human possibilities. For standard history, past religious interiority is relegated to the unreachable and unknowable, perhaps even the irrelevant, but, considered from the point of view of the practical past, the imagining of such interiority offers the promise of self-transcendence.

Any attempt to imagine the past not only has a fictional element but is always mediated by the present, by our own needs, constraints, and lenses. It could never be otherwise. But this need not discourage us since this creation of the past is a way of understanding ourselves through its light. The past does not, and cannot, exist in the form of a precise archive that can be retrieved. Rather, those traces that survive enable a range of possible, imagined pasts. The practical past serves the aims of the present, which is of course the only reality, and so may permit new possibilities for human interiority and even regimes of future action. In imagining the past, then, we reimagine ourselves.

Shinran's milieu

Ironically, while Shinran (alongside Hōnen) stands today as the most revered figure in Japanese Pure Land Buddhism, and one of the standout figures in the entire history of Buddhism, he was not widely known in his own lifetime.[7] Several centuries were to pass before the movement he initiated reached its mature, institutional form as the Jōdo Shinshū (True Pure Land school or Shin Buddhism), but it eventually grew to become the largest denomination in the whole of Japanese Buddhism.[8] Shinran could be understood as taking his master Hōnen's teachings to their logical extreme. In doing so, he developed a radical theology of Other Power, one that some have judged as even falling outside the boundaries of genuine Dharma.

One of the plentiful gifts that Shinran grants us is his historicity. The details of his life story are admittedly sketchy, since few historical sources survive. The most important of these is a hagiography (saint's life) known popularly as the *Godenshō* (*The Biography*), which was written in 1295 by his great-grandson Kakunyo (1270–1351). We also have a series of letters written by his wife, Eshinni (1182–1268?), which were discovered in 1921. And of course we have access to

Shinran's own writings, which, while often focusing on scriptural quotations, offer occasional glimpses into his existential condition, especially through his pastoral letters. In one of them, for instance, he writes: 'My eyes fail me, and besides being utterly forgetful about everything, whatever it may be, I am hardly the person to clarify these matters for others' (*CWS*, p.535).

The historicity of Shinran is in marked contrast to the mythic biographies of many earlier Indian and Chinese teachers. Not that the latter don't have their value: they offer fascinating insights into how the ideal Buddhist was seen and how the archetype of the path was imagined over many centuries. In the case of Shinran, however, through his letters and through his self-searching, it feels as though he is someone we can know, even talk to, despite the many centuries that separate us. We feel that we could take tea with him. One literary critic has noted how 'all history writing requires a fictive or imaginary representation of the past.'[9] Contemplating Shinran as a living person invites us to participate in an imagined interiority, an exercise that has transformative force.

Shinran was born during a chaotic and uncertain time, a time that was beset by much anxiety. There was little or no government control over large parts of the country, and this impacted on the religious milieu. Temples paid their bills through the earnings from tax-exempt estates, often donated by wealthy landowners who wanted to get into the government's good books. But the estates had to be administered. The scholarly and aristocratic monks in charge of the temples saw themselves as above this work, and so recruited and ordained low-ranking, lay priests to fulfil menial tasks such as cooking, cleaning, farming, and so on. But the estates also required protection, and so priest-soldiers (*sōhei*) emerged, recruited from the ranks of the lay priests. As crazy as it might sound, the headquarters of the Tendai sect, on Mount Hiei, became home to so many *sōhei* that it began to resemble an armed camp.

The priest-soldiers were constantly getting into scrapes. They fought with the scholar-monks over who merited precedence, and there were frequent battles between competing temples. Arson was commonplace. The *sōhei* of one temple would torch a rival temple, and of course the rival would retaliate. Bands of *sōhei* would fight each other in temples, on Mount Hiei, or on the streets of the capital.

Grasping the underlying principles of the Dharma was rarely the priority. The lower ranks of the clergy were filled with uneducated, even thuggish, laymen while the higher ranks primarily comprised retired aristocracy. High-ranking people became priests regardless of their understanding of or commitment to the Dharma. This was problematic as some continued to live secular lives, keeping wives or concubines, and politicking.

It was not uncommon for monks who wanted to follow a more spiritual vocation to abandon the imperially sanctioned temple network in order to wander freely through the mountains and countryside, living in small huts, writing poetry, and even sharing the Dharma with the common people. A notable example was Saigyō (1118–1190), known for the long, poetic journeys he took to the north. He wrote, for instance:

> Even a person
> free of passion
> would be moved to sadness:
> autumn evening in a marsh
> where snipe fly up.[10]

There were always monks inspired by devotion towards the Dharma, but they tended to be in the minority and often did not sustain strong ties to the established institutions owing to the constraints that this inevitably imposed.[11]

Real power lay in the hands of the samurai, or warrior class, and especially from the 1150s they began to assert themselves. In 1156, the Hōgen disturbance erupted, which was a dispute between rival members of the imperial court. Two warrior clans who fought in this conflict, the Taira and the Minamoto, ended up as enemies; this provoked the Gempei war, which raged from 1180 to 1185. The Minamoto clan eventually triumphed and, in 1192, the emperor appointed its leader, Yoritomo (1147–1199), as supreme military commander or shogun of Japan. In Kamakura, he set up a tent government (*bakufu*) – basically a military dictatorship – and brought the country to heel.

The Promise of a Sacred World

During the chaos caused by war and by political instability, the welfare of the country was further weakened by a series of natural disasters, the most serious of which was the famine of 1181–1182, when tens of thousands starved to death. These were the circumstances into which Shinran was born. It required little imagination to equate such a state of affairs with the prophesied age of *mappō* (末法) or final Dharma.

Shinran was to push this acute sense of historical crisis towards even more radical conclusions, seeing it as revealing the basic nature of the human condition. *Mappō* was no longer a particular period in history, but revealed the primordial, existential reality. Greed, hatred, and ignorance are the underlying drivers of human behaviour. But the karmic burden caused by our habitual unskilfulness does not render us irredeemable. Amida's compassionate vow was proclaimed precisely to transcend our karma and so enable the liberation of all morally flawed beings. For Shinran, then, the Primal Vow of Amida applies not just to the degenerate time, but has in fact always been responding to the deepest existential call of humanity. It thus symbolizes the ever-present impulse towards transcendence.

Shinran's life

What we know of Shinran's life can be conveniently organized into four phases. The first is his early life and his initiation into Tendai monastic routine. The second is his relatively short period of study and discipleship under Hōnen, which saw him break out of the paradigm of Buddhist practice within which he had been trained thus far. The third period is his exile to Echigo province and his subsequent missionary work in the Kantō region (a zone that in modern times incorporates Tokyo). Finally, the fourth period is his long retirement, from his sixties until his death, when he returned to Kyoto and engaged in extensive literary work.

It is believed that Shinran was born into a minor aristocratic family related to the Fujiwari clan. However, the motives for which he entered the Tendai cloisters of Mount Hiei (Hieizan) at the tender age of nine are not at all certain. While later 'biographies' attribute deep spiritual motives to this step, the reality may have been more pragmatic, perhaps motivated by political or even economic considerations. There are no records of Shinran's life as a Tendai priest, and he himself does not explicitly refer to this period in his own writings. One certain detail, however, comes from the letters of Shinran's wife Eshinni. In a letter to their daughter, Kakushini, she mentions that Shinran was a hall priest or *dōsō* on Hieizan. The *dōsō* were priests of low status who served either at the Constant Practice Meditation Hall (Jōgyō Zanmaidō) or at the Lotus Hall (Hokkedō). These two buildings are located next to one another and are joined by a bridge. The Constant Practice Hall at Hieizan is dedicated to perpetual nembutsu, while the Lotus Hall focuses on *Lotus Sutra* repentance.[12] The constantly walking *samādhi* (*jōgyō zanmai*) is a form of contemplative nembutsu in which, over a period of ninety days, the devout meditator circumambulates a statue dedicated to Amida Buddha while cultivating visualization and recitation.[13] The ultimate goal of the practice is to enter a transcendent vision-world in which one sees directly all the Buddhas of the ten directions. The *dōsō* were especially associated with this intensive discipline.

Taking refuge in the Primal Vow

In 1201, after twenty years on the mountain, Shinran suffered some kind of crisis that caused him to doubt the value of his religious career and even to despair of his own enlightenment. We cannot be certain of the content of this crisis, but, given his later writings, it may have been related to an awareness of his incapacity to fulfil the ideals and principles that he was supposed to exemplify as a monk. An acute sensitivity to his personal shortcomings was to become a signature of Shinran's thought. But his crisis may also have been linked to the corruption he saw around him within the Tendai establishment: the conflicts, the politicking, the disregard for monastic vows. Maybe he realized that he was just not cut out for monastic life. After all, he didn't choose it, and yet his adolescence and early manhood were dedicated to life in the cloister. I wonder, for instance, how he dealt with his sexuality. The fact that he later married suggests that this might have been an unresolved area of his life.

Shinran's crisis led him to take the dramatic step of leaving Hieizan in search of answers. We are told that he embarked on a hundred-day retreat at Rokkakudō Temple in Kyoto, and that on the ninety-fifth day he had a vision. In essence, the vision directed him to seek out Hōnen, who had been teaching exclusive dedication to vocal nembutsu since the 1170s. In a one-page summary of his teachings written just two days before his death, Hōnen counselled: 'Even if you study Śākyamuni's whole teaching, you should still become an ignorant man who doesn't know a word... Never behave as a wise man but single-mindedly recite the nembutsu' (*Sen*, p.13).

Shinran took this advice to heart. His tutelage under Hōnen was to be relatively short-lived, but it was revolutionary in terms of his subsequent religious trajectory. He later wrote: 'I, Gutoku Shinran, disciple of Śākyamuni [Buddha], discarded sundry practices and took refuge in the Primal Vow in 1201' (*CWS*, p.290). While Shinran was not regarded as the most influential of Hōnen's disciples, at least within his own lifetime, he was nevertheless granted permission to copy his central work, the *Selection* (*Senchakushū*), and also to make a portrait of the master, which Hōnen later autographed. These were regarded as great honours. Shinran also relates that Hōnen bestowed upon him the name Shakkū and then later, following a dream, the name Zenshin. He describes Hōnen as 'the eminent founder who had enabled the essence of the Pure Land way to spread vigorously [in Japan]' (*CWS*, p.289). Shinran underlines the fact that Hōnen '[t]urned compassionately towards foolish people, both good and evil' (*CWS*, p.73), which refers to reaching outside establishment Buddhism to those unable to participate in elite forms of practice. This open-handedness was to inform his own ministry. Finally, Shinran makes reference to the 'auspicious signs' that were seen on Hōnen's death in 1212, a clear indicator of the fact that his master had realized rebirth in the Pure Land or *ojō* (往生). In fact, Shinran came to regard Hōnen as an incarnation of Amida Buddha:

Amida Tathāgata, manifesting form in this world,
Appeared as our teacher Genku [Hōnen];
The conditions for teaching having run their course,
He returned to the Pure Land. (*CWS*, p.390)

According to *Tannishō*, Shinran summed up what he learned from Hōnen in the following way: 'As for me, I simply accept and entrust myself to what my revered teacher told me, "Just say the nembutsu and be saved by Amida"; nothing else is involved' (*CWS*, p.662). Through his contact with Hōnen, Shinran gained confidence that, in spite of his failings (or – as he later believed – *because* of them), he was assured of rebirth in the Pure Land. This insight was both liberating and consoling. While it is clear that Shinran continued to regard himself as a faithful disciple of Hōnen for the rest of his life, consecrating him as the seventh master of Shin Buddhism, his mature thought expresses a radically different understanding from his teacher regarding the function of the nembutsu and of Dharma practice in general.[14]

Hōnen propagated his exclusive nembutsu teaching for around thirty years in the Kyoto area. As his following grew, he made enemies within the Buddhist establishment. Despite Hōnen issuing a seven-point pledge to conciliate his opponents, in 1205 monks from the traditional lineages petitioned the cloistered emperor to ban Hōnen's teaching on the basis of nine complaints. They included the following: establishing a new sect without official permission; slighting Śākyamuni Buddha in favour of Amida; denigrating other practices and approaches; rejecting the worship of the *kami* (indigenous gods); denying the efficacy of the precepts and even ethical behaviour; misunderstanding the true meaning of the nembutsu; and sowing disorder in the country (*Sen*, pp.17–18). These were serious charges, and it became clear that the established sects had the emperor's sympathy.

So in 1207, after just six years, Shinran was separated from his master when they were both defrocked and banished from the Kyoto region. They never met again. Shinran was sent to the remote fishing region of Echigo (now Niigata prefecture), a distance of some 550 kilometres from Kyoto, under the criminal name of Fujii Yoshizane. He married and began a family.[15] From this time onwards, Shinran referred to himself as neither monk nor layman (*hisō hizoku* 非僧非俗), concluding that the only thing that mattered was liberation through the nembutsu. Much later, this example created the pattern for a married clergy in Shin Buddhism, as well as other sects.

The Promise of a Sacred World

Shinran recalled his banishment in the following way: '[Hōnen] and a number of his followers, without receiving any deliberation of their [alleged] crimes, were summarily sentenced to death or dispossessed of their monkhood, given [secular] names, and consigned to distant banishment. I was among the latter' (CWS, p.289). We can only imagine the trauma that this banishment entailed – the humiliation, the sense of injustice, and the confusion. Shinran regarded establishment or *kenmitsu* Buddhism as spiritually bankrupt, and his indictment of it pulls no punches when, in later life, he offered the following assessment:

> Monks of Sakyamuni's tradition in the various temples,
> however, lack clear insight into the teaching and are
> ignorant of the distinction between true and provisional;
> and scholars of the Chinese classics in the capital are
> confused about practices and wholly unable to differentiate
> right and wrong paths. (CWS, p.289)

Both Shinran and Hōnen were pardoned in 1211. While his master returned to Kyoto, Shinran instead travelled to the Kantō region, more specifically Hitachi province, where he was to spend more than two decades. He began to gather a sizeable community by establishing modest *dōjō* ('places of practice') in the homes of sangha members. As a result, the Kantō sanghas became the bedrock of Shinran's following. His innovation of using hanging scrolls inscribed with the nembutsu (*myōgō honzon*) as the central object of reverence – rather than a traditional Buddha image – along with his Dharma talks and nembutsu recitation encouraged people from many walks of life to join his budding movement.

Upon his return to Kyoto around 1235 or 1236, Shinran dedicated himself to writing and correspondence. Through letters, he answered questions about doctrine and gave advice on the various issues that arose within his nascent sangha. Among his literary efforts, he completed and revised *True Teaching*, wrote various commentarial texts such as *Notes on the Essentials of Faith Alone* and *Notes on Once-Calling and Many-Calling*, and composed collections of *wasan* (hymns) that communicated the basic themes of his teaching or praised the texts and masters of the Pure Land tradition. For the most part, Shinran wrote in Japanese, which was relatively novel at that time.[16] He died in 1263 at the age of almost ninety.

Chapter Four

The Horizon of the Impossible

> I find that all beings, an ocean of multitudes, have since the beginningless past down to this day, this very moment, been evil and defiled, completely lacking the mind of purity. (*CWS*, p.95)

I cannot get enlightened. There. I said it. For a Buddhist, this sounds like a kind of blasphemy, but it also sounds a little absurd. There is nothing special about me that marks me out as uniquely incapable (although, like many of us, I often think there is). To deny the possibility of enlightenment would seem to deny the essential promise of Buddhism: liberation from all limiting habits that provoke suffering for oneself and others. The liberation from *all* limiting habits? You see what I mean? That sounds like a tall order, especially when each day seems only to confirm how those habits bite hard into my everyday thoughts and action. Can we perceive our own limitedness? Can we transcend it? It seems impossible.

At least on some readings, Buddhism presents a vision of the human being as somehow *perfectible*. If we could only apply ourselves sufficiently, if we could only see through our distorting illusions about who and what we really are, we could achieve some transcendent state of being – nirvana or enlightenment. Self-help books tell us that we have unlimited potential, and that life is about fulfilling that potential – whatever that might mean. The sky is the limit. Shinran's diagnosis, by contrast, is that we are bounded creatures, at times slaves to our calculating, deluded mind. We are not getting better every day, but all too often repeating the same old patterns.

Shinran seems to have agreed with me. He couldn't reach enlightenment either, and is reported to have said that '[i]t is impossible for us, who are possessed of blind passions, to free ourselves from birth-and-death through any practice whatever' (*CWS*, p.663). So there is no practice that we can undertake, no privileged technique that will release us from the prison that is our everyday self. If we depend on our efforts alone, he says, there is no way out of our entrapment. We are all *bonpu* (凡夫, 'foolish beings').

Shinran addresses us urgently and personally out of his own existential raggedness. His call is not theoretical but rooted in his keen awareness of his karmic failings. To underline this point, Shandao, one of Shinran's key inspirations, wrote: 'Know yourself to be a foolish being of karmic evil caught in birth-and-death, ever sinking and ever wandering in transmigration from innumerable kalpas in the past, *with never a condition that would lead to emancipation*' (*CWS*, p.679, emphasis added). This all sounds dispiriting, even defeatist, doesn't it? But Shinran goes further. Not only are we incapable of freeing ourselves from our delusion, but it is precisely our arrogant assurance that we *can* liberate ourselves that impedes us from accepting Amida's compassion. We are our own worst enemy. Shinran cites the following passage:

> In each moment, blind passions intrude a hundred or a
>   thousand times;
> Though some may hope to realize dharma-insight in this Sahā
>   world,
> They will pass kalpas countless as the Ganges' sands in the six
>   courses,
> and still the time of realization will not come. (*CWS*, p.219)

'In each moment, blind passions intrude a hundred or a thousand times.' This passage describes my habitual mind all too well. The flashes of envy, of self-pity, the craving for attention and affirmation, the petty tantrums. And so it goes on. But it is not just my mind that is like this; according to Shinran, such is the human condition. He indicates that we lack the resources to uproot our unskilful impulses. Crucially, it is only when we see deeply into the constraints of our existential predicament that a way forward can emerge through opening ourselves to Other Power.

Paul Ricoeur characterises human existence in terms of its 'primordial disproportion' and as a 'non-coincidence' with ourselves.[1] This disproportion consists in how the constraints of our embodiment contrast with our intuition of something that is infinite, our capacity to imagine something that transcends what we currently are or even could become. Our existential condition is fragile and unstable in the sense that we are the only being that is both greater and less than itself at the same time. We can aspire beyond ourselves but also fall beneath ourselves. In reflecting on our capacity to become aware of our own condition, Ricoeur notes that, 'In order for human finitude to be seen and expressed, a moment that surpasses it must be inherent in the situation, condition, or state of being finite.'[2] So there is something inherently self-transcending in human awareness that reveals itself when we awaken to our limits. It is kind of paradoxical. Shinran's religious vision seems to open up precisely this space. In his very awakening to his own limitations, he invokes something that is, in contrast, infinite: unlimited compassion, generosity, and wisdom.

Ricoeur characterizes our finitude as consisting in a limited or particularized perspective. To be human is to live in the world, and to gaze out upon it, from a bounded viewpoint. More specifically, our finitude is expressed through ethical fragility, which is our persistent tendency to transgress our best standards of conduct by acting in ways that are harmful to ourselves and others. The potential for unskilfulness is an inescapable part of the structure of being human and, far from being transcended, is underlined in the fusion of our horizon with that of Amida Buddha. Through Amida we come both to understand our existential flaws more fully and also, in some sense, to divest ourselves of them. Shinran's thought arises precisely from this tension between the constraints imposed by our finitude and the longing for what is infinite, between limitedness and the limitless, and offers the promise of connection with the superabundance that Amida epitomizes.

The smallness of our being

The French philosopher Pascal wrote: 'Then let us learn our range: we are something but we are not everything [...] the smallness of our being hides from us the sight of the infinite.'[3] In the summer of 1988 I had just completed my first year of a degree in philosophy at the University of Leeds. But I was losing touch with reality. LSD had opened up not the doors of my perception but rather the gates of hell. In one of my semi-conscious fugues, I was walking from Yate back to my parents' farm in Almondsbury, near Bristol, a distance of some nine miles. It was a hot day and I remember that I was wearing espadrilles, footwear entirely unsuited to walking along a tarmac road. Who can say what I was thinking, but I passed a church and, in my desperation, it occurred to me to go inside. Perhaps I would find some clarity there, some solace, some way forward. I had always kept the idea of God in reserve, a possibility to be turned towards in extreme need. So I sat for a while, alone among the wooden pews, miserable, existentially lost.

Some kind parishioner noticed my bedraggled presence and sat down at my side. He asked me if I wanted to pray, but in my distress I couldn't answer. He suggested that we pray together. I can't remember his exact words but they were something like this: 'Oh Lord may this young man find his way forward, may he find peace in You. May he find the Truth.' I was mute, paralyzed, and I started to cry. I was crying because I realized that the words meant nothing to me, that there was no one listening, that I was alone and I always would be. Some years later, I would read the following heart cry from the poet Rilke: 'Who, if I cried out, would hear me among the angels' hierarchies?'[4] This seemed to sum up my situation. My conception of the sacred, at least in the naive way that I had understood it until that point, was completely shattered with no possibility of repair. God was not there, there was no transcendent, nothing sacred, just the cactus land of my own mind. Just the burden of existing. God had ceased to be a 'living option'. Yet this shattering experience turned out to be the beginning of a long road towards recovering what is transcendent, a road that I am still walking, at times uncertainly, at other times with joy. This utter collapse of my self was what permitted me to open my heart to the Other Power, although it would be many years before I could formulate it this way.

We generally don't value broken things, and so often toss them aside as useless. But in the Dharma life we will be broken up, reconstituted, and broken up again. To be human is to be fragile. But this fragility does not make us weak, nor is it something that we can resolve. Rather, through attuning to our own fragility, we can become more sensitive to others. We can begin to understand that we can break them and they can break us. And we do. And they do. And this is part of the risk that is implied by human intimacy. So each of us gets broken into a thousand pieces as we are humbled by our existential fragility, exemplified so poignantly in the myth of Avalokiteśvara. And the Buddha, Dharma, and Sangha put us back together again, but never as before.

Japanese aesthetics embraces the broken in the conviction that to repair it makes the object still more beautiful. *Kintsugi* is the art of repairing broken pottery with gold. Every break is unique and, rather than repairing an item to make it look like new, the technique highlights the 'scars'. In the process of restoring what has been broken, we may create something more resilient, beautiful, and unrepeatable. Awakening to the insufficiency of self-power is a prerequisite for opening up the possibility of entrusting to the transubstantiating power of Amida's vows. Going for refuge to the Three Jewels thus becomes a living option. Amida's merit supervenes upon our karma, transcending its habitual logic, since it belongs to a higher order of conditionality. This higher order could be understood by means of the term *adhiṣṭhāna*, the benevolent power of the enlightened mind, which blesses like a radiance or a perfume that envelops us with inexhaustible sweetness. This blessing sacralizes all perception and all action.

Three approaches to awakening

There are many ways to conceive of and approach the notion of awakening. My preceptor Subhuti has offered a threefold model in order to illustrate how different Buddhist schools have understood the ultimate goal and what this implies in relation to practice.[5] These three approaches, or 'myths' as he calls them, are: self-development, self-surrender, and self-discovery. They are not necessarily mutually exclusive, nor do they exhaust the possible range of models for talking about awakening, but they can give us a convenient starting point in order to clarify some of the distinctive features of Shinran's approach to the 'great matter' (*daiji*, 大事).[6] While I will touch on all three in the brief account below, the main focus will be on the second model or myth: self-surrender.

Self-development

We could say that self-development encapsulates the classic model of the Buddhist path, at least as framed by Western consciousness. It requires striving, sustained effort over decades or even lifetimes, and consists in moving towards ever more refined states of consciousness, wisdom, and compassionate conduct. It is a result of individual endeavour: *we* make the effort, *we* reach the goal. While this approach has been aligned with contemporary notions of personal growth, it is worth saying that even the Pali Canon shows the Buddha drawing on the support of all kinds of forces both terrestrial and celestial.

The self-development model is reflected in such classic teachings as the Noble Eightfold Path. This involves the cultivation of right view, then right attitude, speech, action, livelihood, effort, awareness, and meditation. In cultivating each aspect of the path, we advance towards awakening. For Shinran, the notion of self-development or self-power (*jiriki*) became a stick with which to beat his opponents, even though they never subscribed to such an exclusive approach.[7] Most schools have generally allowed at least some role for influences that supplement self-effort, especially in the context of Mahāyāna Buddhism where devotion to Buddhas and bodhisattvas has always been central.

Self-surrender

Self-surrender is commonly associated with devotion. Shin Buddhism is routinely pigeon-holed as a devotional approach directed at lay people. It may even be disparaged as a 'popular' form of Buddhism that lacks the philosophical profundity or ethical rigour of other schools. It is seen as being about 'faith', which is often unfavourably contrasted with knowledge or wisdom. Faith is often relegated to a condition of believing but

The Promise of a Sacred World

not knowing, even believing in something that cannot be verified. It is frequently qualified by the adjective 'blind'. But faith need not be disqualified as simply a weak substitute for knowledge. It is a valid faculty of intuition in itself. In the words of Jean-Luc Marion, 'Faith does not manage the deficit of evidence – it alone renders the gaze apt to see the excess of the pre-eminent saturated phenomenon, the Revelation.'[8] In other words, faith is the capacity or faculty by means of which we attune to what is ultimate. As Paul Tillich puts it: 'Faith is the state of being ultimately concerned.'[9] Sangharakshita has characterized faith in terms of an affinity between ourselves and the Buddha, between 'what is ultimate in us and what is ultimate in the universe'.[10] It is a kind of sacred resonance, a sensitivity and responsiveness to our ultimate concerns.

At first glance, it might appear that Shin proposes little more than a simple, devotional practice. But it goes much further than that. When we think of devotion, we are perhaps most likely to focus on its affective and aesthetic aspects. But devotion is more than just *feeling*: it inspires action. It consists in aligning ourselves with something that manifests to us as transcendent, tuning into it we might say, so that we begin to resonate with it. We might analyze devotion in terms of two levels. The first is devotion without faith, which is really a form of idolatry and commonly a form of self-intoxication. Here there is no meaningful transformation or existential responsiveness. The second level of devotion acts out faith. It is not necessarily ecstatic, but may be calmer, quieter, more humble. Faith then is a receptivity to what is transcendent, a responsiveness. For Buddhism, faith or *śraddha* is a positive mental event.[11]

Self-surrender suggests that we are the agent – we are the one who does the surrendering – and that the transcendent object of our devotion passively receives our surrender. But it is just the opposite. Out of compassion, Amida reaches out to us. This might be likened to how deity visualization is understood in Tibetan Buddhism. Through our own efforts, we contemplate an image of the Buddha or bodhisattva while, at the same time, the figure reaches out and blesses us, even becomes us. When evoking the mind that is necessary to take us to the Pure Land, Shinran writes that 'The Tathāgata [Buddha] *gives* this sincere mind to all living things [...] This mind manifests the true mind of benefiting others' (*CWS*, p.95).

Consider also the following passage, in which Sangharakshita speaks about the bodhichitta:

> The *bodhichitta* is much more like a sort of higher power
> – the power of Enlightenment, if you like – which works
> through you when you are open and receptive. It's not
> 'yours' in the ordinary sense [...] it's something that takes
> you over.[12]

Jean-Luc Marion offers a way of understanding such a trans-formation by drawing on the analogy of anamorphosis. Anamorphosis is a technique applied in painting whereby a given object only becomes visible when seen from a specific viewpoint. A famous example is *The Ambassadors* (c.1533) by Hans Holbein the Younger in the National Gallery, London. On preliminary viewing, this painting has a greyish, diagonal slash across the bottom of the frame. In anamorphosis, our gaze must 'submit to the demands of the figure to be seen'.[13] In the case of Holbein's painting, when we view it from the appropriate angle, we see that the slash is in fact a human skull, a reminder of death and impermanence. Through surrendering the perspective of the uncommitted spectator and submitting ourselves to the promptings of what seeks to reveal itself, we enable the object to guide us towards it. We shift position, in either space or thought, and the phenomenon becomes visible once our gaze has satisfied the demands of the perspective.

Applying this metaphor to Amida, if we are to respond to Amida's invitation, we need to 'shift our gaze' or, in other words, to activate a new faculty, the faculty of *śraddha* or awakened imagination, which is itself a gift bestowed by Amida. Amida is the activity of enlightenment or the bodhichitta reaching out to us, but we actively resist it by insisting on the priority of our own power. Here the anamorphosis consists in relinquishing the self-development paradigm and relying instead on Other Power. In the words of Jean-Louis Chrétien: 'In the event that cuts us short and puts right every illusion of mastery, the divine is not solely what escapes our comprehension, but also *what advances toward us, seizing us and acting on us* in that very escape.'[14]

Self-discovery

The self-discovery model or paradigm sees awakening as already within us. It is inherent, even our deepest nature. Awakening is therefore something that shows itself, something that emerges. Instead of being apart from us, in some faraway future, awakening is here and now. This immediate moment has sacramental value, nothing is lacking, it is itself the sacred excess. To borrow a wonderful phrase from Bachelard, we could describe it as an aliveness to 'the brilliance of the first openings'.[15] The self-discovery model also underlines how awakening must always be mediated through our embodied, fleshly experience. Sometimes this inherent nature is conceived as a kind of seed or embryo (*tathāgatagarbha*).

Some versions of this teaching even suggest that awakening is inherent, that, in some way, we are *already* Buddhas. Buddha-nature thus highlights the spiritual impulse latent within – that part of us that yearns towards the good, true, and creative – and enshrines this as the primordial ground of human experience.

Zen is typically categorized as a self-discovery approach. Yet Dōgen writes:

> All beings who receive and utilise this water and fire [the Dharma] spread the influence of the Buddha in the original state of experience, so that those who live and talk with them, also, *are all reciprocally endowed with the limitless buddha-virtue*. Expanding and promoting their activity far and wide, they permeate the inside and the outside of the entire universe with the limitless, unceasing, unthinkable, and incalculable Buddha-Dharma.[16]

So we can already see that the dividing line between our efforts and the efforts of others is not absolute; their practice will inevitably influence ours, as ours will influence theirs.

The three orientations just described could be characterized as: (a) 'I become the Buddha', (b) 'the Buddha becomes me', and (c) 'the Buddha is within me' (or 'the Buddha *is* me'). According to these respective models, awakening may be earned, gifted, or inherent. Rarely have any of these models been applied in isolation, and they have often overlapped to differing degrees and in varying combinations. While throughout Buddhist history they have regularly been placed in tension or even opposition, they need not be. None can fully exhaust the mystery of awakening, and so we might reformulate them as three *sacred dimensions* of relation to the 'great matter'. While Shinran's perspective is most likely to be read in terms of the second position, 'the Buddha becomes me', it would also seem to share aspects of the third, that is to say, the Buddha *is* me or, better, the Buddha emerges from within me. I will say more about this in Chapter 13.

Self-surrender or self-collapse?

Self-surrender sounds quite appealing, poetic, even aesthetic. We may have a vision of ourselves prostrating before a Buddha at Bodh Gaya with ghee lamps flickering all around, or solemnly placing our forehead at the feet of the Dalai Lama in rapt devotion. But the self doesn't really want to surrender. It will do anything to avoid it. The habitual self has no interest in giving itself up, and so often 'self-surrender' just becomes another means of confirming and bolstering the self. It may also become a naive handing over of responsibility for oneself to some spiritual authority with all the attendant danger that implies. It is not an anamorphosis but rather a kind of spiritual consumerism or a romantic attachment. This is why utter failure can be helpful. Self-help books teach us that failure is not a bad thing because it builds our character so that we may later succeed. This is the stuff of Hollywood films: we fail at first, things are tough, but then we overcome the challenges and live happily ever after. But according to Shinran we will *always* fail in the project of getting ourselves enlightened because there is something inherently disordered about the project itself. It is a self-centred, self-confirming, acquisitive enterprise. Enlightenment becomes something to be *added on* to the self, rather than something that requires the renunciation, the giving up, even the total collapse of that self. The breaking up of the self is another way of talking about spiritual death, which is essential if we are to realize spiritual rebirth, if we are to realize our identity with Amida Buddha.

When the self has completely exhausted its own efforts and can do no more, we may reach the most creative edge of ourselves. In the words of Wendell Berry:

> It may be that when we no longer know what to do we
> have come to our real work, and that when we no longer
> know which way to go we have come to our real journey.
> The mind that is not baffled is not employed. The impeded
> stream is the one that sings.[17]

The 'Parable of the white path'

Shandao formulated a celebrated parable of the existential predicament known as the 'Parable of the white path', which illustrates the process of reaching the limits of self-power and being drawn forward by the call of Other Power.[18] It concerns a lone traveller who plans to travel hundreds of miles to the west. Unexpectedly, he comes across two rivers blocking his way: one, flowing south, is a torrent of fire; the other, snaking north, is a river of water. Both rivers are just a hundred steps wide, but forbiddingly deep and long. The only way to safety is across a narrow, white path, just a few inches wide, between the rivers. However, the waves of the water constantly rise up and break over the path, submerging it, and the flames from the fiery river scorch it. It would seem impossible to cross over.

It gets worse. As he reaches the bank of the two rivers, the man is assailed by robbers and savage beasts intent on attacking and killing him. He is trapped. Left to his own devices, the traveller will die, but, in his darkest despair, he resolves to try the narrow path, however risky it may seem. At this moment, he hears a voice from the eastern side encouraging him. From the western bank he hears a second voice that beckons him, and so he steps forward on to the path. After just a couple of paces he hears the robbers calling him back, sowing doubt in his mind. 'The path is too dangerous. You are bound to die... better to turn back', they cry. But the traveller pays no attention and firmly proceeds to the western bank where, greeted by kind friends, he rejoices in having overcome the perils that he faced.

Shandao goes on to explain that the eastern bank corresponds to saṃsāra, or the unenlightened condition, which is like a house on fire. The western bank is the Pure Land of Sukhāvatī. The surging waves that wash over the path represent greed, while the flames stand for hatred. The encouraging voice from the eastern bank is Śākyamuni Buddha urging the man forward, while the beckoning voice from the western bank is Amida Buddha. The white path itself stands for the aspiration to be reborn in the Pure Land, which is fragile and vulnerable. The parable repays repeated reflection, but the central message seems to be that the darkest hour will call forth Amida's compassionate light. Unfailingly, Amida responds to the needs of the spiritually destitute.

In reflecting on the paradoxes of the 'Parable of the white path', we could think of the Pure Land as Amida themself, as the horizon of illumined reality, always in front of us but yet beckoning us, bursting towards awareness. Amida's body, as light, extends towards us as compassion, as the path itself. The Pure Land is what is always in the offing, promising itself as a transformation of consciousness, as an opening onto an infinite dimension. It evokes the impossible, which, in the words of John Caputo, 'does not describe the domain of what is, but of what calls'.[19] The impossible is what calls us forward, it is 'something unforeseeable that shatters our horizons of expectation'.[20]

Part 2

Cascade of Blessing

My eyes being hindered by blind passions,
I cannot perceive the light that grasps me;
Yet the great compassion, without tiring,
Illumines me always. (*CWS*, p.385)

Chapter Five

Shared Out in Endless Abundance

Amida has been called 'Buddha of unhindered light filling the ten quarters' [...] This Tathāgata is light. Light is none other than wisdom; wisdom is the form of light. Wisdom is, in addition, formless; hence this Tathāgata is the Buddha of inconceivable light. This Tathāgata fills the countless worlds in the ten quarters, and so is called 'Buddha of boundless light'. (*CWS*, p.486)

Infinite brightness

Amida Buddha never walked this earth, never went on alms round, and never washed feet that were dusty from hours of walking. Amida's form gives itself as an icon by means of which enlightenment is revealed to us. Amida is the source of liberation and of all existential value. Amida is not an object nor even a subject, but more like a flavour or a scent, something subtle: there but not there. Amida is light, and light is what makes visible, what permits perceptions. Light is awareness. Amida is infinite brightness. But Amida's light is not just ordinary awareness, that half-sleep of daily routine in which our revealed world is consumed and even devoured rather than wondered at. Instead, Amida evokes a kind of consecrated awareness, or rather reminds us that all perception is ultimately sacramental. Amida's infinite light, which blesses all with wisdom and compassion, hints at an iconizing awareness, one that is capable of seeing everything as saturated with reality, with supernumerary meaning, an awareness that is constantly giving itself but which can never be fully assimilated. It is always new and yields inexhaustible fruits. Amida gives constantly and without reserve, generously and without the possibility of depletion, like a well that can never be emptied. Amida evokes what one philosopher has called a 'sacramental return', by means of which the extraordinary is revealed through the medium of the ordinary.[1] Amida evokes an awareness that blesses and loves rather than seeks to exploit or destroy.

You may be more accustomed to conceive of the Buddha as a terrestrial being – one who belongs to human history, who walked this earth yet awakened to some extraordinary, transformative insights. The Buddha then is special, yes, but not radically different from us. The Buddha was born, as we are born. He appears to us as more or less comprehensible, recognizable, albeit perhaps much wiser than we are. But Amida is not of this nature. Amida is not the historical Buddha but an archetypal reality that transcends space and time, and became central to much of East Asian Buddhism, often eclipsing the importance of even Śākyamuni himself. Amida or Amitābha is the Buddha of infinite or boundless light. They are also known as Amitāyus, or 'boundless life'. They are sometimes depicted as golden in colour, sometimes as dark red – the colour of the setting sun – and sit in meditative contemplation, radiating light throughout the cosmos, a light that blesses all beings with both wisdom and compassion, without exception and without conditions.

Amida is awakening awareness, the sun lighting up the darkness, the gift of light that impartially and inexhaustibly shines on all. Amida is both infinite light and infinite life. In terms of both space and time Amida calls forth a reality that is beyond measure, beyond limit, beyond reckoning. Amida overflows our perceptual categories. We so readily take light for granted, yet it remains utterly mysterious. Light is indivisible, unbounded, and invisible. Light permits seeing, and so serves as a symbol of consciousness and of wisdom. Light bedazzles us, light reveals. In her short poem 'Bearing the light', Denise Levertov contemplates how raindrops hanging from the branches of a pear tree are lit up by the morning light:

> Rain-diamonds, this winter morning,
> embellish the tangle of unpruned pear-tree twigs;
> each solitaire, placed, it appears, with considered judgement,
> bears the light beneath the rifted clouds –
> the indivisible shared out in endless abundance.[2]

Light is 'shared out in endless abundance' and yet remains indivisible. This is the mystery of light. It is not an object itself but a condition under which objects are seen, by means of which they are able to reveal themselves. Objects 'bear the light'. Light gives life. Light is awakening.

Amida appears as a Buddha although, as Shinran himself wrote, 'Amida's form is altogether impossible to explain' (*CWS*, p.328). Moreover, in the words of my teacher, Sangharakshita, Amida is not just one Buddha among many 'but Buddhahood itself in the most beautiful and adorable form conceivable'.[3] He goes on to say: '[Amida] is wisdom and compassion not only in their fullness but in their overflowingness. He [*sic*] is the most highly transcendent and the most deeply immanent. In him absolute reality manifests as the supreme beauty out of infinite love.'[4] So Amida epitomizes the principle of spiritual awakening, of Buddhahood.

According to the *Larger Pure Land Scripture*, in a lifetime many aeons ago, Amida was known as Dharmākara ('treasure of Dharma').[5] Dharmākara was inspired to renounce his secular power as a king and go forth into the Dharma life as a bodhisattva (awakening being). This meant to tread the path towards awakening not just for his own benefit but for the benefit of all beings. Like all bodhisattvas, Dharmākara made a series of vows that expressed his supreme aspiration. In fact, the *Larger Scripture* mostly comprises variations on the formula of the bodhisattva vow. So inspired is Dharmākara that he vows not only to gain awakening for himself alone but to create a miraculous land, known as a Buddha-field (or Pure Land), which will offer the ideal conditions for all beings to awaken.[6] This land is known as Sukhāvatī: the 'happy land'. Dharmākara pledges to create not just any Buddha-field but one that combines all the qualities of *all* other Buddha-fields in one. He then dedicates five cosmic ages to gathering these qualities together. The Pure Land that he finally assembles can be thought of as the epitome of his untold spiritual merit, accumulated through many aeons of dedicated Dharma practice.

In the *Larger Scripture*, Dharmākara makes a series of forty-eight cosmic vows, which guarantee all kinds of spectacular outcomes once he has gained full awakening.[7] The vows have a conditional structure. In essence, Dharmākara affirms that he only wishes to gain awakening if all his vows are to be fulfilled. The most celebrated of these is the Eighteenth Vow:

> May I not gain possession of perfect awakening if, once I have attained Buddhahood, any among the throng of living beings in the ten regions of the universe should single-mindedly desire to be reborn in my land with joy, with confidence, with gladness, and if they should bring to mind this aspiration for even ten moments of thought and yet not gain rebirth there.[8]

The *Larger Scripture* confirms that Dharmākara *did* go on to gain full awakening, since he became Amitābha Buddha, and consequently all of the vows *have* been fulfilled, including the Eighteenth Vow. This means that rebirth in the Pure Land is assured for those who follow the guidance of the vow. Many of the other vows offer similar guarantees.

Another key vow is the nineteenth, which reads:

> May I not gain possession of perfect awakening if, once I have attained Buddhahood, any among the throng of living beings in the ten regions of the universe resolves to seek awakening, cultivates all the virtues, and single-mindedly aspires to be reborn in my land, and if, when they approached the moment of their death, I did not appear before them, surrounded by a great assembly.[9]

This vow is the source of the belief that Amitābha will come to meet the devotee on his or her deathbed and guide them towards the Pure Land. This dramatic encounter has been widely depicted in classical Japanese *raigō* paintings and enacted through deathbed nembutsu practice. Such practice emphasized the importance of calling on Amitābha at the moment of death. While this interpretation of Pure Land devotion was widespread, Shinran would emphasize the assurance of birth in this present moment as the primary, existential opening.

The cosmic range of Amitābha's vows signals an existential shift away from the individual fulfilment of the bodhisattva path

　　　　　　　　The Promise of a Sacred World

towards a spiritual outlook that places unwavering confidence in the grace of the transcendent Buddha. No longer is it our onerous responsibility to tread the demanding path towards awakening; instead, awakening is fulfilled on our behalf, and we participate in it through our receptivity to Amitābha's inexhaustible compassion. Perhaps it all sounds too easy. We will see below that this deceptively simple narrative hints at some far-reaching existential insights.

The medium of Amitābha's grace is their infinite light, which exerts a transforming influence on those blessed by its all-pervading rays, which is everyone. Through Amitābha's blessing, beings not only feel overjoyed but also begin to turn their lives around. They begin to fathom the true value of their being in the world. This transforming impact is conceptualized in terms of a transfer of merit from Amitābha to all beings. Since Amitābha pursued the bodhisattva ideal for many aeons, they have a lot of merit to go around – an infinite amount, in fact. By means of their measureless light this merit is perpetually gifted to all beings. We are always in the process of receiving and rejoicing in this incalculable blessing.

Amida attained Buddhahood in the infinite past

While Shinran lived in thirteenth-century Japan, Amida's historical origins may be traced back to ancient Indian sources, where they were known as Amitābha. The two main scriptures that recount Amitābha's legend are known as the *Larger* and *Smaller Pure Land Scriptures*, and were probably written in northwest India after 100 CE but became better known through their Chinese translations.[10] A third scripture, popularly known as the *Contemplation Sutra*, recounts a series of contemplative visions that disclose the sublime characteristics of the Pure Land and of Amitābha. This text was composed some time later, perhaps in Central Asia or China.[11] Collectively, these three texts became known as the Pure Land scriptures.

While Amitābha emerges in the Buddhist scriptural record as one among a number of transcendent or archetypal Buddhas and in texts created several centuries after the death of the historical Buddha, even in early Buddhism there was an understanding that there was more than one Buddha. To understand this context, it may help to recap some Buddhist cosmology. According to Indian tradition, the universe is cyclical and passes through periods of evolution and degeneration. This also applies to the rise and fall of the Dharma. In each cosmic cycle, there is a period before the Dharma arises, a period during which a Buddha appears and his teachings hold sway, and then a period of decline and decay. The notion of a decadent age of Dharma (*mappō*) was to become central to Shinran's reliance on Other Power, as we shall see. Given this cyclical view of the universe, it follows that there have been previous Buddhas, perhaps even an infinite number of them. Early Buddhist tradition attests to a Buddha before Śākyamuni (the present Buddha), who in turn was preceded by a long line of Buddhas that dissolve into the legendary mist. Moreover, there will be a future Buddha, known as Maitreya, who will revive the Dharma once it has disappeared once more.

So, even in early Buddhism, we encounter a mythic universe in which there are multiple Buddhas reaching back to the primordial past, not just a single, historical individual who flourished briefly in ancient India. Mahāyāna cosmology expanded this conception of the universe. Rather than there being just one world system, these are now innumerable, extending endlessly through all directions of space. It follows from this that there should be Buddhas in each of these different world systems, not just our own. So for Mahāyāna cosmology, there is not just a lineage of Buddhas reaching back into the primordial past, but multiple Buddhas may exist simultaneously in different universes. These universes may even interpenetrate.

In the *Lotus Sutra*, after recounting the traditional story of his awakening, the Buddha declares: 'It has been immeasurable, boundless hundreds, thousands, ten thousands, millions of nayutas of kalpas since I in fact attained Buddhahood.'[12] This is a spectacular revelation. The Buddha did not get enlightened in the recent past but immeasurably long ago – so long ago that we may as well think of him as eternal. This underscores the idea that the Buddha exemplifies something that is in fact transcendent, a cosmic influence that exists at all times and in all places – a quite different conception from the historically rooted Buddha that is commonly read into the early scriptures. To put this another way, enlightenment is not a moment within the sequence of time as we usually conceive it but rather disrupts that time. The Buddha breaks in on us. The Buddha of the *Lotus Sutra* goes on to say: 'Ever since [gaining awakening] I have been constantly in this saha world, preaching the Law, teaching and converting, and elsewhere I have led and benefited living beings in hundreds, thousands, ten thousands, millions of nayutas and asamkhyas of lands.'[13] This indicates that there is in fact just one Buddha who may manifest at different times, in different places, and in different guises. Moreover, they are an active force continually reaching out across different worlds in order to draw all beings towards awakening. Shinran affirms that Amida is not just one among a number of Buddhas but rather the 'primordial Buddha who embodies the essence of all Buddhas'.[14]

Although he recognizes the value of calling on other Buddhas and suggests that they are basically one, Shinran reserves a special place for Amida, owing to the spectacular scope and content of their vows. He writes, for example, that 'Amida attained Buddhahood in the infinite past [...] took the form of Śākyamuni Buddha and appeared in Gaya' (*CWS*, p.349). Thus Amida epitomizes the principle of awakening itself that may manifest in different places and at different times in the form of 'innumerable personified and accommodated bodies' (*CWS*, p.461).

Shinran differentiates between two kinds or levels of 'Dharma-body' when speaking of the Buddha. The first is identified as the Dharma-body as *suchness* and the second is the Dharma-body as *compassionate means*.[15] Shinran notes that the 'Dharma-body as suchness has neither color nor form; thus, the mind cannot grasp it, nor words describe it. From this oneness was manifested form, called dharma-body as compassionate means.'[16] For Shinran, Amida occupies an intermediate position between the 'Dharma-body as compassionate means' and the formless essence of the Buddha. This mediating position between form and formlessness is reflected in the idea that Amida takes the form of light, and is also known as the 'Tathāgata of unhindered light filling the ten quarters'. Light enables us to see the forms of things just as they are. It is able to illuminate these forms precisely because it is 'itself without color and without form'. As a formless form, we might say, light is the form of the formless par excellence (*CWS*, pp.461–2). Amida is ultimately the formless form of infinite light – a metaphor for wisdom and compassion – that pervades the cosmos.

The Buddha's three bodies

Amitābha's nature can be opened out still further through making use of a later model of the Buddha known as the *trikāya* or three bodies. The first body is the *dharmakāya* or 'body of truth'. Even early Buddhism made a distinction between the Buddha as a human individual and the body of his teachings (*dharmakāya*). For instance, the Pali Canon records the Buddha as saying: 'He who sees the Dharma, sees me.'[17] In addition, *dharmakāya* signified the *qualities* of a Buddha: those things that distinguished him from ordinary, unawakened people. Some Mahāyāna schools integrated the notion that the teachings were the true Dharma-body into the practice of text worship. So listening, reading, or worshipping Dharma texts enables us to contact the Buddha's spiritual charisma.

We can also understand the *dharmakāya* as the principle of enlightenment itself, and even as the ungraspable nature of reality as revealed through all things. Shinran writes:

> *Nirvana* has innumerable names. It is impossible to give them in detail; I will list only a few. Nirvana is called extinction of passions, the uncreated, peaceful happiness, eternal bliss, true reality, dharma-body, dharma-nature, suchness, oneness, and Buddha-nature. Buddha-nature is none other than Tathāgata. This Tathāgata pervades the countless worlds; it fills the hearts and minds of the ocean of all beings. Thus, plants, trees, and land all attain Buddhahood. (*CWS*, p.461)

This image of plants, trees, and land attaining Buddhahood evokes the idea of awakening as something omnipresent, revealing itself to us through everything and in every moment. So we do not exactly attain enlightenment but, rather, enlightenment is the deeper context within which all life unfolds. This reminds me of a startling passage written by Shinran's contemporary, the Zen mystic Dōgen:

> Trees and grasses, wall and fence expound and exalt the Dharma for the sake of ordinary people, sages, and all living beings. Ordinary people, sages, and all living beings in turn preach and exalt the Dharma for the sake of trees, grasses, wall and fence.[18]

The second body of the trio is the *sambhogakāya* or 'body of mutual enjoyment'. We might also understand this as the 'Dharma-body as compassionate means'. The *sambhogakāya* is revealed through the subtle forms of celestial Buddhas. These transcendent beings may be encountered in states of meditation, in visions, or in Buddha-fields. They reveal themselves in order to help us break free of our existential fetters. Amida is this Buddha transcendent, the Buddha in glory, the saturated agent who blesses us, who breaks in on our ignorance. Amida reveals to us the deepest truths of human existence by manifesting as the persona of reality itself.

The final, and most earthly, body is the *nirmāṇakāya* or 'body of transformation'. In the first instance, this is identified with Śākyamuni, the Buddha in the world. For some schools, this Buddha was no more than a phantom, a magic show. Out of compassion, the Buddha incarnated as an ordinary mortal and demonstrated the ideal spiritual life in order to inspire others. He was actually fully awakened all along. Shinran indicates that Śākyamuni was in fact the manifestation of Amida on earth (*CWS*, p.349). The *nirmāṇakāya* might also take other forms besides the human body, such as a book, a statue, or a falling leaf. For Shinran, the most important form taken by the transcendent Buddha is not anthropomorphic but the nembutsu itself. *Namu Amida Butsu* is the Buddha as revealed through sound.

Amida as Buddha-nature

Shinran also understands Amida in relation to the notion of Buddha-nature, the third 'myth' of awakening that was outlined in Chapter 4. According to this model, we have within us the seed of Buddhahood, which, when revealed, enables us to realize that we are not different from the Buddha. Bringing Amida in relation to the idea of Buddha-nature indicates that Amida may be understood as something that is extrinsic to us, reaching towards us from outside, as it were. At the same time, Amida may symbolize something that is *within* us, inherent, which is obscured or buried by the clouds of our delusive tendencies. On this reading, then, Amida is not alien to us but is, rather, our deepest nature. Shinran writes that 'Buddha-nature is Tathāgata (Buddha). This Tathāgata pervades the countless worlds; it fills the hearts and minds of the ocean of all beings' (*CWS*, p.461).

It is common to conceive of Buddha-nature as a kind of metaphysical principle, something abstract, either a potential or a way of talking about an existential fundament that is currently not disclosed to consciousness. What is so compelling about bringing Amida in relation to the idea of Buddha-nature is that it becomes *personified*. Buddha-nature becomes a personal, compassionate force that is seeking to make itself known through us for the benefit of all beings. Soga Ryōjin writes: 'Buddha nature [found as ideal in the self], *must be seen as coming from a spiritual realm beyond the self*. We must, namely, consider it to be a shadow image of the really existing Tathāgata.'[19]

The apparent contradiction between Amida on the one hand being outside us and, on the other, being inside points to the paradoxical nature of awakening and the fact that we are in the realm of myth, metaphor, and poetic truth. Amida is not literally 'out there'. But neither is it adequate to reduce Amida simply to a symbol for our enlightened potential since this would be to coopt Amida into little more than a content of our ego-world. The whole idea of 'inside' and 'outside' has its limits. Amida is the dissolving of our ego-world into a compassionate responsiveness to all life. This hints at a non-dual awareness that goes beyond the hard distinction between subject and object. It is possible then to conceive of Amida as both immanent and transcendent at the same time. While generally the language of Pure Land Buddhism favours transcendent metaphors and images, when taken too literally they may end up reinforcing the dualism that Other Power is concerned to dissolve. In the words of Paul Tillich, religious symbols always point to our ultimate concern, to what we cherish as holy: 'They must express an object that by its very nature transcends everything in the world that is split into subjectivity and objectivity. A real symbol points to an object which never can become an object.'[20]

The illumined image

Amida epitomizes a spiritual reality that can perhaps never be fully known. It cannot be assimilated or trapped by the controlling, egocentric tendency but is, instead, always beyond the horizon calling us, calling on us. It can never be fully known, or fully ours, because it is always in the process of being disclosed and received. It cannot be grasped, only revealed.

Amida can never become an object of our world upon whom, or which, we can fix our masterly gaze. In naming Amida, we do not summon them, we do not capture their reality in the way that we believe ourselves capable of knowing a cup or a shoelace. Rather, Amida gives themself to our intuition as what Jean-Luc Marion has called a 'saturated phenomenon', which 'submerges, exceeds – in short, saturates – the measure of each and every concept. What is given disqualifies every concept.'[21] A saturated phenomenon outstrips our capacity to interpret it. It overflows our categories of classification and so cannot be adequately framed within any particular concept. Amida has this nature. To 'know' Amida requires a reversal of our usual assumptions concerning the acquisition of knowledge. Owing to the excess, an *undoing* of knowledge is needed. This results in a kind of paradoxical knowing that consists in knowing that we do not know, and invites a radical openness and humility. In Shinran's words, 'I have no idea whether the nembutsu is truly the seed for my being born in the Pure Land or whether it is the karmic act for which I must fall into hell' (*CWS*, p.661).

Amida is an inexhaustible reservoir of value that exceeds all attempts to make them fully visible. We do not capture Amida as a constituent of our world, but rather Amida constitutes or reconstitutes us through giving over their incalculable merits. To know Amida means to cooperate with a never-finished process of being configured as inherently fallible and insufficient and yet, at the same time, *transfigured* under the blessing of Amida's infinite light.

While it is relatively easy to understand who Amida is in terms of their mythic narrative, and even in terms of their historical emergence as a focus for Buddhist devotion, it is less easy to pin down who or what Amida signifies in existential or soteriological terms. Myth reaches towards something that cannot be said, towards the invisible. Bultmann argues that living mythically means to believe that 'the world and human life have their ground and their limits in a power which is beyond all that we can calculate or control'.[22]

So what might it mean for us to take the myth of Amida seriously? What is the power beyond that it points towards? The Amida myth encapsulates an orientation, a comportment towards reality, that goes beyond the egocentric will and that serves the aims of compassion. Amida reaches out to us *as though* from outside although, as we have noted, Amida can also be understood as a force latent *within us* that seeks expression, like a seed longing to explode into life. Moreover, Amida may be understood as something that we already are, an existential dimension that is always true, always being revealed, the dimension of our ultimate concern. Lived subjectively, Amida is the impulse towards awakening coming alive within us.

To approach Amida means to abandon our illusory posture as masterly spectators, and open up to a more receptive, decentred perception within which Amida's radiance reveals itself as blessing. It means activating our imagination, adopting a new kind of 'gaze', if you will, which implies nothing less than a conversion of the fictional 'I' that bears this gaze and even its transcendence. Amida reveals the profound depths of reality by means of what Subhuti has called an 'illumined image'. An image of this kind 'carries the mystery of Enlightenment to us so that we may contemplate it and finally realise it'.[23] In calling on Amida, we go for refuge to the Buddha, which is another way of saying that we open ourselves to the principle of awakening and begin to identify ourselves with it.

The imagination transfigures all experience by awakening its symbolic possibilities. Through the image of Amida we glimpse

The Promise of a Sacred World

our own enlightened potential and begin to call this down into the world, into ourselves. We begin to embody Amida. To live within Other Power means to be guided by a compassionate impulse that can never fully belong to us – perhaps we belong to it – an impulse we can never appropriate but that we can serve and so begin to embody through our daily lives.

Chapter Six

The True Intent

> To reveal the true teaching: It is the *Larger Sutra of the Buddha of Immeasurable Life*. The central purport of this sutra is that Amida, by establishing the incomparable Vows, has opened wide the dharma-storehouse, and full of compassion for small, foolish beings, selects and bestows the treasure of virtues [...] Thus, to teach the Tathāgata's Primal Vow is the true intent of this sutra; the Name of the Buddha is its essence. (*CWS*, p.7)

This passage forms the second paragraph of Shinran's most systematic work, *True Teaching*. In it, he sets out his convictions in relation to doctrinal classification and the hierarchy of teachings and texts. For him, the 'true teaching' is unquestionably the *Larger Scripture*, and its primary purpose is to reveal the significance of the Primal Vow, which is the Eighteenth Vow, and the unparalleled virtues inherent in Amida's name. Shinran thus telegraphs his intention to read the entire Buddhist tradition in the light of the *Larger Scripture*, which results in a creative reinterpretation of his textual inheritance and a highly original vision of Dharma practice. For him, the *Larger Scripture* is the visible edge of a gestalt that may be unfolded into the world through his sacred hermeneutics.

Approaching the Pure Land scriptures

As readers and interpreters of the Pure Land scriptures, we find ourselves in very different circumstances from Shinran's, and this will inform the understandings that we come to. We are, for instance, free to pick up a translation of one of the three Pure Land scriptures from an online bookstore (or even to read a free version online) and, unencumbered by traditional interpretive constraints, read it from beginning to end, much like reading a novel. Leaving aside the interpretive strategies that we have learned as part of being modern humans, our way of reading is very different from how Shinran, and indeed any traditional Buddhist, would have approached the texts. First, we probably won't begin with the assumption that we are reading a sacred text. We live in a world that is saturated with words, and where we have access to a seemingly infinite fund of texts both secular and religious. Our relationship with texts is most commonly one of consumption: we seek entertainment or practical knowledge to apply to everyday life. From time to time we read in search of solace or to enlarge the imagination, and this may open a crack through which what is sacred may begin to shine through. The Islamic mystic Suhrawardi wrote: 'The encounter with suprasensory reality can come about through a certain way of reading a written text.'[1] In other words, a text may be the catalyst that opens up for us the sacred dimension of existence. This implies a different style of reading, one informed by the urgency of our ultimate concerns.

What might it be like to read like this? It means to understand texts as messengers of the sacred. They offer us intimations of something transcendent that, while invisible, is nevertheless sensed, like electricity or perfume in a crowd of people. This implies the activation of additional senses, a kind of existential attentiveness, a patient receptivity. Sangharakshita has hinted at a way of reading that does not engage in discursive mental activity, 'so that the import of the sutra, bypassing the rational mind, would be able to penetrate directly to the imaginal faculty of the reader and even to awaken his or her innate Buddha-wisdom'.[2] He suggests that such an approach is particularly relevant to scriptures that speak the language of myth and symbol rather than concepts.

We also read the Pure Land scriptures with the benefit of knowing how they are historically situated. We know that they evolved according to particular circumstances, needs, and interests, and how, through translation, they were often modified or reinterpreted. We now know, for instance, that a number of versions of the Pure Land texts were redacted over time, as ideas developed and consolidated.

The Promise of a Sacred World

They do not speak with a single, coherent voice. For Shinran, however, all of the Buddhist scriptures were Buddha-Dharma, so the question was: how do we make sense of their scope and contradictions? As noted above, Shinran's vision enshrines the *Larger Scripture* as the core text and draws on the other two scriptures either to support or to finesse it. This approach is clearly evident in *Passages on the Types of Birth in the Pure Land Sutras*, where he ranks the three scriptures according to how far they favour the teaching of Other Power (*CWS*, pp.637ff.). He identifies the Eighteenth Vow found in the *Larger Scripture* as the most complete expression of Amida's compassionate promise, and also emphasizes the twenty-second vow, which he glosses as 'The Vow of great love and great compassion' since it is concerned with the aspiration to return to this world in order to help liberate others (*CWS*, p.663). This vow draws out more explicitly the altruistic context of Shinran's Pure Land orientation. He goes on to equate the nineteenth vow with the message of the *Contemplation Scripture*, which 'takes the self-power within the Other Power as its central purport' (*CWS*, p.645). Shinran most definitely regards this as an inferior orientation, since he asserts that 'the kinds of birth in accordance with the *Contemplation Sutra* are all birth into the provisional transformed lands' (*CWS*, p.645). Finally, Shinran reads the *Shorter Scripture* in the light of the twentieth vow, which he interprets as revealing an intermediate orientation. Thus he categorizes the three scriptures in terms of a hierarchy of profundity. We will look at this topic from the point of view of Shinran's own trajectory of religious transformation when we consider his teaching of 'turning through the three vows' (see Chapter 10).

Palimpsestic reading

A palimpsest is a piece of writing material on which the original text has been erased to allow for reuse. Often, traces of the prior text remain or can be detected using specialist techniques.[3] We might say that Shinran intuits that underneath the *Larger Scripture*, and indeed underneath all three Pure Land scriptures, there is a kind of hidden text that expresses its true and essential meaning. It is as though he sees a primordial text, unwritten, of which the visible texts are reflections or expressions, and which is revealed to him through them. This palimpsest is really the direct blessing of Amida himself. I have often had the sensation that Sangharakshita functioned in a similar kind of way, as though there were another level to the text that illuminated the words on the page and that enabled him to interpret their deeper meaning. As though the visible traces were just the imperfect transcription of some transcendent text that, we might say, is fundamentally awakening itself.

Shinran sees a unity and an overarching message in the Pure Land scriptures that is not visible in the texts themselves. Far from it: they show clear points of disagreement that reflect the fact they were not created as a unity. There is nothing to indicate why one of the three texts should be prioritized above the others. There is nothing in the texts to suggest that the Eighteenth Vow is the key not just to the *Larger Scripture* but to all three Pure Land scriptures, and even to the whole of Buddhism itself. But this is what Shinran sees. Of course he didn't come to this understanding alone. The root teachers who catalyzed his Dharmic awakening led him towards this unifying vision, which, ultimately, enabled him to distil the vast heritage of Buddhist wisdom into a 'life regime': the nembutsu.

Shinran approaches the Pure Land scriptures, and indeed the works of revered masters, as palimpsests, which permits him to apply a hermeneutic framework that contrasts between 'an explicit meaning and implicit, hidden, inner meaning' (*CWS*, p.212). This enables him to discern a deeper meaning inherent within the texts and to conclude that 'what is true in the three sutras has as its essence the selected Primal Vow. What is provisional in the three sutras is essentially the practice of various roots of good' (*CWS*, p.221). So, even though two of the scriptures don't even mention the Primal Vow, Shinran determines that it is, nevertheless, their underlying message. Accordingly, the plentiful references to the importance of cultivating skilful action – self-power practice, in other words – are relegated to the 'provisional' teaching of the scriptures.

Scripture as vision-world

Among the distinctive features of Mahāyāna scriptures is the concept of *samādhi* (vision-world). While in some contexts this term refers in a general way to meditation techniques, here it indicates contemplative visualization.[4] The scriptures do not merely describe a vision-world, they *constitute* it through serving as a template for visualization. They are 'blueprints for something to be constructed in the mind'.[5] They are existential dramas in which we participate. To 'read' one of the Pure Land scriptures is to enter the vision-world that it discloses and be transformed in doing so.

The Three Pure Land scriptures evoke a transcendent realm, but it is a realm that also spills over into our own lived world.[6] The narrative of the scriptures takes place within transhistorical or mythic time, and unfolds within an infinite dimension that reflects the vast scope and sacred dignity of their contents. This mythic time and dimension are never closed off from our ordinary sense of time and space, since the two interpenetrate. The scriptures reveal a sacred reality of incalculable Buddhas and innumerable universes. These spectacular and unbounded visions invite us, the reader or participant, into a transformative awareness.

The myth of Dharmākara

The *Larger Scripture* runs to about seventy pages in English translation, and is framed around a dialogue between Śākyamuni Buddha and Ananda, his long-time attendant and disciple.[7] The setting is Vulture's Peak, near the city of Rājagṛha.[8] So far, the scene and characters are familiar from the early Buddhist scriptures. But the primary framing story contains within it a secondary story, which is that of the bodhisattva Dharmākara and his epic path towards becoming Amitābha Buddha (Amida). This story takes place in the ancestral past, during the time of a previous Buddha known as Lokeśvararāja. The bulk of the text is devoted to Dharmākara's bodhisattva vows (*praṇidhāna*), to lavish descriptions of the Pure Land of Sukhāvatī, and to extolling Amitābha Buddha's virtues.

The introductory part of the text focuses on the cosmic scene and the assembly of illustrious beings. In particular, it describes the spiritual trajectory and virtues of the bodhisattvas. We learn that they all follow the same archetypal pattern, which is more or less modelled on what we know of the Buddha's life. Ananda then pops up and points out that the Buddha appears especially radiant, and he wonders whether this is because he is contemplating all other Buddhas. The Buddha doesn't answer directly, but, seemingly pleased with the question, extols some of the virtues of the Buddhas and then goes on to introduce the vows and bodhisattva career of Dharmākara (later Amitābha). He begins by naming a long series of previous Buddhas leading up to Lokeśvararāja ('sovereign monarch of the world').[9] Dharmākara, a king, decides to renounce everything in order to follow the bodhisattva path. He approaches Lokeśvararāja and, after paying his respects, makes a bodhisattva vow, which includes the intention to create a land where all may find happiness and peace and so become liberated. The Buddha then reveals to Dharmākara a vision of all Buddha-fields or Pure Lands. Dharmākara proceeds to spend five cosmic ages contemplating and cultivating the practice necessary to create a Pure Land before returning to the Buddha to proclaim a further set of bodhisattva vows, this time forty-eight in total, which he then adopts, practises, and fulfils. The Buddha then reveals that Dharmākara gained full awakening ten cosmic ages ago, that he dwells in the western region of the universe one hundred thousand million Buddha-fields away, and that his Pure Land is called 'land of peace and happiness' (Sukhāvatī).

The text moves on to evoke the sumptuous mythic geography of the Pure Land and the characteristics of the fabulous beings who dwell there. This is not the place to summarize in detail the adornments of the Pure Land, and there is no substitute for reading the text itself in order to get a sense of its splendour, but touching briefly on some notable features may evoke something of its grandeur. Above all, the Pure Land is bathed in Amitābha's compassionate light, which, according to the twelve epithets of the text, is measureless, boundless, unimpeded, unopposed, flaming, pure, full of joy, full of wisdom, uninterrupted, inconceivable, ineffable, and surpasses the light of the sun and moon (CWS, pp.655ff.). When living beings come into contact with this light, their bodies and minds become supple and gentle, they are filled with joy, and skilful thoughts arise within them.[10] The number of beings coursing in the delights of the Pure Land is immeasurable.

The tree under which Amitābha gained awakening is also to be found in Sukhāvatī, and it is some four million leagues high, while its branches and leaves spread out in all directions for two million leagues (a league is just under 3.5 miles or 5.5 kilometres). A gentle breeze stirs and carries the sounds of the Dharma from this tree to all beings in all realms, and those who hear them are immediately lifted into a state where they will never fall back from the path towards awakening. This world is full of jewelled lotuses, each one of which has a hundred thousand million petals that emit light of every colour. Each flower radiates thirty-six hundred thousand million rays of light, and from each ray of light burst forth thirty-six hundred thousand million buddhas. As you can see, this vision is truly mind-boggling! Such lavish descriptions of the Pure Land fulfil a symbolic function. Images are used to illustrate the principles of interdependence, non-substantiality, and interpenetration. In this way, the Pure Land functions as a kind of encyclopedia of poetic symbols that point towards the truths of the Dharma.

Later on, the text considers why some human beings do not seek rebirth in the Pure Land, and details all the modes of 'evil' to be found in mundane existence and how these may be overcome through dedicated Dharma practice.[11] After bestowing a vision of Sukhāvatī upon Ananda, the Buddha reveals to Maitreya that there are two grades of rebirth in the Pure Land: one for those who have faith and one for those who still harbour doubt about the Buddha's spiritual capacities.[12] The first kind happens by spontaneous rebirth within a lotus flower, whereas the second kind involves the aspirant waiting 500 years in a flying palace without even hearing the Dharma. Significantly, the Buddha makes it clear that *all* bodhisattvas are reborn in the Pure Land, even those from other Buddha-fields. In other words, Sukhāvatī is the summation of *all* Pure Lands. The scripture closes by extolling the benefits of having the opportunity to hear it, and also affirms that it will survive for a hundred years longer than all other Buddhist scriptures.

The message of the *Larger Scripture*

The *Scripture* brings together two orientations towards Dharma practice that would later be differentiated as self-power and Other Power. We see in Dharmākara's bodhisattva career the classic 'path of sages': through his own efforts he builds up incalculable merits, which he then materializes into a Pure Land and gifts to all beings via his guarantee that they can be reborn there. This introduces the second orientation, which is Other Power, although this concept is not explicitly drawn out. Other Power means that we can benefit from the spiritual practice of another, more specifically Dharmākara bodhisattva. Instead of just building up our own merit, which we hope will benefit our future rebirth, we can draw on the immeasurable merits of Amida, which, as it were, trump our merits or transcend our own karmic traces to enable us to be reborn in ideal conditions for awakening. So the path to enlightenment no longer depends solely upon our own efforts. Rather, we can benefit from the aeons of spiritual endeavour of a benevolent Buddha. We might say that this transfer of merits symbolizes all the help we have received, and will receive, from other beings that enables us to flourish.

The *Scripture* also reveals that the Buddha is *transhistorical* or perhaps simply transcendent. They are omnipresent and immanent. Even while Śākyamuni Buddha became enlightened at a particular moment of historical time, he incarnates the principle of Buddhahood that is outside or beyond it. The Buddha transcends a linear conception of history but simultaneously remains constantly available. Shinran himself later equated Amida and Śākyamuni (*CWS*, p.349). He says 'Thus, the reason why Śākyamuni [Buddha] appeared in the world [...] lies solely in teaching this [sutra]' (*CWS*, p.227). From this we could say that the historical manifestation of the Buddha served to reveal their transhistorical reality.

We could understand the story of Dharmākara as symbolizing all of the conditions that have occurred to give birth to this present instant of awareness. We are the inheritors of the entire melange of accumulated conditions that have permitted this moment to reveal itself. A moment that is given and in which we are right now awakening to reality. A moment that has inexhaustible dimensions and possibilities. If our imagination can open up to this mind-boggling legacy, we can begin to savour the sacred excess that saturates this instant.

The Pure Land tradition came to identify Dharmākara's vows as the core message of the *Larger Scripture* and, in turn, of all three

Pure Land scriptures considered as a unity. More specifically, Tanluan singled out the Eighteenth Vow as the essence of the scripture, since it epitomized all the others. Besides this, three other vows came to be seen as of special importance, namely, the seventeenth, nineteenth, and twentieth vows, which together with the Eighteenth Vow form a cluster. The seventeenth vow promises that all Buddhas will praise the name of Amitābha, the nineteenth promises that Amitābha will appear to the believer on his or her deathbed, while the twentieth vow promises rebirth to those who hear the name of Amitābha.

Embraced by all Buddhas

The *Shorter Scripture*[13] runs to about eight pages in English translation and has become a widely used devotional text.[14] Its structure is fairly simple. On this occasion, we find ourselves at Śrāvastī in Prince Jeta's Grove, a favoured resting place of the historical Buddha. We are introduced to the cosmic assembly, which includes 1,250 monks, a wide array of bodhisattvas, as well as countless gods. This time the Buddha's interlocutor is Shariputra, one of his chief disciples. Seemingly out of nowhere, the Buddha begins to tell him about Sukhāvatī, the land of bliss. The Buddha then goes on to describe some of the characteristics of this land. For instance, there are flocks of rare birds that gather to sing six times a day and, with soothing voices, they teach the Dharma. The text introduces Amitābha and the inhabitants of this Pure Land, and exhorts us to aspire to be reborn there. There follows a somewhat lengthy section (around two pages) in which all the Buddhas in all directions praise the merits of Amitābha and of the *Scripture* itself, now referred to as 'Receiving the Protection of all Buddhas'.[15] It is so called because:

> If good men or good women hear this discourse and keep it in mind, or hear the name of all buddhas, these good men and women will all be protected and remembered by all buddhas, they will all become irreversible in their progress toward unsurpassable, complete awakening.[16]

Those who make a vow to be reborn in Sukhāvatī are guaranteed to reach enlightenment once born there. The text closes with Śākyamuni Buddha reflecting on how difficult it was for him to gain unsurpassed awakening and then teach this wisdom to others. The cosmos is in a phase of decay and human beings are in a degenerative state, corrupted by wrong views and beset by all kinds of mental afflictions, which makes awakening especially precarious.

The alternative title of the scripture, 'Embraced by all Buddhas' or 'Receiving the Protection of all Buddhas', indicates that the bodhisattva vows are no longer just a model to be emulated, but are active sources of transformative blessing that offer consolation and safe harbour for all beings. Moreover, while the scripture focuses on Amitābha Buddha, this alternative title indicates that *all* Buddhas have the same liberative powers.

Contemplating the land of bliss

The *Contemplation Scripture*[17] opens with the grisly story of King Ajātaśatru's imprisonment of his father, Bimbisara, and his attempts to starve him to death.[18] Bimbisara's loyal queen, Vaidehī, visits him regularly in prison and spreads a mixture of ghee, honey, and flour on her body and fills her ornaments with grape juice, which she then offers to the king to give him sustenance. After a while, Ajātaśatru discovers this ruse and, enraged, is on the point of murdering his own mother when some wise advisors step in to stop him. Instead, he imprisons Vaidehī who, in desperation, calls on the Buddha for aid. On seeing a vision of the Buddha, she bemoans her fate. What has she done to warrant such an evil son? She begs the Buddha to reveal to her a place where there is no suffering, as she wishes to be reborn there. So the Buddha emits a golden ray that, having encircled the entire universe, comes to rest on the crown of his head and transforms itself into a golden pillar. Vaidehī sees reflected in it all the Pure Lands of the universe. Afterwards, she voices the aspiration to be reborn in Sukhāvatī and wants to know how to contemplate it.

The second part of the scripture comprises a series of exercises that evoke the spiritual world of Sukhāvatī, and culminates in an encounter with Amitābha Buddha (here known as Amitāyus). The visualization guidelines are very detailed and incorporate dazzling imagery. In brief, we begin by visualizing the setting sun. Then, we visualize water in every direction, which freezes and transforms into precious stones to form the 'earth' of the Pure Land. This ground is criss-crossed with golden cords and emits light of 500 colours. Next, we see enormous jewel trees with leaves 25 *yojana*s in length and breadth (a *yojana* may be somewhere between 4 and 9 miles). Their golden blossoms spin like fire-wheels. From the blossoms appear fruits, which transform into jewelled canopies that reflect the Buddha-fields of the entire cosmos. Then, we contemplate the jewel ponds and heavenly musicians. Next we visualize a lotus-flower throne, each petal of which has the colour of a hundred jewels, and is at least 250 *yojana*s in length and breadth. Upon the lotus throne we visualize the golden figure of Amitāyus, flanked right and left by bodhisattvas. The light of Amitāyus blazes in all directions, and on seeing this Buddha we behold all the Buddhas of the cosmos. Finally, we visualize ourselves as being reborn in Sukhāvatī inside a lotus blossom. As the petals of the lotus open, our bodies emit coloured light and we can hear the Buddhas and bodhisattvas preaching the Dharma.

In the final three contemplations, we dwell on the three grades into which beings are reborn in Sukhāvatī. Each grade consists of three sublevels. Rebirth at the highest level of the highest grade results from practising the precepts, cultivating a skilful attitude, studying the scriptures, engaging in regular meditation, and so on. One destined to such rebirth sees Amitābha Buddha and their glorious retinue of bodhisattvas at the time of death and is reborn seated on a diamond throne. Those who have accumulated a more modest stock of merit are destined for rebirth in the middle and lowest forms of the highest grade where they appear on thrones of purple and gold and just gold respectively.

As our stock of merit diminishes, the privileges with which we will be reborn into the Pure Land become more restricted. However, even those who have no merit at all, and who have even committed one of the five grave offences, will still attain rebirth if they call on Amitābha at the moment of death, albeit at the lowest form of the lowest grade. They will be reborn enclosed within golden lotuses, which, after ten great aeons have passed, will finally burst open. Avalokiteśvara and Mahāsthāmaprāpta will then instruct them on the interdependent nature of all phenomena and the purification of unskilful actions. Thus, while on one level embracing the principle of karma, the *Contemplation Scripture* also allows for its transcendence owing to the unconditional nature of Amitābha's compassion and their transfer of merit.

The logic behind contemplating the Buddha as a spiritual exercise is laid out in connection with the eighth meditation:

> The body of all the buddhas, all the tathāgatas, is the realm of reality, and they enter into the focused minds of all living beings. Therefore, when you focus your mind on the Buddha, your mind takes on the thirty-two major physical characteristics of the Buddha. When your mind creates the Buddha, your mind becomes the Buddha. The ocean of all the perfectly awakened buddhas arises from the focused mind.[19]

As the teaching concludes, Queen Vaidehī and her 500 maidens are blessed by a vision of Amitāyus and their attendant bodhisattvas in Sukhāvatī, and the Buddha assures them that they will all be reborn there. The *Scripture* also offers some alternative names for itself, including *Purification and Elimination of Karmic Hindrances for the Attainment of Birth in the Presence of all Buddhas*. This underlines that Buddha contemplation is seen as a means to transcend karma on the basis of Other Power.

What is the Pure Land?

On the surface, the Pure Land would seem like a kind of fairy tale, a cosmic fantasy that is a world away from the practical cares of daily life. Couched as it is in supersaturated imagery, impossible dimensions, and incalculable time, it may even seem a little garish. What are we to make of it? What is the Pure Land? Can we really be reborn there? Does it really have jewel trees? Does it have bathing ponds of pure and fragrant water?

The Pure Land is a myth – not in the sense of an untruth, far from it. Paul Ricoeur points out that 'If we interpret myth literally we misinterpret it. For myth is essentially symbolic.'[20] The symbolic function of a myth, he argues, is to reveal the bond between human beings and what they consider sacred.[21] The sacred in itself, he argues, is always 'floating', which I take to mean that it has no prescribed form but it may be evoked by means of myth and ritual. So myth has the capacity to express in symbolic language what we consider sacred. Moreover, it discloses 'new and unprecedented worlds, an opening on to other possible worlds'.[22] Through myth, then, we may open out for ourselves a world that transcends the limits of the ordinary mind and so begin to inhabit a dimension of enhanced value and significance. James Hollis proposes that myth 'bridges from the unknown to the knower and helps the human stand in some sort of meaningful relationship to mystery'.[23]

Sangharakshita has defined a Pure Land or Buddha-field as '[t]he sphere of spiritual influence of one particular Buddha'.[24] To put this the other way around, we could say that, if we are within the sphere of influence of a particular Buddha, then we are in their Pure Land. The Pure Land is not necessarily an external, material world, but rather a spiritual dimension that we can begin to inhabit as we open ourselves to the blessing of Amitābha. Shinran offers an intriguing reflection in relation to the inside-or-outsideness of the Pure Land when he writes: 'Hence we know that when we reach the Buddha-land of happiness, we unfailingly disclose Buddha-nature' (*CWS*, p.202). Buddha-nature is normally seen as a potential within us; something that can come alive within us as we become spiritually sensitized, like a seed that grows and then flowers. Yet Shinran appears to be saying that awakening to our Buddha-nature is in fact the same as being reborn in the Pure Land. Perhaps we could say then that the Pure Land is neither inside nor outside of us but both or, even better, that the Pure Land discloses to us the promise of a sacred world. This in turn offers us a glimpse of ultimate fulfilment.

To offer a different perspective, Sangharakshita has also proposed that 'Sukhāvatī may therefore be thought of as *a kind of cosmic sangha*, unthinkably vaster and infinitely more perfect than the institution which is as it were its shadow here on earth.'[25] This suggests that, instead of being a place, the Pure Land expresses a *relation*, even the spirit of *kalyāṇa mitratā* or spiritual friendship.

In the *Vimalakīrti Nirdeśa*, another renowned Mahāyāna scripture, the Pure Land is declared to be *this very world*.[26] We see it as impure owing to our distorting perceptions and afflictions. Amida and the Pure Land are not really separate from one another, neither are they separate from us. To enter the Pure Land is to enter into Amida's body, even to be reconstituted by Amida *as* Amida. It means to be welcomed *into* Amida, but not in such a way that submerges or dismembers us. Rather, we become more fully connected to others as we realize our solidarity with them, as we awaken to our shared cares, fears, and longings. As Shinran puts it:

> When a foolish being of delusion and defilement awakens shinjin,
> He realizes that birth-and-death is itself nirvana;
> Without fail he reaches the land of immeasurable light
> And universally guides sentient beings to enlightenment.
> (*CWS*, p.72)

Chapter Seven

All with the Same Mind

The masters of India in the west, who explained the teaching
  in treatises,
And the eminent monks of China and Japan,
Clarified the Great Sage's true intent in appearing in the
  world,
And revealed that Amida's Primal Vow accords with the
  nature of beings. (*CWS*, p.70)

Shinran's Dharmic vision didn't come from nowhere. Through
his monastic training he had access to a spectacular treasure
trove of Dharma riches that informed his mature thought and
provided him with a textual vocabulary with which to bring
to life his liberative vision. In this and the following chapter, I
show how Shinran built his understanding of the Dharma on
the insights and authority of previous masters, most notably his
immediate root teacher, Hōnen. Through meticulous selection
and inspired reinterpretation, Shinran formulated a novel and
compelling orientation towards Buddhist living. This arose from
his conviction that the *Larger Scripture* is the pre-eminent text,
the Eighteenth Vow is its essential message, and the recitation
of the name of Amida Buddha is the consecrated act.

Dimensions of lineage

Like many religious traditions, Buddhism has accorded great
importance to lineage. Shinran was no different. I am no different.
When the Triratna Buddhist Order was formed in the late 1960s,

it was not affiliated with a traditional school. But this doesn't mean that lineage is irrelevant. I was ordained into this Order by my preceptor Subhuti 'with loyalty to my teachers'.[1] Subhuti was himself ordained by Urgyen Sangharakshita, the founder of our Order. Sangharakshita, in turn, was ordained as a monk in India and also had a number of noted Tibetan teachers. They had their own teachers and preceptors, and so the lineage stretches back even to the Buddha himself. I have already mentioned that, in the early 1990s, Sangharakshita drew on the Tibetan image of the Refuge Tree to symbolize the lineage of our emerging tradition. Really he wanted to say that we are the inheritors of the entire Buddhist legacy, the 'eternal legacy' as he once named it. In placing specific figures on the Tree, he calls our attention to them. Shinran is one of those figures.

Lineage has been especially important in East Asian Buddhism, where it has served, at least in part, to underpin the credentials of a particular school or teacher. We could think of lineage as a kind of transmission of *kalyāṇa mitratā* or spiritual friendship. It is a stream of blessing that flows from the past towards the present. At the same time, lineages are a kind of fiction, since they reduce what is often a complex, even messy, inheritance into a neat, linear transmission. In this sense, through canonizing key figures and teachings, a lineage becomes an imaginative representation of spiritual heritage. This may lend a semblance of authority and coherence to what was often a somewhat disorderly evolution. Lineage sanctifies the past in relation to the concerns of the present.

Lineage can be conceived in a range of ways. So far I have pointed towards the lineage of *kalyāṇa mitratā*, the fiction of an unbroken sequence of teachers transmitting the Dharma, which began with the Buddha and cascades down towards us today. Sangharakshita pointed out four dimensions of lineage: inspiration, institutions, ideas, and practices. We might also add textual and hermeneutic lineage, both of which become important themes in Shinran's religious universe.

Lineage highlights our sources of inspiration and guidance. This invites a sense of gratitude for having received and being part of a living river of transmission. It also confers a responsibility to honour the lineage and to relay it faithfully. Lineage is a living out

The Promise of a Sacred World

of the principle of conditionality and especially interconnection. We reflect on the Dharma in relation to a certain lineage horizon (even if that is a secular one), and this shapes the kinds of understandings that we will produce. Our way of seeing the Dharma is situated within a particular lineage and a specific body of sources. In a sense, our lineage is everyone who has marked our lives, especially for the better. For this reason, we might say that lineage in itself articulates the principle of Other Power. Eminent texts and revered teachers function as Other Power, and through opening ourselves to them we absorb their *kalyāṇa mitratā*, their *adhiṣṭhāna*, which rains down upon us like purifying nectar.

So what was Shinran's lineage? What would his Refuge Tree look like? While Shinran considered himself a faithful disciple of Hōnen, his Dharmic inheritance was much more complex than that. He was born in Japan almost 1600 years after the death of the historical Buddha. Just as we are, Shinran was historically, culturally, linguistically, and religiously distanced from the roots of Buddhism. We have already seen that his formative years were spent as a workaday Tendai monk on Hieizan. Just like us, he was heir to a bewildering array of Buddhist texts and teachings. But Shinran had no way of knowing that those teachings and texts had evolved over many centuries, and had to reconcile them all as originating with the Buddha. His teachings emerge as a creative response to this prodigious and conflicting legacy.

Curating the Dharma

Indian Buddhist texts and teachings were transmitted to China not systematically but piecemeal. The order in which they were translated often bore no relationship to their order of composition; later works sometimes appeared before the earlier ones on which they were based or to which they responded. The inherited teachings were shorn of their historical and doctrinal context. This left Chinese interpreters with a headache. How did they all hang together?

The volume and complexity of this incoming Buddhist material inspired novel hermeneutic strategies known as *panjiao* (doctrinal classification or taxonomy). *Panjiao* serve as means to curate a vast and disparate array of texts. These *panjiao* systems ranked texts and teachings hierarchically, especially in accordance with their seeming profundity and the stage of the Buddha's teaching career at which they were supposed to have been preached. *Panjiao* applied the Mahāyāna teaching of *skilful means*, enabling Chinese Buddhists to interpret each teaching as a corrective to overcome the shortcomings of the teaching that preceded it. This can be linked to the *Lotus Sutra*'s teaching of *ekayana* or 'one way', which asserts that there is ultimately only one kind of awakening, available to all. However, owing to the differing capacities of beings, the compassionate Buddha formulated numerous teachings to communicate this. So how and on what basis did Shinran categorize the eternal legacy? What was Shinran's *panjiao*?

As we have already seen, Shinran identified the three Pure Land scriptures as containing the most profound message of Buddhism. Second, he conceived of these sacred texts as having an underlying unity that cohered in the *Larger Scripture*, the keystone text. Third, he interpreted the fundamental message of the *Larger Scripture* to be Amida Buddha's Primal Vow. Finally, from the vast heritage of scriptures, commentaries, and Dharma transmission, Shinran concluded that the nembutsu was the consecrated practice and was singled out for all. How did he get to this exclusive position, and how did he defend it?

Imagined discipleship

Shinran went forth from his monastic context and embraced an exclusive approach to the Dharma that had no historical precedent. In consequence, he stepped outside the established boundaries of lineage. Later, he constructed his own relatively simple lineage chart, partly based on a model that Hōnen had created.[2] There are just seven figures in the chart, but they span a period of more than a thousand years. In his *Shōshinge*, Shinran names the following as the Pure Land root teachers (*honshi*, 本師):[3]

1. Nāgārjuna (India, c.150 CE)
2. Vasubandhu (India, fl. fourth–fifth century)
3. Tanluan (China, c.488–554)

4. Daochuo (China, 562–645)
5. Shandao (China, 613–681)
6. Genshin (Japan, 942–1017)
7. Hōnen (Japan, 1133–1212)

Through this lineage model, Shinran places himself at the feet of eminent figures, texts, and orientations that were central to his understanding of the Dharma and the essential message of the *Larger Scripture*. But the figures he selected don't form an unbroken sequence of teachers and disciples. As you can see, huge stretches of time separate some of the masters. So the lineage that Shinran created was more a cascade of inspiration than a direct transmission. He highlights philosophical and doctrinal affinity rather than historical continuity. It is an exercise in imagined discipleship.

Shinran saw himself not as an innovator but as a faithful servant of tradition. According to *Tannishō*, he said: 'when I expound the Tathāgata's Dharma to sentient beings in the ten directions, I am only speaking as the Tathāgata's representative. [I] [...] do not propagate any new Dharma at all.'[4] But we can't take this humble reverence at face value. In his *Shōshinge* (*Hymn of True Faith*) and the *Kōsō wasan* (*Hymns in Praise of Eminent Monks*), Shinran presents the seven root teachers and traces out a doctrinal continuity between them and the *Larger Scripture*. Most importantly, they 'Clarified the Great Sage's [the Buddha's] true intent in appearing in the world' (*CWS*, p.70). But, while revering his root teachers as Buddhas who have enabled him to grasp the true message of the Dharma, Shinran also reinterprets their teachings. He draws on his own insights into the *Larger Scripture* to mould their ideas into a coherent whole that reflects his palimpsestic style of reading. Yet he never undermines their authority. In summarizing the importance of his chosen root teachers, Shinran wrote:

> Through their treatises and commentaries, these masters, *all*
>   *with the same mind,*
> Save the countless beings of utter defilement and evil.
> All people of the present, both monk and lay,
> Should rely wholly on the teachings of these venerable
>   masters. (*CWS*, p.309, emphasis added)

Given the vast differences in culture, language, and Dharmic inheritance that separate these figures, it seems a stretch, to say the least, to believe that they wrote 'with the same mind'. Yet this is what Shinran sees. It was as though their writings formed a great stack of tracing paper, each one superimposing itself over the other, and through all of them Shinran discerns the radiant light of an underlying gestalt. This light is, of course, Amida Buddha's wisdom and compassion that reveal themselves in and through everything. We might say that Shinran sees in his root teachers a transcendental unity that lends coherence to their apparently inconsistent viewpoints.

While he recommends that we 'should rely wholly on the teachings of these venerable masters', Shinran uses careful selection and reinterpretation to enable them to speak for his own doctrinal innovations. He thus converts lineage into a hermeneutic principle. By situating himself amidst a body of eminent texts and revered masters, he saturates himself in their blessing and authority. Through writing within it and about it, Shinran both constructs and affirms his imagined lineage. At no stage does he claim to be doing anything original, far from it, but rather he writes in dialogue with, or under the guidance of, the texts of his lineage. In his mind, this lineage, and ultimately Amida Buddha, shines through him. The structure of *True Teaching* reflects this. Shinran immerses himself within selected texts while, at the same time, curating their content in order to give voice to his own religious imagination.

The Indian masters: Nāgārjuna and Vasubandhu

By selecting two Indian masters, Shinran roots his lineage in the birthplace of Buddhism. Moreover, Nāgārjuna (fl. c.150–250 CE) and Vasubandhu (fl. fourth or fifth century CE) are giants of Buddhist history. Calling down their *adhiṣṭhāna* lends gravitas to his proposition. We now know that they probably weren't the authors of the sacred texts attributed to them by the Pure Land tradition.

On the face of it, Nāgārjuna would seem a little out of place in a discussion about Pure Land. Yet he is credited with a treatise known as *Commentary on the Ten Bodhisattva Stages* (hereafter *Ten*

Stages), which 'distinguished the paths of difficult and easy practice' (*CWS*, p.362).[5] This juxtaposition of approaches became central to prioritizing the nembutsu, which was equated with the easy path. According to Shinran, Nāgārjuna taught that 'the moment one thinks on Amida's Primal Vow, one is naturally brought to enter the stage of the definitely settled' (*CWS*, p.71). Moreover, in a *wasan* (hymn or verse) Shinran proclaims that Nāgārjuna praised the Pure Land in various works and 'wholeheartedly recommended the nembutsu to all' (*CWS*, p.362). Thus, from texts attributed to Nāgārjuna, Shinran solicits an endorsement for an exclusive approach to nembutsu.

In fact, the chapter on 'easy practice' from *Ten Stages* endorses the chanting of the names of any one of a host of Buddhas and bodhisattvas, together with their lavish reverence and praise, as means to attain the stage of non-retrogression (*avaivartika*). In other words, it recommends supreme worship (*pūjā*):

> If you say the names of the Buddhas such as Amida, as well as those of the great bodhisattvas, while holding them single-heartedly in mind, you will also attain the stage of non-retrogression. *There are various Buddhas, including Amida*, whom you should reverently worship and whose names you should say.[6]

This inclusive message is clear from passages that Shinran himself cites in *True Teaching* (*CWS*, pp.22–3). Even so, he takes the text to say that keeping in mind the name of Amida Buddha is singled out for special attention. He does this because he is convinced that Amida Buddha's vows have unique priority. They trump everything. Elsewhere, he writes:

> [T]he reason that the myriad Buddhas have come into their various worlds is that they take preaching the power of Amida's vow and liberating all sentient beings as their most fundamental intention (*hongai* 本懐). Therefore, this [message] is called the direct preaching for which the myriad Buddhas appeared in the world.[7]

This passage makes clear that the primordial function of *all* Buddhas is to preach the power of Amida's vow. In light of this, all other teachings are classified as provisional and serve to draw beings to 'enter the great treasure ocean of true and real virtue' (*CWS*, p.486), which is Amida Buddha's vow.

The Pure Land tradition credits Vasubandhu, the second Indian master, as the author of the *Treatise on the Pure Land* (hereafter *Treatise*). This is a brief manual of contemplation exercises that centre on Amida Buddha and his Pure Land.[8] In the *Shōshinge*, Shinran praises Vasubandhu for going for refuge to Amida Buddha and goes on to comment: 'Based on the sutras, he made the true and real apparent and clarified the great vow of crosswise transcendence.'[9] Although the term 'crosswise transcendence' (*ōchō* 横超) came to play a significant role in Shinran's thought, the *Treatise* does not mention it (it was incorporated into the Pure Land vocabulary by Shandao). Shinran's teaching favours the 'crosswise transcendence' above the 'lengthwise transcendence'. To transcend lengthwise refers to standard Mahāyāna teaching. This means to follow the path of individual striving towards awakening, a path that may require many lifetimes to complete. Transcending crosswise, by contrast, 'is the true teaching based on the fulfilment of the [Primal] Vow, which embodies the perfectly consummate true reality [...] in the space of an instant, one swiftly transcends and realizes the supreme, perfect, true enlightenment' (*CWS*, p.114).

In its auto-commentary, the *Treatise* states: 'Upon *seeing* that Buddha, the bodhisattva who has not yet realised the pure mind will ultimately attain the realisation of the dharma-body of equality.'[10] In other words, visualization of the Buddha is indicated as the means to trigger awakening. Despite the fact that this passage specifies *seeing* the Buddha, Shinran reads it as extolling the power of the vow to lift us out of the entrapment that is the cycle of rebirth. He thus relocates the impetus towards awakening within Amida's vow instead of the practitioner's effort. He also reimagines the encounter with Amida Buddha. Instead of requiring contemplative mastery, this encounter consists in simply *hearing* Amida's name.

Tanluan and Other Power

The Chinese teacher Tanluan (c.488–554) wrote a *Commentary on the Treatise on Birth*,[11] a sophisticated analysis of the *Treatise* attributed to Vasubandhu. This became one of Shinran's key inspirations, and he cites it extensively.[12] Among the important ideas introduced there are the application of the term 'Other Power' to the compassionate intervention of Amida Buddha and the twofold transfer of merit.[13] Shinran in turn developed these ideas.

Tanluan's first contribution is his clarification of the term 'Other Power'. The *Commentary* begins by affirming the distinction drawn in *Ten Stages* between two types of path or practice: easy and difficult. He then equates them with self-power (Ch. *zili*, Jp. *jiriki* 自力) and Other Power (Ch. *tali*, Jp. *tariki* 他力) respectively. He goes on to highlight various shortcomings of the self-power approach, among which is the fact that it 'lacks the support of Other Power'.[14] For this reason, it is likened to journeying overland on foot. In contrast:

> In the path of easy practice, one aspires to be born in the
> Pure Land by solely entrusting oneself to the Buddha as
> the cause. Allowing oneself to be carried by the *power of the
> Buddha's Vow*, one duly attains birth in the Land of Purity.
> Supported by the *Buddha's power*, one immediately enters
> the group of the truly settled of the Mahāyāna.[15]

The easy practice is like being carried across the sea on a ship. Tanluan equates Other Power with trusting in Amida Buddha's vows and aspiring to be reborn in their Pure Land where the conditions to realize awakening are ideal. If we entrust to the Buddha *as the cause*, then the *Buddha's power* (願力) will carry us forward. Tanluan uses several near-synonyms to hint at a transformative influence that goes beyond self-directed effort. Over time, and especially for Shinran, Other Power became the signature term. Besides firmly linking the notion of Other Power with Amida Buddha's vows, Tanluan also ranked Other Power in a position that was clearly superior to self-power. Thus Shinran praises Tanluan by affirming that '[h]e shows that the cause and attainment of birth in the fulfilled land lie in the Vow' (*CWS*, p.72).

Tanluan's second contribution is the twofold merit transfer (*ekō* 回向), known as turning *away* and turning *towards*. Tanluan defines the two aspects as follows:

> The outgoing aspect is when one takes one's own merits, directs them toward and bequeaths them upon all sentient beings aspiring to be born together in Amida Buddha's Pure Land of peace and bliss. The returning aspect is when one, having been born in that land, attains the fulfilment of the power of expedient means through completion of shamatha and vipashyana and enters into the dense forest of birth-and-death, teaching all sentient beings, together turning them toward the Buddhist path. (*CWS*, p.72)

This passage lays out a conception of merit transfer that is more or less familiar. We, the aspirant, gift the fruits of our skilful karma for the benefit of others. But here the transference is *twofold*. First, we dedicate our merits to help not just ourselves but all beings find rebirth in the Pure Land. In these ideal conditions, awakening is fulfilled through the supportive power of Amida's vows. Second, once enlightened, we return to the world of suffering to liberate others. So Tanluan clarifies that the aspiration towards the Pure Land is underpinned by an altruistic motive. Longing for the Pure Land could readily become self-centred and even turn into a kind of flight from the frustrations and messiness of life as we know it. In emphasizing the theme of turning *towards*, we root our aspiration to the Pure Land within the compassionate heart of the bodhisattva ideal.

Shinran was clearly inspired by this altruistic vision of merit transfer, and develops it in the light of his understanding of Other Power. In the *Shōshinge*, Shinran praises Tanluan because he taught that 'Our going and returning, *directed to us by Amida*, come about through Other Power' (*CWS*, p.72, emphasis added). Moreover, *True Teaching* opens with the following statement: '*Amida's directing of virtue* (*ekō*) to sentient beings has two aspects: the aspect for our going forth to the Pure Land and the aspect for our return to this world' (*CWS*, p.72, emphasis added). These quotations show that Shinran reinterpreted Tanluan's insight into the two aspects of merit transfer. Given his general reading of the human condition, that is to say that we are enmeshed in greed, hatred, and delusion, we are hardly likely to collect sufficient merit to favour even our own rebirth in the Pure Land, not to speak of benefiting others. So Shinran comes to the view that merit transference is not a practice carried out by us *bonbu* (since our own merit is feeble), but rather describes how Amida Buddha's compassion intervenes in the world to draw all beings towards his Pure Land. Although this stance may be the most unique and revolutionary feature of Shinran's thought, and is central to the message of *True Teaching*, he claims that Tanluan was the one who first clarified it.

In his rendering of the fulfilment passage of the Eighteenth Vow, Shinran affirms that the transfer of merit is, properly speaking, a gift from Amida Buddha:

> All sentient beings, as they hear the Name, realize even one thought-moment of shinjin and joy, *which is directed to them from Amida's sincere mind*, and aspiring to be born in that land, they then attain birth and dwell in the stage of nonretrogression. (*CWS*, p.80, emphasis added)

So while Shinran was inspired by Tanluan's work in clarifying that the two aspects of merit transfer are the working of Amida Buddha, this view is actually Shinran's original interpretation.

Daochuo (562–645)

Daochuo determined how difficult it is to fulfil the Path of Sages,
And reveals that only passage through the Pure Land gate is possible for us.
He criticizes self-power endeavour in the myriad good practices,
And encourages us solely to say the fulfilled Name embodying true virtue.

With kind concern he teaches the three characteristics of
   entrusting and non-entrusting,
Compassionately guiding all identically, whether they live
   when the dharma survives as but form, when in its last
   stage, or when it has become extinct. (*CWS*, p.72)

Daochuo was a scholar of the *Parinirvāṇa Sūtra* who later adopted
the Pure Land orientation. He shared the widely held view that
the Dharma had entered its last age (*mofa, mappō*) and so was in
terminal decline. As a consequence, he believed that the traditional
means of gaining awakening – what he called 'the path of sages'
(*shengdao*) – was no longer realistic, and that '[t]he Gateway of
the Pure Land [*jingtumen*] is the only one through which we can
pass [to Enlightenment].'[16] He therefore classified all Buddhist
teachings into just two categories: those that promote entrance to
the Pure Land and those that don't. In order to ground his own
teachings, Hōnen went on to make good use of this schema (*Sen*,
pp.58ff.). In commenting on traditional, self-power approaches to
enlightenment, Daochuo goes further and boldly asserts that 'Until
now, however, neither monk nor layperson has ever been able to
reach these goals' (*Sen*, p.57). In other words, not only is the Pure
Land approach the most appropriate for the age of final Dharma
but it is the *only* approach that actually works.

Daochuo combined the teachings of the *Larger Scripture* and the
Contemplation Scripture. In doing so, he argued that, owing to the
power of Amida's vows, beings of the lowest spiritual capacity were
precisely those singled out as capable of birth in the Pure Land.

Shandao (613–681)

Shandao alone in his time clarified the Buddha's true intent;
Sorrowing at the plight of meditative and non meditative
   practicers and people of grave evil,
He reveals that Amida's light and Name are the causes of
   birth. (*CWS*, p.73)

Shandao was Daochuo's most important disciple.[17] He continued
to emphasize the age of degeneration and, along with it, a decline

The Promise of a Sacred World

in human spiritual capacity.[18] He stressed that the Pure Land sutras were proclaimed *especially* to meet the needs of his degenerate age, and was concerned to engage those who felt spiritually impoverished, including the unlettered. Consequently, Shandao's message is sympathetic to the lay orientation, emphasizing the urgency of seeking rebirth in the Pure Land through the power of Amida's vows. He promoted verbal nembutsu (*nianfo*) as the method most suited to degenerate beings of the final age.[19] His revered work, *Commentary on the Contemplation Sutra*,[20] is cited extensively by both Hōnen and Shinran and exercised a decisive influence on both.

Besides stressing the practice of recitation, Shandao emphasized the importance of unshakeable trust in Amida's saving powers. Following a passage in the *Contemplation Scripture*, this trust or faith is described in terms of cultivating a 'threefold mind': (1) a most sincere mind (至心); (2) a profound or deep mind (深心); and (3) a mind that vows to direct all actions towards rebirth in the Pure Land (欲生).[21] Shandao explains the sincere mind as being *genuine*, even humble: 'one should not outwardly manifest the aspects of being wise, good and diligent while inwardly embracing vanity and falsehood' (*Sen*, p.99). Without this spirit of integrity, the value of our outward religious acts is degraded, if not disqualified. Shandao analyzes the profound mind according to two aspects. First, we must cultivate the conviction that we are 'an ordinary sinful being involved in transmigration [...] tumbling in this stream of cyclic rebirth, unable to find the karmic conditions for escape' (*Sen*, p.101). Second, we must nurture a deep trust that Amida Buddha can – and will – exercise his compassionate power to grasp us, if we entrust ourselves to him 'without doubt or reservation' (*Sen*, p.101). The final aspect of the threefold mind refers to merit transfer; in this context, merits are transferred specifically towards rebirth in the Pure Land, rather than to any other end.

Shinran engages in extended discussions on the topic of the three minds.[22] In *True Teaching*, he poses the question of whether the three minds as taught in the *Larger Scripture* and the three minds taught in the *Contemplation Scripture* are the same or different. He returns to his distinction between the explicit and implicit meanings of the scriptures, and comments that, in the *Contemplation Scripture*, 'the three minds that beings awaken are all minds of self-benefit that are individually different and not the mind that is single, which arises from [Amida's] benefiting others' (*CWS*, p.212). In other words, they exemplify a self-power approach. The implicit meaning of the *Scripture*, however, 'refers to disclosing the Tathāgata's universal Vow and revealing the mind that is single, to which [practisers of the three minds] are led through [Amida's] benefiting others' (*CWS*, p.212). So the implicit meaning points towards Other Power.

Shinran goes on to address the question of whether the mind that is single as elaborated in the *Shorter Scripture* is the same as the three minds discussed in the other two scriptures. He defines 'the mind that is single' (*isshin* 一心) in the following way: '"Single" means nondual. "Mind" is a term for the true and real' (*CWS*, p.227). Reading all three texts as having an underlying, *implicit* meaning, Shinran concludes that the three minds are really just one mind. But this mind is not cultivated by us. Rather, it is Amida Buddha's mind working through us. He writes: 'The Threefold mind is the mind that is single; the mind that is single is the diamondlike true mind' (*CWS*, p.114). This mind is gifted to us by Amida Buddha.

Chapter Eight

The True Essence of the Pure Land Way

> The nembutsu is the refined practice that was long ago adopted from among twenty-one billion practices. The manifold practices are the coarse ones that were, among the twenty-one billion, already rejected [...] Further the nembutsu is the practice specified in the Original Vow [of Amida Buddha]. (*Sen*, p.98)

In Japan, the Pure Land orientation was first popularized within the Tendai school as part of a curriculum that combined teachings and practices drawn from a wide array of traditional sources.[1] The nembutsu was also propagated by less conventional figures. Kūya (903–972), for instance, was a wandering monk or *hijiri* (聖) who danced and sang. During the Kamakura period, institutions emerged that were dedicated exclusively to the Pure Land orientation, a development that was unprecedented in the history of Mahāyāna Buddhism. In this chapter, we meet Shinran's two final root teachers, both Japanese masters, in order to appreciate how their teachings prepared the ground for his distinctive approach.

Genshin (942–1017)

> Genshin, having broadly elucidated the teachings of
>   Śākyamuni's lifetime,
> Wholeheartedly took refuge in the land of peace and urges all
>   to do so. (*CWS*, p.73)

Genshin (942–1017) trained within Tendai but developed a close affinity with the Pure Land orientation. He lived on

Hieizan where, amongst other things, he formed part of a mini-sangha devoted to Amida practices called 'The Fellowship of the Twenty-Five Samādhis' (*nijūgo zanmaie*). This fellowship observed an intensive retreat on the fifteenth of each month dedicated to a version of Buddha contemplation that focused on Amida (*nembutsu zanmai*). The retreat consisted in reading aloud the entire *Larger Scripture*. After completing each section, the participants recited the nembutsu one hundred times while circumambulating an image of Amida, then transferred the merits accumulated and recited verses of praise. To close the retreat, they dedicated their merits towards seeing Amida at the moment of death. The explicit goal of the group was to enable participants to attain birth in the Pure Land. This was to be accomplished by encouraging each other and, when the moment of death came, to help the dying member to maintain the correct attitude since rebirth in the Pure Land depended on it. This implied constantly watching over the dying person in shifts, reciting the nembutsu for them, and attending to their practical needs. When the person arrives at the moment of death, all should gather together, chant the nembutsu, and recite prayers.[2]

Essentials of Birth in the Pure Land

Genshin laid out this pattern of practice as part of his renowned *Essentials of Birth in the Pure Land* (*Ōjōyōshū*), completed in 985, which was to become a Pure Land classic as well as a notable work of Japanese literature. In this tour de force, Genshin drew on virtually the entire Chinese Buddhist canon. In doing so, he introduced ideas from Chinese masters that proved crucial in the development of Japanese Pure Land thought and practice. Through his systematization of a wealth of doctrinal and practical teachings, he created a fund that later thinkers could draw from. He also highlighted the efficacy of vocal nembutsu and the possibility of Pure Land salvation for the ordinary person.

In *Essentials of Birth*, Genshin follows a fivefold approach to nembutsu practice as recommended in Vasubandhu's *Treatise on the Pure Land*, namely: veneration, praise, aspiration, contemplation, and dedication. *Veneration* consists in the worship of Amida Buddha through prostrations and other forms of reverence. Nembutsu *praise* consists in singing devotional verses to Amida Buddha, not unlike the *anuttara- pūjā* or supreme worship. *Aspiration* means not only to fervently desire rebirth in the Pure Land but to combine this with the cultivation of the bodhichitta, the aspiration to help all beings reach awakening. Genshin recommends that we affirm the bodhisattva vow using the following verse:

> However innumerable beings are, I vow to save them;
> However inexhaustible the passions are, I vow to extinguish them;
> However immeasurable the Dharmas are, I vow to master them;
> However incomparable the Buddha truth is, I vow to attain it.[3]

Following Tanluan, Genshin reconceives the scope of the bodhichitta. Instead of aspiring to lead all beings to awakening, it becomes the aspiration to lead all beings to the Pure Land, where they can then awaken.

Nembutsu *contemplation* covers a range of ways of recollecting Amida Buddha of descending degrees of complexity. The most elaborate form involves contemplating the forty-two notable marks of Amida Buddha, such as their topknot and the dharmachakras on the soles of their feet. This requires considerable skill in visualization. The next level incorporates both the contemplation of Amida Buddha's appearance and also their ultimate nature. Finally, in simplified Buddha-contemplation, Genshin offers a series of easier practices that include visualizing Amida's wisdom-eye, imagining one's own rebirth in the Pure Land, and, most significantly, just calling Amida to mind and going for refuge to them. He describes this last approach in the following terms:

> If there are those who are incapable of contemplating (*kannen*) the Buddha-marks, they should single-mindedly call and think on the Buddha (*shōnen*), while dwelling and taking refuge in them, on [Amida's] coming to welcome them, or on rebirth [in the Pure Land] [...] Whether walking, standing, sitting, or lying, while speaking or in silence, whatever you

may be doing, always keep the thought in your breast like a starving man thinks of food or a thirsting man seeks water. Bow your head, raise your hands, or lift up your voice calling the sacred name. But whatever your outer acts may be, keep the thought (*nen*) constantly in your heart.[4]

This passage recommends calling on Amida Buddha, basically vocal nembutsu, which offers a form of practice suited to the ordinary person. Finally, nembutsu *dedication* consisted in dedicating all the merits of nembutsu practice to the rebirth of oneself and others in the Pure Land.

Genshin summarizes the repertoire of practices that he considers essential for rebirth in the Pure Land in the following way: 'They are arousing the bodhichitta, guarding the three kinds of conduct, deep faith, sincerity, and constant nembutsu, then in accord with our longing and dedication of merit we will assuredly be reborn in the Land of Utter Bliss.'[5] It is clear that Genshin recommended vocal nembutsu as part of a broad programme of Pure Land devotion rather than as an exclusive practice. But he was keen to stress the ease of nembutsu recitation and how it could be fulfilled by everyone since it did not require esoteric knowledge or special training:

anyone, man or woman, noble or commoner, whether walking, standing, sitting or lying, and regardless of time, place, or any other circumstance, can practise it without difficulty; moreover, it can be utilised even for seeking rebirth at the approach of death. Therefore nembutsu is unsurpassed.[6]

Raigō: descending to welcome

Like most religious orientations, Pure Land Buddhism has been concerned about death and the afterlife. At least partly for this reason, deathbed nembutsu (*rinjū nembutsu*) became an important emphasis. It derives from a passage in the *Contemplation Scripture* that says that Amida Buddha, together with a host of bodhisattvas, will descend to welcome (*raigō* 来迎) the devout person at the moment of their death and escort them to the Pure Land. This dramatic and joyful moment became a popular subject of Japanese Buddhist art.

The *Contemplation Scripture* describes in lavish detail the spectacular drama that unfolds before aspirants to the Pure Land at the moment of death, and how each will be reborn according to their karma as well as how the *raigō* that each receives is determined by their respective spiritual merits. For instance, a practitioner of the highest grade will be greeted by Amida Buddha together with their principal bodhisattvas and a spectacular retinue of buddhas, monks, and devas. Then:

> The Bodhisattva Avalokiteśvara will be bearing a diamond platform, and will appear before the practitioner together with the Bodhisattva Mahāsthāmaprāpta. The Buddha Amitābha will illuminate the practitioner's body with a great flood of light and, together with all the bodhisattvas, extend his hands in welcome. Avalokiteśvara and Mahāsthāmaprāpta, along with countless other bodhisattvas, will praise and encourage the practitioner. When the practitioner sees all of this, they will jump for joy. They will seat themselves on the diamond platform and, following after the Buddha, instantly be born in that buddha-field.[7]

Once born into the Pure Land, aspirants see Amida Buddha and the bodhisattvas in all their glory. They also hear the Dharma preached by the jewel trees and realize mind-boggling insights. Simultaneously, they visit and pay homage to all the Buddhas in all the universes, and receive from each of them a guarantee of future enlightenment.

Genshin was the first Japanese Buddhist to focus on and write about *raigō*. Through his initiative, and his Amida fellowship, it rapidly assumed a central role in Japanese Buddhism and more specifically in death rites.[8] It is notable that Genshin himself, in an expression of polite humility, expected the lowest rank of birth in the Pure Land. Without Amida Buddha's compassionate intervention, the accumulation of unskilful acts of such a person means that they are destined for rebirth in one of the three unfortunate states (*duggati*), where they will experience immeasurable suffering for many aeons.[9] Such a person, who is really all of us, should sincerely and continuously intone 'Homage to Amida Buddha' (*Namu Amida Butsu*) ten times at the moment of death. This act wipes out evil karma and, as the person dies, they see a golden lotus flower and are reborn within a lotus-bud in Sukhāvatī. After twelve great kalpas (a great kalpa is 1.344 trillion years!), the lotus bud finally opens, and Avalokiteśvara and Mahāsthāmaprāpta arrive to teach the reborn person the Dharma. On hearing it, the devotee rejoices and awakens the aspiration for supreme enlightenment.

But this emphasis on preparation for death and the moment of death results in various problems. First, it is future-oriented. So instead of being concerned with the present – about awakening right now – practice focuses on preparing for the future, when birth in the Pure Land will be possible. This results in a kind of postponement of true Dharma life until the moment of death, and so everything we do before then is relegated to preliminary status. Second, it requires a very specific attitude at the moment of death, which not all may be able to engender or sustain. What happens, for instance, if someone develops dementia on their journey towards death? What happens if they become anxious and confused? What happens if they die in violent circumstances? This last consideration was especially important for the warrior class.

Placing so much importance on the moments before death provokes a high degree of stress. The circumstances of death are impossible to control, and so the likelihood of rebirth in the Pure Land is precarious. In one tale, a devout monk is reborn as a snake despite his assiduous practice of the nembutsu. Why? At the moment of death, he becomes distracted by thinking about who will inherit his vinegar bottle.[10] In turn, this death anxiety multiplied the grief of relatives and friends owing to uncertainty about the postmortem fate of the deceased.

Such considerations resulted in extreme solutions. Most prevalent seems to have been a neurotic merit-making aimed at producing a surfeit through millions of recitations of the nembutsu. It was hoped that this would enable the devout to meet death with the requisite calm (although it could not assure it). Thus the aspiration for a favourable death seemed to demand an unrelenting approach to practice that was contaminated with anxiety, since there was no guarantee that it would result in *raigō*. A still more extreme response was religious suicide. If the moment and circumstances of death are normally unpredictable, better to decide these circumstances oneself and so precipitate birth in the Pure Land by burning oneself alive or drowning oneself.[11]

Shinran came to a radical interpretation of Amida Buddha's welcoming descent known as 'spontaneous *raigō*' (*ji raigō*). This was based on his understanding that assurance of birth in the Pure Land is not something that happens at death but within *life* (*sokutoku ōjō*), that is to say, at the moment of genuinely entrusting ourselves to Amida Buddha's compassion. In commenting on a passage written by a fellow disciple, Shinran notes:

> *Come of themselves to welcome*: *of themselves* (*ji*) means 'in person'. Amida and a vast and numberless saintly host [...] *appear in person to be alongside and always* protect those who have realized true and real shinjin, at all times and in all places; hence the word 'themselves'. (*CWS*, p.453)

This does not negate the possibility of rebirth in the Pure Land after death, but clarifies that the cause of birth is *not* our death-proximate karma. It is our trust in Amida's vows.

Hōnen (1133–1212) and universal nembutsu recitation

> Master Genku [Hōnen], well-versed in the Buddha's teaching,
> Turned compassionately to foolish people, both good and evil;
> Establishing in this remote land the teaching and realization
>   that are the true essence of the Pure Land way. (*CWS*, p.73)

The seminal moment in the emergence of Pure Land as a distinctive form of Mahāyāna practice was when Hōnen began to propagate nembutsu recitation as the *universal* means of attaining birth in the Pure Land.[12] He rejected the received wisdom that complex and difficult practices were more spiritually advantageous and that monastic life was indispensable for liberation. This opened a religious path for the ordinary person and, in doing so, dimmed the aura of monastic supremacy. The universal scope of his approach is expressed in the following passage:

> It is therefore clear that since the nembutsu is easy, it is open to *everyone*, while the various other practices are not open to people of all capacities because they are difficult. Was it not in order to bring all sentient beings *without exception* to birth that he [Dharmākara/Amida] in his original vow cast aside the difficult practice and selected the easy one? (*Sen*, p.77, emphasis added)

While Hōnen is sometimes characterized as teaching *exclusive* nembutsu practice (*senju nembutsu*), this quotation shows that he admitted other possibilities, albeit only for people of superior capacities.[13] *Just* nembutsu (*tada nembutsu*) might more accurately describe his perspective. In other words, nothing else is needed.[14]

Orphaned at an early age, Hōnen entered a local temple before training as a Tendai priest on Hieizan. Notwithstanding his later thought and practice, he continued to regard himself as a faithful monk for the rest of his life, following and transmitting the precepts, and even dying in his Tendai robes.[15] On Hieizan, Hōnen followed a pattern of Pure Land practices that included nembutsu contemplation (*nembutsu zammai*). He also studied the writings of the Chinese master Shandao, which convinced him that nembutsu recitation (as opposed to visualization and related ritual ceremonies) should be adopted above all other practices.[16] Although we can't be exact, it has been estimated that Hōnen may have recited the nembutsu as many as 70,000 times per day,[17] which would have taken up most of his waking hours.

In 1175, Hōnen underwent a spiritual awakening. After twenty-five years, he left Hieizan and set up a hermitage near Kyoto, where he began to attract followers. During this period he compiled his eminent work, the *Selection* (*Senchakushū*),[18] which collected passages from scriptures and commentaries arranged to reflect his particular vision of Pure Land doctrine and practice (a model that Shinran himself came to follow in *True Teaching*). In it, Hōnen declares that the Pure Land way is the *only* valid means of liberation given the dire conditions of *mappō*. In this period of the decline of the Dharma, Hōnen was convinced that it is virtually impossible for beings to gain spiritual liberation through their own efforts alone (or self-power, *jiriki*). In other words, it is not possible to pursue the classic bodhisattva path – what Daochuo had called the 'path of sages'. In the time of *mappō*, this is the 'difficult path'. Teachings belonging to the 'gate of the Pure Land', by contrast, preach reliance on the Other Power (*tariki*) of Amida Buddha. Through Amida's transfer of merit, as embodied in their bodhisattva vows, we are assured of immediate rebirth in the Pure Land at death, which then provides the perfect environment for attaining full awakening. This is the 'easy path' and is ideally suited to the degenerate age.

In this way, Hōnen formulated a simple yet compelling system of doctrinal classification and evaluation. Rather than getting bogged down in the intricacies of *panjiao*, which attempted to square the circle by assigning all scriptures to different phases of the Buddha's life, now all teachings were assigned to one of just two categories: the Dharma-gate of the sages or the Pure Land Dharma-gate. Moreover, these categories were linked to the conviction that the world had entered *mappō*, a time in which most of the true teachings have been lost and the spiritual capacities of sentient beings have degenerated. Consequently, the scriptures and doctrines that centre on gaining enlightenment through learning and discipline – the Dharma-gate of the sages – are no longer practicable. Only the teachings on rebirth in the Pure Land remain potent.

The right and miscellaneous practices

Hōnen follows Shandao in sorting all practices into the categories of 'right' and 'miscellaneous' (*Sen*, pp.64–9). The five right practices are as follows:

1. Sutra-chanting (of the three Pure Land scriptures)
2. Contemplation (of the blessings of the Pure Land)
3. Reverence (bowing to Amida Buddha)
4. Reciting the name (of Amida)
5. Giving praise and offerings (to Amida)[19]

The miscellaneous practices comprise any manifestation of the five right practices that is *not* directed towards Amida Buddha, together with all other Dharma practices, such as giving, practising the precepts, and so on. First, Hōnen selects the right practices above the miscellaneous practices. Then, within the five right practices, he selects the right established act, which is chanting the nembutsu, as paramount while the other four forms of practice are relegated as auxiliary acts.

To justify his selection of the right practices above the miscellaneous practices, Hōnen, again following Shandao, makes a series of five contrasts. First, the right practices promote an intimate relation with Amida, whereas the miscellaneous practices result in estrangement. Second, the right practices promote a near relation with the Buddha, whereas the miscellaneous practices result in a distant, far relation. Third, the right practices promote a perpetual or incessant awareness of Amida Buddha, whereas the miscellaneous practices result only in an intermittent awareness. Fourth, the right practices automatically result in a process of the transference of merit towards birth in the Pure Land, whereas the miscellaneous practices only serve this function if the practitioner expressly intends it. Hōnen asserts that, even if someone fulfilling one of the right practices does not consciously direct their merits towards the attainment of birth, this transference will happen anyway. Citing Shandao, he argues that: '"Namu" means "to take refuge". It also means "to desire to transfer one's merits". "Amida Butsu" is the practice. For this reason, one can surely attain Rebirth [by reciting it].'[20] Finally, in the fifth contrast, the right practices are considered 'pure' in the sense that they lead directly to rebirth in the Pure Land. The miscellaneous practices, however, do not directly favour such rebirth, but instead lead to 'the realms of human and heavenly beings, to the three vehicles, or to [birth in other] pure lands' (*Sen*, pp.68–9).

The right established act

Based on this system of classification, and combined with his convictions concerning *mappō*, Hōnen concluded that the practice of nembutsu recitation was the right established act, and so the superlative means to accomplish liberation. Moreover, it works universally for all beings:

> Why should anyone cast aside the exclusive and right
> practice, by which a hundred out of a hundred obtain birth,
> and stubbornly clinging to the miscellaneous practices,
> by which not even one out of a thousand attain birth?
> Practitioners ought seriously to ponder this. (*Sen*, p.71)

Interpreting a passage from the *Contemplation Sutra*, he glosses the instruction to 'single-mindedly concentrate' on the Buddha as indicating that we ought to leave aside all other spiritual practices and *only* recite the nembutsu (*Sen*, pp.84–5). The simplicity of recitation means that *everyone* can be blessed by Amida's compassionate light. This includes the lowly and spiritually destitute. Referring to those who have committed one of the 'five heinous acts',[21] Hōnen writes: 'Only the power of the nembutsu can destroy these kinds of sins. Therefore, it was for the sake of the most wicked and inferior people that the highest Dharma of the supremely good practice [i.e. the nembutsu] was expounded' (*Sen*, p.122). Those who continue to pursue other practices, however, will remain in darkness (*Sen*, p.98). For Hōnen 'The nembutsu is the refined practice that was long ago adopted from among twenty-one billion practices' (*Sen*, p.98), whereas the miscellaneous practices were rejected. Hōnen's position is tantamount to a rejection of *all* other forms of practice besides nembutsu recitation. Little wonder that it proved highly controversial and even incited angry condemnation that would result in his exile.

According to Hōnen, Amida Buddha selected the nembutsu as the right established act, and this is the true significance of the Eighteenth or Primal Vow. In order to justify this view, he makes a further set of contrasts: between inferior and superior and between difficult and easy (*Sen*, p.76). The nembutsu is regarded as superior, as it is 'the container into which all of [Amida's] uncountable virtues have flowed' (*Sen*, p.76). All other practices, by contrast, produce only 'a limited portion of merit and virtue' (*Sen*, p.76). To illustrate this point he employs the analogy of the word 'house', which includes within itself all the various constituents of a house

– rafters, beams, pillars, and so on – but does not include their names. Thus the nembutsu expresses the principle of synecdoche, where a part may stand for the whole or the whole may stand for a part, as it epitomizes and calls forth Amida's incalculable merit.

With regard to difficult and easy practice, Hōnen affirms that the nembutsu is easy whereas all other practices are difficult. He reasons that, if the Primal Vow had required us to fulfil more demanding practices, very few people would be able to attain birth in the Pure Land. For this reason, Amida 'moved with an impartial compassion and wishing to save all beings universally [...] chose the single practice of uttering the Nembutsu' (*Sen*, p.78). This reasoning is compelling since, if Amida Buddha is truly compassionate, and so wants to help all beings, why would Amida require them to carry out difficult practices in order to merit aid?

An obvious objection to Hōnen is that, if the nembutsu is the ultimate message of the Buddha, why did he teach so many other practices and approaches? All exclusive approaches face this same problem. Hōnen argues that 'those practices were expounded only in order eventually to bring all sentient beings simply to recite the name of Amida Buddha' (*Sen*, p.84). In other words, they were taught so that they could then be abandoned in favour of nembutsu recitation. This argument is reminiscent of the 'Parable of the magic city' found in the *Lotus Sutra*, which is used to justify why the Buddha initially taught the 'lesser path' of individual enlightenment even though his true message consisted in the bodhisattva path.[22]

Elsewhere, Hōnen argues that the miscellaneous practices were taught as provisional, skilful means taking into account the karmic affinities of various beings (*Sen*, p.89). In addition, through the expounding of the miscellaneous practices, the relative shallowness and depth of their spiritual aspiration is revealed. Hōnen goes on to reinterpret the significance of the three classes of rebirth in the Pure Land as expounded in the *Larger Scripture*. Their distinguishing characteristic is no longer *which* practices they follow and with what attitude, since all should now focus exclusively on the nembutsu, but rather *how many* repetitions they complete (*Sen*, p.90). Those belonging to the superior class recite the nembutsu a minimum of 30,000 times a day.

Hōnen emphasizes constant and lifelong vocal recitation of the nembutsu, since it is charged with the incalculable merit of Amida and so dissolves away bad karma. By means of the nembutsu, Amida transfers to us the untold merit that they accumulated throughout their bodhisattva path. In addition, recitation establishes an intimate, devotional bond, a mutual care and concern between the devout and Amida. To support this claim, Hōnen cites a rather beautiful and mystical passage from Shandao:

> When sentient beings arouse themselves to practise and always recite with their lips the name of the Buddha, the Buddha will hear them. When they constantly and reverently bow down to the Buddha with their bodies, the Buddha will see them. When they constantly think of the Buddha in their hearts, the Buddha will know them. *When sentient beings remember the Buddha, the Buddha also remembers them.* In these three acts, the Buddha and sentient beings are not separate from each other. Hence, they are called the intimate karmic relations. (*Sen*, p.67, emphasis added)

For Hōnen, vocal nembutsu does not just burn off bad karma but also establishes a resonance, an intimate, loving, and saving connection with Amida Buddha.

Hōnen turned away from some aspects of deathbed nembutsu practice, since he reconceived the causal basis of *raigō* in terms of Other Power. The conventional view was that the practitioner's determined focus at the moment of death *causes* Amida and their attendants to descend in welcome. But for Hōnen it was the other way around: that is to say, Amida comes to welcome the dying practitioner because of the nembutsu that person has chanted all along. Moreover, it is Amida's revelation before them that in fact enables the dying person to sustain mindfulness, be filled with joy, and so renounce saṃsāra in favour of the Pure Land.[23] In short, Hōnen understood deathbed nembutsu as entrusting oneself to Amida's compassion rather than contriving liberation through the transaction of the requisite rituals.

Hōnen normalized a devotional orientation to Dharma practice that did away with dependence on monastic life and clerical intercession. Since liberation no longer required decades of sequestered Dharma study, mastery of classical Chinese, and dominion over a complex repertoire of ritual technologies, it was now within the reach of ordinary people – not just the religious professionals. The vocal nembutsu was a practice that anyone anywhere could apply. It required no special training or resources. For this reason, Hōnen's version of Pure Land practice was destined to become a layperson's Buddhism.

Hōnen's exclusivism, which Shinran would reaffirm, may seem to strike an intolerant tone. It certainly jars with a universalist vision of Buddhism. Yet Hōnen is doing no more than underline a basic truth: in order to achieve depth, we need to limit our range. Sangharakshita puts it like this:

> For commitment to be strong it has, in a sense, to be
> narrow. It is only through intensity of commitment and
> practice that you achieve any results. You will not achieve
> that intensity if you try to follow different teachers and
> their different teachings and practices, at the same time.[24]

Given constraints of time, energy, and capacity, we cannot study everything. Worse, multiple approaches may conflict and so give rise to confusion rather than deeper understanding. So should we abandon all other practices?

Both Hōnen and Shinran warn against trying to hedge our bets through following other approaches, at least if we think we can achieve awakening that way. If we really saw into Other Power, we would realize that hedging our bets reveals our persistent attachment to self-power. The nembutsu itself is not something that we practise to achieve a goal. Rather, it expresses an appreciation of how we have, in some sense, already achieved it through Amida's boundless compassion. But we don't, and can't, see into our ego-clinging all at once. We need to be constantly watchful for it.

The emphasis on just nembutsu invites us to reconsider the true purpose of practice. It is not simply a question of abandoning all other practices, but rather one of questioning the mindset that thinks self-generated effort leads to awakening. It also challenges us to investigate the source of the impulse towards practice. Put another way, what is the origin of our urge to go for refuge? The nembutsu becomes the purifying gem, the catalyst for an interior revolution. On my reading, just nembutsu is not about doing one thing only, but rather about seeing that everything radiates from the nembutsu. The nembutsu is the source of practice. These are topics that we will take up more fully in Part 3.

Part 3

Other Power

It is a matter of neither practice nor good acts, neither sudden attainment nor gradual attainment, neither meditative practice nor nonmeditative practice, neither right contemplation nor wrong contemplation, neither thought nor no-thought, neither daily life nor the moment of death, neither many-calling nor once-calling. It is simply shinjin that is inconceivable, inexplicable, and indescribable. It is like the medicine that eradicates all poisons. The medicine of the Tathāgata's Vow destroys the poisons of our wisdom and foolishness. (*CWS*, p.107)

Chapter Nine

Great Practice Is No Practice

> The nembutsu, for its practicers, is not a practice or a good act.
> Since it is not performed out of one's own designs, it is not a
> practice. Since it is not good done through one's own calculation,
> it is not a good act. Because it arises wholly from Other Power
> and is free of self-power, for the practicer, it is not a practice or a
> good act. (*CWS*, p.665)

Namu Amida Butsu. Shinran came to the startling conclusion that
the ego-driven will is not, and never can be, the instrument of
liberation. It is not even the agent of sincere practice since, when
such a will is at work, any practice that it propels is essentially
useless, tainted by its selfish purposes. Whatever self-power
practice we might take up is ultimately futile, since it will be the
product of 'calculation' (*hakarai*) (*CWS*, p.526). Moreover, any belief
that our individual practice is sufficient or even contributory in
bringing about our liberation is, in Shinran's eyes, an expression
of deluded pride. Since we are ignorant beings, everything we
do just enmeshes us deeper in the mire of saṃsāra (*CWS*, pp.312,
525–6). While this picture may at first glance seem discouraging,
for Shinran the humble acknowledgement of our incorrigible status
turns out to be the beginning of an authentic Dharma life. So who
or what could be the agent of our liberation?

For Hōnen, the practice of the nembutsu is the cause of rebirth
in the Pure Land; it *invokes* Amida's Primal Vow, as it is 'charged'
with his incalculable merit. To 'activate' the power of Amida's
vows, we need only cooperate through honouring the nembutsu.
There is, if you like, a kind of bargain. According to Shinran,

however, chanting the nembutsu does not occasion our rebirth in the Pure Land. Why? Because he affirms that such a rebirth has, in a sense, *already* been guaranteed. The nembutsu is intoned not in the hope of earning liberation but out of superabundant joy, as a kind of confirmation. It is an expression of gratitude for already having been 'grasped never to be abandoned' by the compassionate Buddha (*CWS*, p.527). Reciting the nembutsu is neither a spiritual practice nor a 'good act' in the conventional sense, but rather an upwelling within oneself of Other Power. This does not mean that we should abandon recitation altogether, but underlines that the spiritual impulse – such as it is – is gifted by Amida, who practises *through* us. Ultimately, the function of this 'practice' is not to earn our liberation but to enact it.

Shinran's teachings turn everything upside down. On the surface, his views might seem to provoke a kind of spiritual paralysis, a dumbfounded fugue. What then do we actually *do*? What is the meaning and purpose of Dharma practice? In this chapter, I show that, despite differences in approach, Shinran shares some underlying affinities with his contemporary Dōgen in terms of their vision of Dharma practice or, as we shall see, 'no-practice'. In doing so, I affirm the prestige of both as offering profound insights into the Dharma, especially the nature of conditionality, the structure of human awareness, and the meaning of awakening.

To understand how Shinran came to envision the meaning and function of Dharma practice, it will help to go right back to early Buddhism and learn something of the origins of the nembutsu. We need also to review the general Buddhist vision of human beings – their obstacles and their possibilities. In this way, we may begin to trust that, rather than dismissing the entire Buddhist tradition as now obsolete, Shinran's conception of Dharma practice proposes a faithful, even ecstatic, surplus of Buddha devotion. This surplus overflows in grateful astonishment at the plenitude of Amida's wisdom and compassion.

Contemplating the Buddha

As conceived by Shinran, the nembutsu seems improbably remote from the teaching of the historical Buddha and the Pali

Canon. But its origins can be traced back that far. The idea of remembrance or recollection of the Buddha (*Buddhānusmṛti*) is found in the earliest texts. Instead of imagining enlightenment in the abstract, it is contemplated through the *person* of the Buddha, who becomes a kind of icon. Through contemplating his qualities, we may begin to approach and even incarnate the awakened mind. A conspicuous early example of what we would now describe as Buddha contemplation is found in the final text of the *Sutta-Nipāta*, where we are introduced to Pingiya, a faithful follower of the Buddha who recites a beautiful and moving hymn in which he praises his absent master.

> I cannot stay away from him even for a moment, brahman, from Gotama [the Buddha] of great understanding, of great intelligence, who taught me the doctrine which is instantaneous, immediate, the destruction of craving, without distress, the likeness of which does not exist anywhere. I see him with my mind as if with my eye, being vigilant day and night, brahman. I pass the night revering him. For that very reason I think there is no staying away from him. My faith and rapture, (and mindfulness) do not go away from the teaching of Gotama. In whatever direction the one of great wisdom goes, in that very direction I bow down.[1]

Here we have, in germinal form, the recollection of the absent Buddha, which both expresses devotion towards him and serves as a means to connect with the underlying nature of the enlightened mind. We could also refer to this practice or contemplation as a form of going for refuge to the Buddha, going for refuge being the most fundamental expression of commitment.

A more developed form of Buddha contemplation is found in the devotional chant known as the *Buddhavandana*, in which we call to mind a series of eight qualities of the Buddha:

> That Blessed One is such since he is accomplished, fully enlightened, endowed with [clear] vision and [virtuous] conduct, sublime, the knower of worlds, the incomparable

leader of men to be tamed, the teacher of gods and men, enlightened and blessed.[2]

This practice was incorporated into a series of six recollections that also included the Dharma and the Sangha (the Three Jewels). Contemplation or recollection of the Buddha assumed more visual and dramatic forms too. By the second century CE, texts emerged that presented detailed instructions on how to contemplate both the qualities and the appearance of the Buddha in their cosmic, archetypal manifestations. The earliest recorded text of this sort is the *Pratyutpanna Samādhi Sūtra*, which teaches 'the meditation in which the Buddhas of the present all stand before one'. The *Sūtra* uses Amitābha as an example and instructs that, with a firm basis in keeping the precepts, we should go to a secluded place and call to mind Amitābha Buddha in the western quarter. We should reflect that a thousand million myriad Buddha-fields away is Amitābha's land called Sukhāvatī, where they are preaching the Dharma right now in the midst of an incalculable throng of bodhisattvas. The Buddha should be constantly called to mind over a period of a day and a night, or for seven days and nights. After seven days, we will see the Buddha, if not in a waking state then in a dream.[3] In this vision, Buddha Amitābha explains that, to be reborn in their land, we must call them to mind constantly with this intention. The Buddha of the *Sūtra* then explains:

> [T]hese bodhisattvas [...] should always call him [Amitābha] to mind in this way: 'The Buddha's body is endowed with all the thirty-two marks, he radiates light, he is fine and upstanding beyond compare, in the midst of the assembly of monks he preaches the sutras, and the sutras he preaches are of indestructible form.'[4]

So this version of *Buddhānusmṛti* combines 'calling to mind' the Buddha, contemplation, devotion, and aspiration to be born in the Pure Land. It also emphasizes contemplating the Buddha in their ultimate aspect, that is to say, as a manifestation of *śūnyatā*:

When they reflect on the Buddha they ought not to reflect on [them as] an existing thing, nor should they have [the notion: 'It is something'] set up by me. As they would conceive of emptiness so should they reflect on the Buddha standing there, like a precious gem set on beryl.[5]

In Chinese, *Buddhānusmṛti* is rendered as *nianfo*, in which the element *nian* comes to refer *both* to thinking about the Buddha (*fo*) and to reciting his name. In the longer and shorter Pure Land sutras, invocation of the Buddha's name is not recommended explicitly. Instead, the texts exhort us to call Amida Buddha to mind with the desire to be born in their Pure Land.[6] In addition, the importance of *hearing* the Buddha's name is highlighted. The seventeenth vow states that the Buddhas of the ten quarters will recite Amida's name. One way to interpret this is that, when we recite Amida's name, we *join* the Buddhas of the ten quarters (*CWS*, p.532). The recitation of the name is first mentioned explicitly in the *Contemplation Sutra*, where it is recommended to those eligible for only the lowest grades of rebirth in the Pure Land. If someone is incapable of contemplating the Buddha owing to acute suffering at the moment of death, or if they have lived a grossly unskilful life, they should say the name. This will enable them to be born in the Pure Land, albeit at the lowest grade.[7] From what we have seen so far, we can identify four methods of *nianfo*:

1. Recollection of the Buddha
2. Hearing the name of the Buddha
3. Calling or praising the name of the Buddha (vocal invocation)[8]
4. Visualizing and contemplating the Buddha

All these methods were previously applied to other Buddhas, not just Amida. However, owing to Amida Buddha's paramount importance in East Asia, *nianfo* came to be associated specifically with them.

Hōnen and Shinran derive their justification for an *exclusive* focus on the vocal nembutsu (*nianfo*) from Shandao. Shandao had selected invoking and praising Amida as the 'right and determining action', which he outlines in the following way:

With single-minded attention, be attentive (*nian*) of the
name of Amida. Whether walking or standing, sitting or
lying, without consideration of the length of time, at each
single instant (*nian-nian*) not let[ting] it go, this is called the
right and determining action.[9]

It is not clear to what extent Shandao prioritized vocal nembutsu.
It is probable that he subscribed to a broader conception of
Buddha contemplation and encouraged vocal nembutsu only
for those unsuited to more exacting practices.[10] For Hōnen and
Shinran, however, the more complex aspects of contemplation,
including visualization, were set aside in favour of just *saying* the
name (nembutsu), which becomes the right established act. The
name functions as a kind of epitome of Amida Buddha and their
qualities, as well as revealing the Primal Vow.

The treasure ocean of virtues

Shinran exalts nembutsu recitation as 'great practice'. In the
chapter on practice (*gyō*) in *True Teaching*, he declares:

> This practice, embodying all good acts and possessing all
> roots of virtue, is perfect and most rapid in bringing about
> birth. It is the treasure ocean of virtues that is suchness
> or true reality. For this reason, it is called great practice.
> (*CWS*, p.13)

So the nembutsu is the means through which we come to
understand the ultimate nature of reality, and so call forth all the
inexhaustible qualities of awakening. He goes on to say that the
practice of nembutsu arises from the vow of great compassion,
which is Amida Buddha's seventeenth vow. This vow specifies
hearing the name rather than saying it but the two come to be seen as
one, especially when interpreted in the light of the Eighteenth Vow.
The seventeenth vow goes like this: 'If, when I attain Buddhahood,
the countless Buddhas throughout the worlds in the ten quarters
do not all praise and say my Name, may I not attain the supreme
enlightenment' (*CWS*, p.13).

It may seem curious that Amida, as part of their aspiration towards awakening, wants all Buddhas to praise them and say their name. It sounds a bit vain, doesn't it? But what might it mean that all the Buddhas proclaim Amida's name? We could answer that it means to call forth the awakening mind and to share it throughout the cosmos. To hear the name means to receive the perpetual blessing of the Buddha. The nembutsu *is* Amida Buddha, and through it all their spiritual virtues are called forth. Through it, Amida becomes real. Through it, Amida proliferates compassion and wisdom throughout the universe. After offering a series of scriptural 'proofs' as to the pre-eminent value of the nembutsu, Shinran concludes that 'saying the Name breaks through all the ignorance of sentient beings and fulfils all their aspirations. Saying the Name is the right act, supreme, true, and excellent' (*CWS*, p.17).

Later in the same chapter, Shinran cites a Chinese master, Yuanchao, who comments:

> Needless to say, our Buddha Amida grasps beings with
> the Name. Thus, as we hear it with our ears and say it with
> our lips, exalted virtues without limit grasp and pervade
> our hearts and minds. It becomes ever after the seed of our
> Buddhahood, all at once sweeping away a koti of kalpas
> of heavy karmic evil, and we attain the realization of the
> supreme enlightenment. (*CWS*, p.48)

At the same time, Shinran emphasizes that 'great practice' is not just mechanical repetition. He distinguishes between outer and inner causes for rebirth in the Pure Land, and also between direct and indirect causes. The outer causes are the nembutsu, which is the direct cause, and Amida Buddha's infinite light, which is the indirect cause. The inner cause is shinjin or wholehearted entrusting (see Chapter 10), without which 'one will not reach the land of light' (*CWS*, p.54). Shinran insists that all of these causes are gifted to us by Amida Buddha, and confirms that saying the nembutsu 'embodies the Primal Vow, in which the nembutsu was selected and adopted' (*CWS*, p.237). Elsewhere, he underlines that great practice is not the dedication of our own merits towards rebirth in the Pure Land, but rather 'It is the fulfilled practice that

Amida directs to beings out of great compassion, and therefore is called "not-directing virtue [on the part of beings]'" (*CWS*, p.298). In other words, the nembutsu as cause for rebirth is 'powered' by Amida's inexhaustible virtues, which are gifted to us through the nembutsu. It is this transfer of merits from Amida Buddha to us, rather than our own karmic impetus, that assures our birth in the Pure Land.

In relation to how we should carry out the 'great practice', Shinran reassures us that there is no set number of times that we ought to recite the nembutsu, nor is there a particular time or occasion when it should be voiced:

> Since we have been given this Vow by the Tathāgata, we can take any occasion in daily life for saying the Name and need not wait to recite it at the very end of life; we should simply give ourselves up totally to the entrusting with sincere mind of the Tathāgata. (*CWS*, p.494)

The possibility of saying the nembutsu according to self-power remains, but this is not great practice and will not lead to rebirth in the Pure Land. In order for the nembutsu to be elevated to great practice it needs to be 'given' by Amida Buddha, which means that we carry it out in the confidence that Amida's compassion is working within us and through us. In this way, it calls us towards awakening. Shinran insists that 'The nembutsu of Amida's Primal Vow is not our practice, it is not our good' (*CWS*, p.555). How so? Because its value depends not on us but rather on Amida Buddha's incalculable merits.

Shinran affirms that we *should* say the name, but equally this must be accompanied by shinjin. Accordingly, someone who entrusts to Amida Buddha and undertakes to say the nembutsu is sure to be reborn in the Pure Land (*CWS*, p.539). In *Notes on Once-Calling and Many-Calling*, Shinran allows that it may even be sufficient to say the name just *once* in order to be assured of birth: 'In entrusting ourselves to the Tathāgata's Primal Vow and saying the Name once, necessarily, without seeking it, we are made to receive the supreme virtues, and without knowing it, we acquire the great and vast benefit' (*CWS*, p.481).

Shinran's 'rejection' of deathbed nembutsu

Where earlier generations of Pure Land devotees had relied heavily on deathbed nembutsu, and Hōnen offered a somewhat ambiguous stance, Shinran completely reinterprets its meaning. This arises from his reimagining of the function of the nembutsu and the meaning of the instant of birth (*ojō*) in the Pure Land. He points out:

> The practicer of true shinjin, however, abides in the stage of the truly settled, for he or she has already been grasped, never to be abandoned. There is no need to wait in anticipation for the moment of death, no need to rely on Amida's coming. *At the time shinjin becomes settled, birth too becomes settled*; there is no need for the deathbed rites that prepare one for Amida's coming. (*CWS*, p.523, emphasis added)

Shinran goes further. *Raigō*, Amida's welcome with a host of bodhisattvas, actually unfolds within the *present* life:

> Amida and a vast and numberless saintly host, consisting of innumerable manifestation-bodies of Buddhas, of Avalokiteśvara, and of Mahāsthāmaprāpta, appear in person to be alongside and always protect those who have realized true and real shinjin, at all times and in all places. (*CWS*, p.453)

He affirms that deathbed nembutsu is redundant for persons who have realized shinjin. Rather, it serves as a last resort for those who have not yet done so:

> Those whose shinjin has become true and real – this being the benefit of the Vow – have been grasped, never to be abandoned; hence they do not depend on Amida's coming at the moment of death. The person whose shinjin has not yet become settled awaits the moment of death in anticipation of Amida's coming. (*CWS*, p.549)

Thus Shinran resolves any uncertainty about assurance of birth in the Pure Land by designating the arising of shinjin as the liberative crux. This move also banishes any legalism associated with building up stocks of merit through reciting the nembutsu with the aim of transferring the merit accrued to future birth in the Pure Land. In this way, Shinran transformed practice from being a calculated investment in future salvation into the enactment of a profound, existential conversion.

Practice as realization

It is standard to contrast the devotional orientation of Shin Buddhism, and its emphasis on the nembutsu, with the aesthetic, contemplative approach of Zen, and its emphasis on sitting meditation. For many casual observers, Zen manifests the idyllic vision of Buddhist practice: simplicity, discipline, silence, and inner peace. Shin Buddhists, by contrast, since they don't meditate but only chant, seem to transgress the orientalist projection. Yet there are striking parallels. Dōgen, who is credited as the founder of Sōtō Zen, was an exact contemporary of Shinran, although there is no evidence that they knew each other or even that they knew *of* each other. Despite their apparent incommensurability, Shinran's approach to nembutsu reveals surprising overlaps with Dōgen's vision of zazen.[11] We might propose that Shinran rejected nembutsu in the same way that Dōgen rejected meditation. Hang on, you may think, didn't they precisely reject everything else and, instead, accept the nembutsu and zazen respectively?

It is not received wisdom to read Shinran's teaching as a negation of nembutsu nor, for that matter, is Dōgen's teaching usually characterized as a rejection of meditation. Quite the opposite. Shinran is believed to have taught 'faith' in nembutsu practice, while Dōgen insisted on meditation as the key spiritual discipline. But, despite the fact that Shinran and Dōgen used the terms 'nembutsu' and 'meditation' respectively, both were engaged in an enterprise that completely reimagined the meanings of these terms and the 'practices' that they referred to. In doing so, both overturned established models of authentic Dharma practice.

Both Shinran and Dōgen rejected all existing Buddhist practices in order to propose activities that were, strictly speaking, 'no practice'. In other words, they could not be appropriated in terms of self-directed effort that has liberation as its goal. They could not be conceived in this way because both Shinran and Dōgen were convinced that, in a sense, the goal of enlightenment had already been achieved. This, in turn, was how they resolved the relationship between practice and awakening. For both, practice does not lead towards awakening but expresses it or is even coterminous with it. At the same time, there are some important differences between their respective visions.

Dōgen did not accept *mappō* as Shinran did. Rather, we are told, he was puzzled by the doctrine of inherent enlightenment (*hongaku*), which was prevalent within the Tendai school during his formative years. If we are all inherently awakened, he wondered, why have teachers down the ages emphasized the need for spiritual practice? Dōgen resolved this dilemma through developing a novel understanding of the relationship between meditation and awakening, known as the 'oneness of practice and realization' (*shushō ittō*):

> To think practice and realization are not one is a non-Buddhist view. In the Buddha Dharma, practice and realization are one and the same. As your present practice is practice in realization, your initial negotiation of the Way is in itself the whole of original realization [...] practice points directly to original realization.[12]

Practice is not a means to an end but *manifests* that end. Awakening is neither a fruit of the past nor a hope for the future, but perpetually reveals itself in the present. Awakening cannot be attained because it does not arise at an instant in time but rather points to a reality that stands outside time as we normally conceive of it.

Shinran's predicament was slightly different from Dōgen's, although his solution was really quite similar. First, he was imbued with the deep pessimism of *mappō* thought, which spoke to his own existential condition, his sense of radical insufficiency. He had concluded that, in this degenerate age, the path of sages (i.e. the path of self-power) is beyond the capacities of human beings. Even reciting the nembutsu cannot serve to liberate us, as it expresses calculation or egocentric clinging. Moreover, for Shinran, *mappō* does not just describe a contingent, historical epoch, but reveals an ever-present existential truth concerning human limitedness. So his problem might be stated like this: if we are ignorant beings trapped by our ego-clinging, how can we ever become otherwise, since all our actions are confirmations of that ignorant clinging? We are pinned inside ourselves. On the surface, Shinran's answer is through Other Power, which reaches out to us as though from outside. It breaks open our limitedness and supplants our egocentric tendency with *bodhichitta*, or Amida's compassionate will. He notes that:

> it is through Amida's design that we come to say the nembutsu with the belief that, saved by the inconceivable working of the Tathāgata's great Vow of great Compassion, we will part from birth-and-death. This being realized, *our calculation is not in the least involved.* (*CWS*, p.667, emphasis added)

Shinran's radical valorization of the nembutsu unfastens it from the strictures of human will (self-power) and reformulates it as expressing the confirmation of the 'definitely assured state'. The nembutsu is no longer a means through which we come to identify ourselves with Amida's mind, or through which we accumulate merit, or even a means that facilitates our liberation. Rather, the nembutsu confirms and celebrates that we have, in a sense, always already attained liberation. The nembutsu irrupts as the mental, verbal, and even physical manifestation of Amida's compassionate working through us.[13] Consequently, it is not a practice but rather the spontaneous revelation of Amida's vow.

The question for Shinran, as it was for Dōgen, was not how to attain enlightenment but rather how to recognize and disclose it. Consequently, practice comprises two aspects: (1) a recognition of our primordial enlightenment and (2) the functioning of that enlightenment within everyday life. These two aspects do not amount to practices at all, at least in the instrumental sense, since they in no way contribute towards our enlightenment. For Shinran, the moment of recognition is shinjin, which itself does not arise through self-directed practice but is primordially gifted. Moreover, the practical expression of enlightenment in our daily life is the nembutsu. We recite the nembutsu not to achieve any goal but rather as the spontaneous expression of joy at realizing that we are 'equal to the Buddhas' and always have been. And this despite the fact that, in the very same instant, we are 'possessed of blind passions'. So the nembutsu is intended not to serve the purposes of the egocentric will but rather to actualize what transcends that will. This is what Shinran terms 'great practice'.

While Dōgen asserted that meditation and enlightenment are one, Shinran affirmed that nembutsu and shinjin are one. Nembutsu does not give rise to shinjin: it reveals it. In shinjin, we realize that we are equal to all the Buddhas. 'There is no shinjin separate from nembutsu [...] there can be no nembutsu separate from shinjin. Both should be understood as Amida's Vow. Nembutsu and shinjin on our part are themselves the manifestations of the Vow' (CWS, p.538). Shinjin and nembutsu would seem then to be coterminous. However, Shinran's perspective is still more complex and unsettling. He came to believe that our moral failings are not the impediment to liberation that traditional Buddhism has consistently asserted. He argued that ethically compromised individuals – that is to say, all of us – are precisely the focus of Amida's concern. It is precisely the delusion of our own righteousness that holds us back from fully accepting the scope of the vow. He firmly believed that '[e]ven the good person is born in the Pure Land, so without question is the person who is evil' (CWS, p.663).

Thus shinjin consists in a dual realization: on the one hand, we wake up to the fact that our mind is identical to that of Amida Buddha, that is to say, it is inherently connected to the impulses of wisdom and compassion. But, on the other, we also see that we are foolish beings (bonpu). This creates a perpetual tension or paradox as we oscillate between one aspect of the insight and the other – at times in despair, at times smug. Remembering that our mind is intimately connected to the Buddha mind consoles and reassures us but may also lead to self-inflation, ego appropriation, and disdain for practice. At the same time, constantly waking up to our incorrigible shortcomings reaffirms our gratitude and indebtedness to Amida, and instils within us a deep humility that offsets the danger of complacency. An excessive focus on our human inadequacy may lead us into doubt and despair, which is why Shinran emphasizes that it is precisely for us, flawed beings, that Amida formulated his vow:

> When I consider deeply the Vow of Amida, which arose
> from five kalpas of profound thought, I realize that it
> was entirely for the sake of myself alone! Then how I am
> filled with gratitude for the Primal Vow, in which Amida
> resolved to save me, though I am burdened with such
> heavy karma. (*CWS*, p.679)

Shinjin is not cultivated through individual effort but entrusted to us by Amida Buddha through their compassionate transfer of merit (*ekō*). In other words, Amida grants not only assurance of rebirth in the Pure Land but also the confidence to trust in that fact. Shinjin is not something that the individual nurtures, it is a blessing *bestowed* by Amida. In fact, it is precisely when we truly abandon believing that we can liberate ourselves that we realize that Amida's light is shining upon us and always has been (*CWS*, pp.79–80). For this reason, it arises 'altogether without one's own working' (*CWS*, p.525). Shinran writes:

> when we entrust ourselves to the inconceivable working of
> the Vow, taking it as essential, the inconceivable working
> of the Name is also included; the inconceivable working of
> the Vow and that of the Name are one, with no distinction
> whatever. (*CWS*, p.663)

In other words, Amida's vow reveals itself through the nembutsu and so, in this way, the saying of the nembutsu is coterminous with the realization of being assured of rebirth in the Pure Land, even with enlightenment itself. Shinjin, it seems to me, can never become a prior fact that we can stand back and admire, but rather it is always being revealed in the present.

For Shinran, then, the nembutsu is not a practice in the conventional sense because, first of all, it is not the product of our egocentric will and, second, it does not lead anywhere. It has no goal in mind, since it confirms and reveals that the goal has, in a sense, already been fulfilled. At the same time, the utterance of the nembutsu does not erase our deluded mind. In a way, it actually confirms it. But it also contains this foolish mind within an infinitely larger universe – the bodhisattva ideal, the bodhichitta, universal compassion. The person through whom the nembutsu is uttered becomes a conduit for, even a revelation of, the Primal Vow – a visible manifestation of Amida Buddha's compassionate working on earth. This also means that it converts the person who says the nembutsu *into* Other Power.

The Other Power perspective thus invites me to joyfully *receive* Dharma practice, rather than fabricating it and then anxiously pushing it along. Practice is gifted to me rather than driven by me. What a relief. So often my impulse to practise is quite feeble and easily derailed. But there is a stronger impetus that is beyond me and that wants to reveal itself through me. I can set aside my fretful striving because sincere practice does not arise from my self-directed will. This also engenders a sense of abundance and gratitude. Rather than feeling that all my efforts go against the grain of my habitual self, I am instead aligning with something that wants to make itself known within and through me.

But it is not that I shouldn't do *anything*. I don't think that I should abandon meditation, devotion, or ethical practice, and just binge on popcorn and online TV. Rather, the Other Power perspective encourages a turning about in how I understand the driving force that grounds practice, as well as fomenting a new understanding of its purpose. The motive is now not so goal-oriented. It is less future-oriented. The impulse to practise is less ego-centred because practice is given rather than contrived. As a consequence, I cannot really practise improperly since such practice doesn't depend on 'me', at least not the me that I normally identify with. Other Power points to a revolution in motivation and intention.

Chapter Ten

Shinjin: The Diamond-Like True Mind

> Great shinjin is the superlative means for attaining longevity and deathlessness. It is the wondrous way to awaken aspiration for the pure and rejection of the defiled. It is the straightforward mind directed to us through the selected Vow. It is shinjin that actualizes Amida's profound and vast benefiting of others. It is true mind that is diamondlike and indestructible [...] It is the true cause of attaining great nirvana. (*CWS*, p.79)

Shinjin is the central mystery and ultimate concern of Shinran's religious universe. It is the axis on which Shin Buddhism revolves, the normative disposition of the sincere and transformed practitioner. Through shinjin, 'we, who are like bits of tile and pebbles, are turned into gold' (*CWS*, pp.459–60). We are spiritualized, raised up, even to the level of being equal to the Buddhas.

While it has been common in some popular and comparative works to render shinjin as 'faith', such a translation is not just inadequate but misleading for a term that is so resonant and multivalent. There is no simple definition that can capture what shinjin points towards. Instead, we are required to enter the universe of meaning where this term makes sense. While the translations 'true entrusting', 'entrusting heart', or 'surety' offer some indications, no single word or phrase can capture shinjin's many shades of meaning, several of which will be highlighted below. Translated more freely, shinjin might even be rendered as 'letting go' or 'letting *through*'.

The gift of shinjin

According to Shinran, shinjin does not arise through self-power, but consists in Amida gifting us an intimate connection with their own mind (or in becoming aware that Amida has *already* done so). This gives rise to a state of serene confidence. Shinjin becomes actualized through the invocation of the nembutsu (*Namu Amida Butsu*). Shinjin and nembutsu are therefore coterminous; it is not that we realize shinjin and then recite the nembutsu, nor that we recite the nembutsu to bring about shinjin but, instead, the two emerge together as expressions of Amida's working through us. Perhaps we could say that shinjin is the subjectively experienced assurance of being grasped by Amida never to be abandoned, whereas the nembutsu is the objective sign of that assurance. The arising of shinjin is not an event that happens in linear time, but one that discloses itself when that time is ruptured, that is to say when the egocentric habit gives way and allows the possibility of a new mode of functioning. This consists in a kind of rebirth or conversion in which our self-serving effort is superseded by Other Power, an influence that seems to come from outside or beyond us. It does not form part of nor can it be appropriated by the habitual self. Rather, it transcends that self to disclose the compassionate orientation that Amida embodies.

Shinjin is not faith because, first of all, it has no object and, second, it is not an action of the self. Through shinjin our subjectivity becomes identified with Amida Buddha. Despite this, we remain entrenched in our foolish ways. Shinjin does not release us from our stupidity but rather intensifies our awareness of it while, at the same time, offering us the assurance that we are destined to become fully enlightened. Birth in the Pure Land is no longer deferred until the moment of death but, rather, fulfilled proleptically in the arising of shinjin as we come to the joyful awareness that we are 'truly settled'.

Shinjin, the nembutsu, our birth in the Pure Land, and our eventual enlightenment are all undergirded by Amida's unfathomable transference of merit (*ekō*). The exclusive source of spiritual value and liberation is this immense merit that Amida gathered over incalculable lifetimes of practice, and its transfer to us is guaranteed by the *Larger Scripture*, which confirms that Amida fulfilled their aspiration towards complete enlightenment. Amida's transfer of merit is really the transfer of their own mind or nature to all beings without exception. This equips beings with the necessary attitude to call on Amida and so be reborn in their Pure Land. As Shinran puts it: 'whether with regard to practice or to shinjin, there is nothing whatever that has not been fulfilled through Amida Tathāgata's directing of virtue to beings out of his pure Vow-mind' (*CWS*, p.93).

At the same time, through the arising of shinjin, we enter into a kind of double or contradictory awareness: on the one hand we experience joy as we recognize our essential identity with Amida. On the other, we feel still more keenly the constraints of our samsaric boundedness, which in turn provokes an ethical reformation. As we further explore the resonances of shinjin, we will see that it leads us to re-evaluate key notions like going for refuge, bodhichitta, and Buddha-nature. Ironically, although Shinran presents shinjin as the 'easy path', he also makes it clear that 'the genuine *difficulty* is realizing true and real shinjin' (*CWS*, p.79, emphasis added). This is because it is so difficult for us to let go of the workings of self-power. In other words, it is difficult to surrender the ego-cherishing attitude.

Shinjin as real going for refuge

The fundamental practice of any Buddhist is to go for refuge to the Three Jewels. This means to place the Buddha, Dharma, and Sangha at the centre of one's life. Going for refuge is usually conceived as an act of individual choice and will, and is expressed through a commitment to ethics, meditation, devotion, and the aspiration towards awakening. It is most commonly understood in terms of self-power. Shinran makes clear reference to going for refuge in relation both to shinjin and to the recitation of nembutsu. The nembutsu in its very structure encapsulates the principle of going for refuge to the Buddha. But Shinran puts forward a radical understanding of the *source* of going for refuge. For him, going for refuge is not an action of the ego-directed will but is, rather, informed by a higher principle as personified in Amida.

Amida goes for refuge *through* us. Or perhaps we could say that Amida transfers to us the momentum of their own going for refuge. In other words, the impulse to practise is not a property of the mundane will but the irruption of something transcendent. Sangharakshita has likened the arising of shinjin to what he terms 'real going for refuge':

> In view of the fact that Śākyamuni the historical Buddha and Amitābha the 'archetypal' or even transcendental Buddha are ultimately identical, and the fact that real Going for Refuge and the path of dependence on the 'other power' *are in principle synonymous*, it should therefore not be difficult for followers of the Jōdo Shinshū to recognise the absolute centrality for the Buddhist life of the act of Going for Refuge.[1]

Subhuti makes a link between real going for refuge and the 'Dharma-niyama', which can be understood as a transcendental order of conditionality, one that supersedes the logic of the ego-directed will. In real going for refuge, the influence of the Dharma-niyama becomes decisive: 'the sense of separate agency is seen as an illusory construct [...] There then emerges a spontaneous flow of increasingly non-egoistic volitions that unfailingly result in skilful activity.'[2] This can be likened to the arising of shinjin, in which the source of spiritual direction is no longer the self-preoccupied will but the mind of Amida transferred to us. We might say that Amida is the *persona* of the Dharma-niyama.

The three minds in one

One of the main ways in which Shinran talks about shinjin is in terms of three minds (*sanshin*) or attitudes. This analysis follows the structure of the Primal Vow (the Eighteenth Vow) of the *Larger Scripture*. The three are: sincere mind, deep mind (or deeply entrusting mind), and aspiring mind (more specifically, the aspiration to be reborn in the Pure Land). In earlier interpretations, these three minds were seen as the responsibility of the individual practitioner (our side of the bargain if you like). But for Shinran, since self-power is redundant, the threefold mind is given or transferred by Amida. Another way to put this is that the three minds imply the transcendence of our ordinary, ego-clinging tendencies and the arising of a new kind of motivation and orientation. This new orientation seems to enter into us from outside because it does not belong within the reach of our habitual awareness. Rather, it disrupts this awareness. Shinran tends to emphasize the three minds as in fact being just a single mind, which is of course the mind of the Buddha Amida (*CWS*, p.112).

Shinran defines sincere mind (*shishin*) as 'that which is true, real, and sincere, the heart of Amida Tathāgata' (*CWS*, p.474). This underscores how the source of the sincere mind is not us but rather Amida. As long as we are entangled in the machinations of self-power, we are incapable of sincerity. A key aspect of sincere mind, then, is waking up to ourselves as ethically compromised, blinkered human beings whose self-contaminated efforts can never bring about liberation (*CWS*, p.493). Shinran quotes Shandao as saying, '[w]e should not express outwardly signs of wisdom, goodness, or diligence, for inwardly we are possessed of falsity' (*CWS*, p.84). This humble recognition of our insufficiency enables us to embrace practice on the basis of Other Power, in which we joyfully recognize that Amida has transferred to us their incalculable spiritual merits. Sincere mind is Amida's working through us. Moreover, the arising of sincere mind moves us to cultivate closer relationships with teachers and companions in the Dharma life and, at the same time, to distance ourselves from those people who are not working to reform their ethical conduct (*CWS*, p.554).

Deep mind (*jinshin*), or deeply entrusting mind, seems to overlap with sincere mind and is characterized by two aspects. The first is to recognize that we are foolish beings trapped in the endless karmic cycle of birth and death, without any hope of escape through our own efforts. The second aspect is to believe deeply that Amida Buddha's forty-eight vows embrace all beings, and so enable us to trust that we will be reborn in the Pure Land. In addition, it is to believe deeply and decidedly that all the Buddhas throughout the ten directions, innumerable as the sands of the River Ganges, give their witness to and encourage all foolish beings to attain birth without exception.

The aspiring mind (*yokushō*) longs to be reborn in the Pure Land. However, for Shinran, '"aspire for birth" is the command of the Tathāgata calling to and summoning the multitudes of all beings' (*CWS*, p.103). In other words, the aspiration originates with Amida Buddha, not with us. The aspiring mind also seeks rebirth within the endless round in order to help other beings: 'after being born in that land, one now awakens great compassion and reenters birth-and-death to teach and guide sentient beings; this too is "directing virtue"' (*CWS*, p.91, citing Shandao). Shinran emphasizes that the three minds are ultimately just one, and this is the manifestation of the true and real mind of the Buddha within us:

> Truly we know that although the terms 'sincere mind',
> 'entrusting', and 'aspiration for birth' differ, their
> significance is the same. Why? Because these three minds
> are already completely untainted by the hindrance of doubt.
> *They are therefore the true and real mind that is single.* This is
> called the diamondlike true mind. The diamondlike true
> mind is true and real shinjin. (*CWS*, p.107, emphasis added)

In affirming that the threefold mind is really just a single mind, Shinran underlines the absence of doubt as being a central characteristic: 'after true shinjin has become settled in us, even if Buddhas like Amida or Śākyamuni should fill the skies and proclaim that Śākyamuni's teaching and Amida's Primal Vow are false, we will not have even one moment of doubt' (*CWS*, p.91, citing Shandao). This indicates that, once it has arisen, shinjin is unshakeable.

Something *promised*

An obvious way to understand shinjin is through the notion of bodhichitta or 'awakening mind', which Sangharakshita has described as the altruistic dimension of going for refuge.[3] The arising of the bodhichitta refers to the moment when an ordinary person transforms into a bodhisattva because they are now motivated by the aspiration to gain enlightenment not just for themselves alone, but also for the benefit of all beings. It is sometimes said that they aspire to guide all beings towards enlightenment. To put this another way, they begin to see that their own process of spiritual liberation is intimately connected to the liberation of all beings; the two are not separate. The bodhichitta is regarded as supremely precious, and is praised in the most lavish terms. The *Bodhicaryavatara*, a poetic evocation of the bodhisattva path, describes the arising of the bodhichitta in the following way:

> From the moment that he takes on that Mind to release the
> limitless realm of beings, with a resolve that cannot be
> turned back,
> From that moment on, though he may doze off or be
> distracted many times, uninterrupted streams of merit like
> the bursting sky continuously pour forth.[4]

The arising of the bodhichitta has something of the miraculous about it, a will that seems to arise from beyond oneself, the presence of which is inexplicable and mysterious.

In the context of the *Larger Scripture*, the forty-eight vows of Amida give voice to the bodhichitta. We could say that through shinjin our path becomes, in a sense, the recapitulation of Dharmākara's cosmic path towards enlightenment. While in traditional Mahāyāna Buddhism the bodhichitta is seen as arising through the individual, it is not exactly a personal will and certainly not an ego-directed impulse. As Sangharakshita puts it:

> It is the bodhicitta that possesses individuals. And those
> of whom the bodhichitta takes possession, as it were, those
> in whom this bodhicitta arises, or within whom it manifests,
> become bodhisattvas. They live, that is to say, for the sake
> of Enlightenment; they strive to actualise, for the benefit of
> all, the highest potentialities that the universe contains [...]
> You get the sense of something vast, cosmic, sublime, which
> descends into and penetrates and possesses those who are
> receptive to it.[5]

This description of the bodhichitta sounds very much like the arising of shinjin. In traditional Mahāyāna, however, the bodhichitta is regarded, at least in some sense, as generated by the individual practitioner, who then seeks to strengthen and realize it through the bodhisattva path. One of the grounds upon which Hōnen's teaching was condemned was on account of his rejection of the cultivation of bodhichitta. He believed that, flawed beings as we are, we are incapable of giving rise to such a sublime aspiration, and so he downplayed its significance. In Shinran's teaching, the bodhichitta is restored but has a distinct origin. We don't cultivate the bodhichitta. Instead, it is given to us in the arising of shinjin. Through shinjin, Amida's bodhichitta is transferred to us or reveals itself within us and through us. Shinran notes: 'You should know that this shinjin is bestowed through the compassionate means of Śākyamuni, Amida, and all the Buddhas in the quarters' (*CWS*, p.527). For Shinran, the bodhichitta does not belong to the apparatus of the self but, rather, emerges precisely in its transcendence, understood as a compassionate will entering into awareness as though from outside.

The fact that Shinran refers to a person in whom shinjin has arisen as a 'definitely-settled bodhisattva' (*CWS*, p.594) underscores the link between shinjin and bodhichitta. Not only are persons of shinjin definitely settled bodhisattvas, but they are also 'equal to Buddhas' since it is certain that they will go on to fulfil complete awakening. Here Shinran's proleptic language is evident: he is prepared to grant the full status of equivalence to the person of shinjin even though they have yet to fulfil the path to complete awakening. This is in part because awakening is seen as dynamic and emergent rather than as belonging to a fixed moment in time.

Another obvious reference for understanding the nature of shinjin is Buddha-nature. According to this idea, deep within us we have the potential to become awakened. But it lies dormant, like a seed waiting to burst into life. In Shinran's thought, through the bestowal of shinjin Amida Buddha is actively communicating to us. In other words, Buddha-nature is not a dormant seed but an active, personal force, or even mind, that seeks expression in and through us:

> Buddha-nature is great shinjin. Why? Because through
> shinjin the bodhisattva-mahasattva has acquired all the
> paramitas from charity to wisdom. *All sentient beings will*

The Promise of a Sacred World

without fail ultimately realize great shinjin. Therefore it is taught, 'All sentient beings are possessed of Buddha-nature.' Great shinjin is none other than Buddha-nature. Buddha-nature is Tathāgata.[6]

We will look at this topic in more detail when considering jinen or 'naturalness'.

The nature of shinjin might also be understood in the light of an 'event', especially as characterized by the philosopher John Caputo. For Caputo, an event is not something that happens, but rather something that is going on *in* what happens, something that is seeking to make itself known *through* what happens.[7] An event is 'ever restless, on the move, seeking new forms to assume'.[8] Events are never finished or fully formed. They are never present but 'draw us out into the future, calling us hither. Events are provocations and promises.'[9] Caputo goes on to characterize an event in the following way: 'Think of a fortuitous visitation by something that we did not invite, the arrival of something unexpected, unforeseeable, unprogrammable, uncontrollable, and even unwarranted. We did not do anything to produce, earn, or deserve it.'[10] Caputo cites the French philosopher Badiou, who talks about a kind of 'laicised grace' that is revealed, or given, through an event. This grace is 'beyond any principle of the management or calculation of existence'.[11] It transcends the calculation of the ego, we might say. An event in this sense is something exceptional that has a transformative and galvanizing impact upon us. It happens *to* us, overtaking and disrupting our ego-subjectivity.

Caputo differentiates an event from 'names'. Names, like shinjin or Amida, give 'temporary shelter' to events, but events themselves are uncontainable and irreducible. An event cannot be confined to the strictures of any particular concept or name. It overflows them. A name can never be the equivalent of the event that it signals and so should never be taken on its own level, that is to say, literally. An event is characterized by *excess*, in the sense that it overtakes us, breaking free of the moorings of the ego. An event is not our own doing; in other words, it is not provoked by the ego but rather is something visited upon us. For Caputo, an event 'is not so much something present as something coming, something stirring, something signalling us from afar, something waiting for us to catch up, something inviting, promising, provoking, and, let us say [...] something *promised*.'[12] This analysis of the mysterious and elusive nature of the event seems to evoke something of the ungraspable, transcendent, even miraculous nature of shinjin.

Turning through the three vows

Shinran's critique of the ego-directed quest for liberation strikes with great force. That the source of all our bondage and suffering cannot, at the same time, serve to liberate us from itself makes compelling sense. In light of this, Other Power, some sort of impulse that transcends the ordinary mind, is necessary. But Shinran's solution provokes a problem of method: how is shinjin activated or realized?

While this may seem like a problem specific to Shinran's theology, it arises, in some guise or other, in many Buddhist models of the goal. For instance, following the logic of the path of sages, if we begin as ignorant beings, how can we ever step outside of that ignorance? Shinran's answer is Other Power: a factor that enters into awareness from a dimension that is beyond the reaches of the ordinary self. This solves the problem from one side. But if no self-directed effort can contribute to the arising of shinjin, how does Other Power even begin to work through us? How to get out of the trap of ego-directed practice?

We can tease out several responses to this dilemma in Shinran's writings. On the surface, his most direct answer as to how shinjin arises is through reciting the nembutsu. We have already seen that to recite the nembutsu is not to do a practice that brings about our liberation, but rather one that expresses or reveals that liberation. So this would seem to imply that shinjin has in fact already arisen, and that the nembutsu is intoned as a joyful confirmation of this. However, Shinran does seem to allow the possibility of recitation without shinjin. Given that we can recite mechanically or insincerely, just reciting the nembutsu is not in itself evidence of the arising of shinjin.

A blunt response to the problem of how shinjin arises might be to point out that the question itself reveals the persistence of the calculating mind. Our doubts about shinjin and about being grasped by Amida reveal our egocentric clinging, our resistance to letting go of self-power. Shinran offers various strategies to alleviate this sort of doubt. First, if our inveterate unskilfulness makes us doubt that we are worthy of Amida's compassion, he consoles us that the fundamental intention of Amida's vow 'is the evil person's attainment of Buddhahood. Hence, evil persons who entrust themselves to Other Power are precisely the ones who possess the true cause of birth' (*CWS*, p.663).

So it is our very imperfection that assures that we have been grasped by Amida. Other Power is an active, compassionate force reaching out to us with the sole intention of freeing us from suffering. But through our misguided reliance on self-power, we stubbornly impede its influence. In order to realize shinjin, it is not that we need to do or develop anything in particular. We just need to stop blocking the way to Amida's constant blessing. It seems alluring to see compassion not just as an abstract possibility but rather as an active, personal force that reaches out to us. But we are still left with the question: how do we stop blocking Amida's compassionate influence?

One way is revealed through Shinran's own trajectory. Having lived a cloistered life as a Tendai monk for around twenty years, observing all the requisite practices, it dawned on him that these efforts had amounted to nothing. He had got nowhere and was, spiritually speaking, lost. It was only on the basis of this deep sensitivity to his insufficiency, to the self-defeating nature of self-power, that he was able to renounce his attachment to it and so open himself to something beyond. He went on to distinguish between two kinds of persons: those for whom self-power remains a viable option, and those for whom it has ceased to be practicable. He clearly assigned himself to the second category. Thus it is not so much that he tries to convince anyone of the merits of Other Power but, rather, that for him self-power was no longer a living option. His *only* option was through shinjin. Shinran testifies to his process of transformation in the following way:

> Thus I, Gutoku Shinran [...] departed everlastingly from the temporary gate of the myriad practices and various good

acts and left forever the birth attained beneath the twin sala trees. Turning about, I entered the 'true' gate of the root of good and the root of virtue, and wholeheartedly awakened the mind leading to the birth that is noncomprehensible.

Nevertheless, I have now decisively departed from the 'true' gate of provisional means and, [my self-power] overturned, have entered the ocean of the selected Vow. Having swiftly become free of the mind leading to the birth that is noncomprehensible, I am assured of attaining the birth that is inconceivable. How truly profound in intent is the Vow that beings ultimately attain birth! (*CWS*, p.240)

This transformative process is characterized in terms of 'turning through the three vows' (*sangan tennyu*), and is laid out in the final chapter of *True Teaching*. It consists in a going forth from self-power (nineteenth vow), to self-power within Other Power (twentieth vow), to absolute Other Power (Eighteenth Vow). Shinran then correlates each stage and vow with one of the three Pure Land sutras. The nineteenth vow is called 'birth attained beneath the twin sala trees' because the aspirant, following the path of sages, the difficult path, seeks to emulate the life of Śākyamuni Buddha, who passed into final nirvana under twin sala trees. This vow is also known as the vow of 'appearing at the time of death', as it promises that Amida Buddha, with an illustrious retinue, will greet assiduous practitioners *in extremis* and welcome them into the Pure Land. Overwhelmed by fear and unable to see the Pure Land, the aspirant calls out desperately to the Buddha, only to end up in the 'land of sloth' (*CWS*, p.211). Nevertheless, the nineteenth vow serves to encourage the follower of the path of sages to seek out Amida Buddha's compassion. This vow is correlated with the *Contemplation Sutra*.

The follower of the twentieth vow abandons all other practices in order to focus exclusively on the nembutsu and so direct the merit gained towards birth in the Pure Land. However, practice according to this vow is still contaminated by self-power. Shinran warns that 'Sages of the Mahāyāna and Hinayana and all good people make the auspicious Name of the Primal Vow their own root of good; hence, they cannot give rise to shinjin and do not apprehend the Buddha's wisdom' (*CWS*, p.240). Such people 'have been enveloped in self-attachment unawares, and do not approach fellow practicers and true teachers' (*CWS*, p.239). Such a person practises self-power within Other Power, and is therefore destined to be reborn in the 'land of doubt' (*CWS*, p.239), where they, while living a very comfortable existence, do not see or hear the Buddha for 500 years. Despite its limitations, Shinran sees merit in this path since it brings us closer to the ultimate mode of practice, whereby we come to abandon our futile, ego-driven efforts to attain birth. So the twentieth vow is a skilful means to lead us to embrace the logic of the Primal or Eighteenth Vow. The twentieth vow is correlated with the *Shorter Scripture*.

Only the practitioner who embraces the Primal Vow can be sure of future enlightenment and be 'truly settled'. The turning through the three vows illustrates a process of gradual transformation and awakening to Other Power. It shows a process of transcending ego-directed practice and an opening up to a higher source of value and direction, as epitomized in Amida's Eighteenth Vow. Shinran does not argue that everyone must follow this sequence, but rather encourages us to embrace Other Power at once.

Shinran writes that '[s]aying the Name is constant mindfulness. Constant mindfulness is right-mindedness. Right-mindedness is the true act [that brings about birth in the Pure Land]' (*CWS*, p.298). We could say that shinjin is mindfulness of the liberative moment. It is not so much that shinjin has arisen (in the ordinary sense, like the sun rose today) but rather that it is always arising: the present moment is hierophanic. This shifts attention away from persistent doubt towards a radical attentiveness to how shinjin is revealing itself right now, at every moment. Since there is no sequence of actions by which we may enter into the life of shinjin, it must arise abruptly, disrupting our ordinary notion of time and conditionality.

We could also say that shinjin entails an attitude of deep listening, which will enable us to begin to hear how Amida is constantly calling out to us, drawing us towards the Pure Land. As Shinran puts it, to '"Hear" means to hear the Primal Vow and be free of doubt. Further, it indicates shinjin' (*CWS*, p.474). The idea of radical attentiveness or radical listening is suggestive of Heidegger's notion of *Gelassenheit* – 'releasement' or 'letting be', which is a kind of transcendence of the will as we normally conceive it but not a state of passivity. It is not something that we can bring about but rather something that we *allow*.[13] Releasement lies beyond the domain of activity and passivity because it does not belong to the domain of the will as we normally understand it. In a sentence reminiscent of Shinran, Heidegger writes, 'The transition out of willing into releasement is what seems to me to be the genuine difficulty.'[14] He goes on to say that releasement consists in 'letting ourselves into an involvement'.[15]

Still further, we might say that to realize shinjin is to find oneself already situated within a new horizon of existence, one in which the logic of Other Power is given rather than chosen. As Dennis Hirota puts it: 'It may be said that Shinran's term "to realize shinjin" (*shinjin gyakutoku*) signifies not the subjective state of an individual but the arising of a new world of meaning in which one comes to carry on one's life.'[16] Shinjin does not entail submitting oneself to an alien will but consists in an *attunement* to a deeper sense of reality. We could even say that it consists in attuning to a more authentic version of ourselves: a version that, at least at times, 'forgets the self', to borrow a phrase from Dōgen. Shinran himself is less concerned to expound a method for cultivating shinjin than he is to affirm and open out a mode of being in which liberation is *already* manifest. He therefore tends to assume shinjin as the basis of his teaching rather than argue for it. For this reason, many of his teachings have the intention to reassure more than to convince.

Entangled in a net of doubt

Shinran's teachings on the existential priority of shinjin are at least partly intended to dissolve anxiety about whether or not our birth in the Pure Land is assured. But persistent doubts seem inevitable. Has shinjin arisen or hasn't it? How can we be sure? In some moments we might feel confident and at other times we may start to panic, fearing that shinjin is not yet settled. Our anxiety is likely to impel us to grasp once again after self-power. This lack of stable, enduring confidence is precisely a sign of *not* having realized shinjin. Shinran cautions that 'if in this lifetime still you are entangled in a net of doubt, then unavoidably you must pass once more in the stream of birth-and-death' (*CWS*, p.4). But while Shinran admonishes us against indulging doubts, this is easier said than done.

The issue of the integrity of shinjin was a problem even in Shinran's own day. In one of his letters, for instance, he laments that followers in Hitachi and Shimotsuke have come under the spell of Jishin (Shinran's eldest son). Jishin, it would seem, was teaching in a way that Shinran had not authorized. Shinran comments of his followers: 'all were shaken at heart and went so far as to cast away all those wholly dependable, authoritative writings which I exhausted my strength in copying out in great numbers to send to them' (*CWS*, p.575). Earlier in the same letter, Shinran comments that '[p]eople who had been saying for many years that their birth was firmly settled have, in the same manner as Jishin, all spoken falsehoods' (*CWS*, p.575). In another letter he laments how the fact that 'their shinjin was not genuine has become manifest' (*CWS*, p.569), owing to how readily they have been shaken from their trust in Shinran's teachings.

Shinran's attitude to doubt seems to be simply to caution against it. For instance, he writes: 'You simply should not fall into doubts over the different things that people say. Simply give yourself up to Tathāgata's Vow; avoid calculating in any way' (*CWS*, p.537). But how? Above all, we cannot fully entrust to Other Power while we remain committed to a vision of our own perfectibility. We need to see deeply into our human limits, and this implies a profound going forth. In this case, the going forth is not material, which might mean letting go of certain possessions and so on, but rather a letting go of self-power as an adequate instrument for fulfilling the promise of awakening. It involves deeply letting go of the delusion that we can liberate ourselves. The Shin perspective signals an *internal* going forth by means of which we abandon the false autonomy of the ego-directed will. We might also say that it is going forth from the secular mind and adopting the religious mind, which is of course the mind of Amida Buddha or the bodhichitta. The central practice in this going forth from the secular mind is an increasingly deeper insight into our own karmic boundedness, which then enables the possibility of opening ourselves to the embrace of Amida's compassion. Through the nembutsu, we open ourselves to a higher source of orientation and confidence.

So can we ever be sure if shinjin has become settled or not? Or will we always be left guessing? While Shinran outlines some of the psychological characteristics of someone in whom shinjin has arisen, notably joy and gratitude, he also confesses that even he doesn't always feel those emotions. He says of the person in whom shinjin is not yet settled that they 'will continue to drift, even without being misled by anyone, for he does not abide among the truly settled' (*CWS*, p.531). So we can assume that, if we fit this description, our shinjin is not yet settled.

Shinran encourages the person who feels uncertain about shinjin to say the name *aspiring* for birth, while the person who feels that their birth is settled should say the name out of gratitude and in order to benefit others. It is useless to try to determine if our saying of the nembutsu is great practice or not, that is to say, whether our shinjin is truly settled or not. We should just dedicate ourselves to the nembutsu. Worrying about whether we have settled shinjin is just another manifestation of the calculating mind. Elsewhere Shinran writes: 'Saying the Name, one will attain birth in the Pure Land of bliss *without fail*; this is because birth through the nembutsu is brought about by the Buddha's Primal Vow.'[17] These comments seem to indicate that saying the name will *without fail* lead to birth in the Pure Land. Yet elsewhere Shinran rejects this idea, recognizing that the nembutsu can be recited in the absence of genuine shinjin. I read the remark here as serving a transformative purpose. We should proceed *as though* this is how things are and, sooner or later, genuine shinjin will begin to fill out our nembutsu. To express the idea paradoxically, an aspect of shinjin is abandoning the anxiety over whether or not shinjin has arisen and just focusing instead on the nembutsu in a spirit of gratitude. Further, Shinran exhorts: 'Hear and reflect on the truth that one is grasped never to be abandoned [...] and let there be no wavering or apprehension' (*CWS*, p.303). This suggests that one antidote to doubt is constantly to recall Amida Buddha's compassion. This returns to the idea of deep listening and *Gelassenheit*. In a *wasan*, Shinran reassures us:

> Those who say the Name in self-power, whether meditative or
>   non-meditative –
> Having indeed taken refuge in the Vow that beings ultimately
>   attain birth –
> Will spontaneously, even without being taught,
> Turn about and enter the gate of suchness. (*CWS*, p.343)

These people are constantly illumined

In the light of shinjin, all secular human hierarchies are dissolved. Shinjin makes no distinction between noble or humble, monk or lay, man or woman, old or young. Not even does our degree of ethical purity or mundane goodness determine or inform the arising of shinjin. Rather than any mundane status or accomplishment, what ennobles us is shinjin itself:

> Śākyamuni rejoices in persons of shinjin, saying, 'They
> are my true companions.' Persons of shinjin are the true
> disciples of the Buddha; they are the ones who abide in
> right-mindedness. Since they have been grasped never to be
> abandoned, they are said to have attained the diamondlike
> mind. They are called 'the best among the best', 'excellent
> persons', 'wondrous, excellent persons', 'the very finest
> persons', 'rare persons'. (*CWS*, p.526)

Shinran was concerned to minister to the marginalized rather than just the privileged sectors of society, but he also redefined these categories according to a spiritual hierarchy. Shinran identified himself with the masses who occupied the lowest rungs of society and who were regarded conventionally as 'evil people', 'who are like stones and tiles and pebbles' (*CWS*, p.459).

   In commenting on the phrase 'These people are constantly illumined', Shinran writes:

These people: *these* is used in contrast with 'non-'. People of true and real shinjin are called 'these people'. Those who are empty and transitory, full of doubt and vacillation, are 'non-persons'. 'Non-persons' are rejected as not being persons; they are people of falsity. 'These people' are true persons. (*CWS*, p.479)

During Shinran's time, the term 'non-person' (*hinin* 非人) was a dismissive label assigned to beggars and others who had been rejected or isolated from all levels of the social hierarchy, a bit like the concept of untouchable. Shinran insists, however, that the person of shinjin is a 'good person', whereas it is those who do not entrust themselves to the Primal Vow, but instead persist in doubt and ego-directed practice, who are the 'non-persons'. This completely overturns the conventional logic of the ruling order. Little wonder that Shinran's teachings were unpopular with the authorities. For Shinran, no matter how privileged and powerful we might be according to the secular order, in the absence of shinjin, we remain a 'non-person' or an 'evil person'. However, no matter how reviled as a 'non-person' or excluded from the social hierarchy the person of shinjin may be, they remain a 'true person'. Through shinjin, 'we, who are like bits of tile and pebbles, are turned into gold' (*CWS*, pp.459–60). This perspective is reminiscent of the Buddha's redefinition of the term 'brahmin' in the Pali Canon, in which he challenges the notion that one is a brahmin (the most worthy of people) simply owing to reasons of birth: 'When all the chains are shattered, when there is no more agitation, and a man [*sic*] has freed himself and thrown off his shackles – this is the person I call a brahmin.'[18] In other words, the truly worthy person is the enlightened one.

Chapter Eleven

Evil Transforming into Good

> Maddened beyond control by blind passions, we do things
> we should not and say things we should not and think things
> we should not. But if a person is deceitful in his relations with
> others, doing what he should not and saying what he should
> not because he thinks it will not hinder his birth, then it is not an
> instance of being maddened by passion. Since he purposely does
> these things, they are simply misdeeds that should never have
> been done. (*CWS*, p.547)

We are fallible, erring creatures. We cause harm to ourselves
and to others, and, even in our attempts to purify or transform
ourselves, we fall into unskilfulness. We can't seem to help
ourselves. According to the Pure Land myth, it is precisely for
this reason that Amida made their great vows to help us. Given
Shinran's perspective on Other Power, the question arises: what
place is there for ethics within his spiritual vision? Is striving to
live ethically just another head of the hydra that is the calculating
mind? If self-power is discredited, this raises important questions
for any kind of intentional ethics and might even suggest that
ethics doesn't really matter.

On the one hand, the template of Dharmākara bodhisattva's
life underlines that a compassionate orientation towards the
needs of others is the essence of the path to awakening. On the
other hand, if our enlightenment is assured through shinjin,
there would appear to be no need to follow ethical norms as they
serve no purpose in procuring liberation. At the extreme, this
latter perspective opened the door to 'unhindered evil' (*zōaku*

muge) or 'unbridled indulgence' (*Hōitsu muzan*), the idea that one not only could but even should act in unskilful ways because to follow ethical norms would be to cling to self-power and so not trust fully in Amida's vow. As we will see, Shinran was bedevilled by such casuistry in his own lifetime, but always resolutely affirmed the importance of skilful conduct. We should act skilfully not as a means to favour our rebirth in the Pure Land but, rather, to express our gratitude for already having been guaranteed liberation. Shinran also recognized that, as radically insufficient beings, we will inevitably act unskilfully again and again. Far from being a barrier to our liberation, this insufficiency moves us both to rely upon Other Power and also to empathize with the karmic limitations of others.

The ethics of karma

Conventional Buddhist ethics rests on the notions of conditionality and, more specifically, karma. According to karma, if we act on the basis of unskilful impulses, that is to say, greed, hatred, and delusion, we will heap up suffering for ourselves. By contrast, if we act according to skilful impulses, that is, generosity, benevolence, and clear seeing, we will reap the commensurate rewards. More specifically, according to Buddhist tradition, we will heap up merit, which is a kind of spiritual capital that favours a good rebirth after the current life. The idea of merit is actually built into Shinran's Other Power perspective since Amida amassed enormous quantities of spiritual merit through their intensive practice over many kalpas. It is this merit that Amida transfers to all beings in order to benefit them and facilitate their birth in the Pure Land. The Pure Land is itself the summation of Amida's merit.

Karma informs the kinds of habits we develop, and colours our subjective experience of the world. In turn, this influences how others behave towards us. This is nothing mystical but something that, if we pay attention, we can see directly in our experience. Karma is generally aligned with a gradualistic model of transformation:

Do not underestimate evil, (thinking) 'It will not approach me.' A water-pot becomes full by the (constant) falling of drops of water. (Similarly) the spiritually immature person little by little fills themself with evil.

Do not underestimate good, (thinking) 'It will not approach me.' A water-pot becomes full by the (constant) falling of drops of water. (Similarly) the wise person little by little fills themself with good.[1]

In classic Buddhist models of the path, ethics is the foundation for all other spiritual practice since it stimulates a greater sensibility towards oneself and others. It is also commonly understood as a preparatory stage, laying the ground for a more decisive transformation that arises through *vipaśyanā* or clear seeing. In following such models, Subhuti frames the Dharma life as consisting in a shift from the mundane to the transcendental path,[2] which may be characterized as 'a movement from a consciousness dominated by the illusion of an ultimately real self to one that has no such illusion'.[3] Through honouring karma and cultivating skilful conduct, 'One consciously subordinates one's ego identity to ethical and spiritual principles, recognising them as serving one's own best interests. In effect, one uses self-interest to slowly transcend selfishness.'[4]

On the basis of skilful action, we facilitate mental states that are less contaminated by selfishness, and this enables us finally to see through the illusory character of the 'self' that we constantly defend and serve. In this shift, we become an *ārya*, or noble one, and now, instead of being driven by self-interest, we operate under the blessing of 'a stream of non-egoic volitions'.[5] These volitions are no longer governed by karma but are guided by the Dharma-niyama, the transcendent mode of conditionality: the enlightened mind.

Even a good person attains birth

Shinran offers little specific guidance in relation to ethics, and his insistence that 'Even a good person attains birth in the Pure Land, so it goes without saying that an evil person will' (*CWS*, p.663), if taken too literally, might give the impression that acting unethically actually *favours* our liberation by Amida. This would be a truly perverse teaching! But Shinran is being contrarian to make a point, and is just *reversing* the logic of a well-worn Pure Land teaching (i.e. that even an evil person can be reborn in the Pure Land owing to the power of Amida's vows). As Shinran goes on to say, 'good people' cling to their own virtue and so remain stubbornly attached to self-power, believing themselves capable of bringing about their own liberation. This means that it is much more difficult for them to embrace the true meaning of Other Power. He underlines that '[i]t is impossible for us, who are possessed of blind passions, to free ourselves from birth-and-death through any practice whatever' (*CWS*, p.663). So attachment to mundane 'goodness' becomes an obstacle to liberation, since the true cause comes from Amida, not from our contrived actions, no matter how seemingly punctilious they may be. To put this another way, liberation consists in *transcending* karma, not just in honouring it.

The purpose of Amida's Primal Vow is to help 'evil people' (*akunin* 悪人) reach the Pure Land. However, this is by no means automatic, as they still need to abandon self-power and embrace Other Power. Moreover, the reason why they are born in the Pure Land is not *because* they are evil but because they are more likely to have recognized their moral fallibility and, for this reason, to trust in a higher source of value. At the same time, Shinran insists that 'no good acts are required, because no good surpasses the nembutsu. Nor need they despair of the evil they commit, for no evil can obstruct the working of Amida's Primal Vow' (*CWS*, p.661). While this might seem to suggest a neglect of ethics as superfluous, more properly, it underlines how liberation transcends our ordinary categories of goodness. Amida epitomizes a mode of conditionality that goes beyond karma and its consequences.

Shinran's analysis of moral agency is certainly at odds with contemporary humanistic models of free will. On his reading, we overestimate our moral autonomy and liberty since, most of the time, we succumb to the impetus of our karmic conditioning. So it is not just a question of deciding to act ethically but, rather, one of learning to see how our actions are embedded in a false notion of self, which in turn causes us to act in destructive ways. Merely imitating right conduct is more likely to reinforce ego-clinging than to transcend it. For this reason, Shinran steered away from the unqualified imposition of moral prescriptions. He points out that 'From the very beginning sentient beings, who are filled with blind passions, lack a mind true and real, a heart of purity, for they are possessed of defilements, evil, and wrong views' (*CWS*, p.493). What we require, then, is the entrance of an influence or factor that transcends the ordinary mind.

In Shinran's vision, all human action is conditioned by past karma. We assume that we have freedom to make moral deliberations, but in fact our perceptions, judgements, and decision-making are constrained in countless ways – psychologically, culturally, socially, and so on. Moreover, our immersion in self-preoccupied motivation means that our karmically driven actions will tend to bind us still further to saṃsāra.

According to Shinran, our tendency to have confidence in self-power and karma shows that we doubt Amida's Primal Vow. As a consequence, while we are still assured of birth in the Pure Land, it will be in the least propitious circumstances, where we will pass 'long years and kalpas' (*CWS*, p.413):

> People who, doubting the inconceivable Buddha-wisdom,
> Rely on their practice of the root of good and the root of virtue
> Are born in the borderland or the realm of indolence and
>   pride;
> Hence, they fail to realize great love and great compassion.
>   (*CWS*, p.414)

This hymn also makes it clear that our doubting of the Primal Vow will impede our capacity to give rise to compassionate action.

I often get trapped in thinking that, if I purify myself through skilful action, then I may become worthy enough so as not to feel inadequate. No one will be able to criticize me, and I won't feel like I am backsliding. But the philosopher Levinas blows a hole in any aspiration to moral perfection, since he argues that we can never become ethically unassailable. To put it another way, we can never justify ourselves through being compassionate such that we reach a point where no one could possibly reproach us and we could not reproach ourselves. Why? First, he proposes that we have a responsibility to others, without concern for reciprocity.[6] So our responsibility to others is *one-sided*. It is not a contract, not a quid pro quo, but comes from our side exclusively. Moreover, our responsibility to the other never diminishes but always expands. How can this be? Responsibility increases each time we assume it, and so there is always more that we can do to help others. This means we will always fall short. We can never make ourselves worthy through altruistic action because our concern for others is *infinite*. Besides, responding to the needs of one person implies that we cannot meet the needs of another. We have to choose. So there is no point at which we can say that we have done enough.

Shinran's approach to ethics rests on similar considerations. Self-power can never produce a situation where we are beyond stain. The delusion that we can purify ourselves is further evidence of our own calculation, our desire to measure out liberation in spoonfuls of goodness. Liberation does not result from a certain quantity of goodness, but consists in a transformation of perspective and relation. This does not give us a licence to abandon ethics, but highlights that any kind of moral superiority or smugness is unseemly.

The mind to save sentient beings

As already noted, Shinran equates shinjin with bodhichitta, which is the altruistic aspiration to seek awakening for the benefit of all beings. He writes:

> The mind that aspires for Buddhahood is the mind to save sentient beings. The mind to save sentient beings is the mind to grasp sentient beings and bring them to birth in the Pure Land of peace. This mind is the mind aspiring for great enlightenment. This mind is the mind of great compassion. (*CWS*, p.113)

This indicates that a dimension of shinjin is the aspiration to liberate others from suffering and, more specifically, to assist them to be reborn in the Pure Land. The person of shinjin functions within an intrinsically ethical and compassionate frame of reference. It follows that such a person would have no reason or justification to deliberately cause harm to others. While we remain subject to blind passions, it is inevitable that we will hurt others, but the fact that we have been grasped by Amida's compassion, that we are destined for enlightenment, should never be used to justify acting in harmful ways. Such reasoning can only ever express the calculating mind.

The person of shinjin increasingly aligns with compassionate activity, which serves the needs of beings. Especially, this activity draws others towards their own shinjin. But this is not an ego-driven vanity project. Given that shinjin is bestowed upon us, the impulse that arises to help others is itself a manifestation of Amida's unfathomable practice. We do not generate the mind to save sentient beings but, rather, it is part of the mind that Amida has gifted to us. So, for Shinran, living in shinjin is to live under the guidance of an impulse that aspires not only towards self-benefit (attaining Buddhahood oneself) but also to the benefit of others (drawing them towards Buddhahood).

While seeking birth in the Pure Land may on the surface express a rather self-concerned desire to escape from the sordid compromises of saṃsāra, it is part of a greater aspiration, which is to put oneself at the service of others. For Shinran, the purpose of birth in the Pure Land is to encounter the most favourable possible conditions to become awakened and then to plunge back into saṃsāra in order to help other beings to become liberated. For this reason, it is said that there is not even one person who fulfils the aspiration to be reborn in the Pure Land who remains there. As Shinran puts it:

> Concerning the directing of virtue through the power of the Primal Vow, the Tathāgata's directing of virtue has two aspects: the directing of virtue in the aspect for our going forth to the Pure Land and the directing of virtue in the aspect for our return to this world. (CWS, p.633)

Shinran lists 'constantly practising great compassion' as one of ten benefits that accrue from entering the path of shinjin in the present life (*CWS*, p.112). In other words, the life of shinjin inspires action that helps to direct others towards the Pure Land. But such activity has its limitations, especially when compared with the compassionate working that takes place after the attainment of Buddhahood:

> Compassion in the Pure Land Path should be understood as first attaining Buddhahood quickly through saying the nembutsu and, with the mind of great love and compassion, freely benefiting sentient beings as one wishes.
>
> However much love and pity we may feel in our present lives, it is hard to save others as we wish; hence, such compassion remains unfulfilled. Only the saying of the nembutsu, then, is the mind of great compassion that is thoroughgoing. (*CWS*, p.663)

This makes clear that the first duty of dedicated practitioners is to say the nembutsu since, taking a long-term view, the most effective way that they may benefit other beings is through becoming awakened and then acting from that basis to offer those beings wise help.

In addition, the mind of shinjin draws all beings towards the nembutsu: 'If these people encourage each other and bring others to say the name, they are all called "people who practise great compassion"' (*CWS*, p.119).

In one of his hymns, Shinran writes:

> Persons who enter Amida's directing of virtue to beings
> And realize the mind that seeks to attain Buddhahood
> Completely abandon their self-power directing of merit,
> Thus benefiting sentient beings boundlessly. (*CWS*, p.404)

To abandon self-power practice is a compassionate act since, in embracing Other Power, we enable the conditions for our own liberation. If we enable these conditions, we can then respond effectively to the needs of others. In Shinran's thought, benefiting others means to inspire them to go for refuge to Amida and so embrace the Primal Vow. More specifically, it means to promote nembutsu practice (or non-practice) as he understood it. But it may also include conferring worldly benefits in order to ease discomfort or suffering within the present life. In one of his pastoral letters, for instance, Shinran writes: 'I hope that everyone will, deeply entrusting themselves to the nembutsu, and firmly embracing prayers [for peace in the world] in their hearts, together say the nembutsu' (CWS, p.560). He goes on to say that 'it would be splendid if all people who say the nembutsu [...] do so not with thoughts of themselves, but for the sake of the imperial court and for the sake of the people of the country' (CWS, p.560). He advises those who are uncertain about their birth in the Pure Land to focus on nembutsu recitation for their own benefit, whereas those who feel that their own birth is settled should recite in gratitude for Amida's benevolence and express the following wish: 'May there be peace in the world, and may the Buddha's teachings spread!' (CWS, p.560).

These remarks make it clear that the context for nembutsu recitation, and indeed of Shinran's entire approach to the Buddhist path, is universal compassion and universal awakening. Amida's own mythic life story confirms this: Amida aspired to become awakened in order to benefit all beings, and all of their actions served this purpose. It is clear that Shinran's vision of nembutsu expressed a concern for the benefit of all, not just oneself. In a letter, he instructed, 'if you simply pray for the people in society who are in error and desire to lead them into Amida's Vow, it will be a response out of gratitude for the Buddha's benevolence' (CWS, p.570).

Rejecting the evil of this world

Shinjin brings about a change of heart, which then permeates our ethical sensibility. This moves us to renounce unskilful action. Shinran writes: 'In people who have long heard the Buddha's Name and said the nembutsu, surely there are signs of rejecting the evil of this world and signs of their desire to cast off the evil in themselves' (CWS, p.553). Further, shinjin brings about the renunciation of worldly values: 'That people seek to stop doing wrong as the heart moves them, although earlier they gave thought to such things and committed them as their minds dictated, is surely a sign of having rejected this world' (*CWS*, pp.553–4). The arising of shinjin inspires a withdrawal from self-preoccupied concerns and norms. Moreover, one's scale of human value undergoes a radical change. Instead of evaluating others and oneself in terms of social status, influence, wealth, or some other worldly measure, the key factor is now shinjin. Those in whom shinjin has arisen are more highly esteemed than those who continue to pursue worldly ends and those who pursue spiritual ends but on a basis of self-power. 'Signs of long years of saying the nembutsu and aspiring for birth can be seen in the change in the heart that had been bad and in the deep warmth for friends and fellow-practicers' (*CWS*, p.551). This underlines how the solace and gratitude that the nembutsu practitioner is blessed with lead to a softening of the heart and a deeper appreciation and love towards brothers and sisters in the Dharma life.

Moreover, in relation to those who attack or undermine the Dharma and nembutsu practice, Shinran exhorts patience and compassion: 'Teachers of the past have stated that practicers of the nembutsu should act with compassion for those who commit such obstruction, feel pity for them, and earnestly say the nembutsu, thereby helping those who seek to hinder them' (*CWS*, p.564). Elsewhere, Shinran comments that '[t]o say *namu Amida butsu* is to repent all the karmic evil one has committed since the beginningless past' (*CWS*, p.504). This points to how, in entering into the life of shinjin and nembutsu, we become more sensitive to the harm that we have caused others due to our clumsy, self-serving actions. This sensitivity manifests through a spontaneous urge to repent our past unskilful conduct and to live in a way that honours the compassionate gift that we have received. Shinran elaborates on this transformation in the following terms:

> Formerly you were drunk with the wine of ignorance and
> had a liking only for the three poisons of greed, anger,
> and folly, but since you have begun to hear the Buddha's
> Vow you have gradually awakened from the drunkenness
> of ignorance, gradually rejected the three poisons, and
> come to prefer at all times the medicine of Amida Buddha.
> (*CWS*, p.553)

A change of heart

Shinran believed that persons of shinjin will naturally renounce unskilful acts insofar as they are capable of recognizing them. Yet early in the evolution of the nembutsu movement, even before Shinran started teaching, some followers had begun to distort the Other Power teachings. We have seen how Hōnen and Shinran were banished after the exclusive nembutsu practice was condemned as sponsoring licentiousness, amongst other supposed outrages. While both were later pardoned, the problem by no means went away. We can see in Shinran's pastoral letters, written in the latter stages of his life, that he was dealing with obstinate problems in relation to ethical antinomianism on the part of some influential followers. Shinran's judgement on such conduct was unequivocal:

> I have heard that, knowing nothing of the scriptures or of the true foundation of the Pure Land teaching, you are telling people who are appallingly self-indulgent and lacking in shame that a person should do evil just as he or she desires. This is absolutely wrong. (*CWS*, p.547)

The arising of shinjin in no way licenses deliberate wrongdoing. Someone who acts in such a way shows that they have grasped nothing of what Amida's benevolence and wisdom really signify. Shinran emphasizes that the arising of shinjin prompts a deep turning about inside us that inspires a moral reformation, such that 'Even that person who has been inclined to steal will naturally undergo a change of heart' (*CWS*, p.547). Unskilful conduct should be abandoned not because this will make us worthy of birth in the Pure Land but because unskilfulness causes harm. Moreover, if there is no evidence of a change of heart, and a corresponding reform of ethical conduct, this itself is a sign that someone has not entered into shinjin at all. In reproving those who were condoning ethical delinquency, Shinran wrote:

> One must seek to cast off the evil of this world and to cease doing wretched deeds; this is what it means to reject the world and to live the nembutsu [...] When has it ever been

said that one should act in accordance with one's mind and heart, which are evil? You, who are totally ignorant of the sutras and commentaries and ignorant of the Tathāgata's words, must never instruct others in this way. (*CWS*, p.547)

The fact that Amida made a compassionate vow to intervene in the lives of human beings by drawing them towards awakening is no justification for those beings to wantonly engage in unskilful actions that cause harm. Instead, the arising of shinjin exerts a purifying influence, which begins to permeate our ethical awareness and results in a greater ethical sensitivity and scrupulousness. Shinran remains keenly aware, however, of our persistent ethical fragility:

> Human beings are such that, maddened by the passions of greed, we desire to possess; maddened by the passions of anger, we hate that which should not be hated, seeking to go against the law of cause and effect; led astray by the passions of ignorance, we do what should not even be thought. But the person who *purposely* thinks and does what he or she should not, saying that it is permissible because of the Buddha's wondrous Vow to save the foolish being, does not truly desire to reject the world, nor does such a one consciously feel himself a being of karmic evil. (*CWS*, p.550, emphasis added)

The perspective presented here is nuanced. Shinran recognizes that persons of shinjin will continue to break the precepts since they are still 'maddened by the passions', and so will repeatedly lose awareness and act unskilfully. But this is quite different from choosing to cause harm to others, which should never be condoned. The justification that we may act unskilfully, since our rebirth in the Pure Land depends only on Amida's transference of merit and not on our own good karma, is no more than the obstinate scheming of the calculating mind. Someone disposed to act in this way lacks sincerity and is embroiled in mundane goals and values. They have no aspiration to reject the world and embrace the transcendent. Moreover, they have not seen into their own nature as a being of 'karmic evil'. A more natural response to seeing this nature is repentance, humility, and the urge to seek out Amida's compassion through the nembutsu. It can make no psychological sense to think that one has received a supremely compassionate gift and, as a consequence, choose to act in a way that undermines the content and origin of that gift. Shinran employs the analogy of drunkenness and of taking poison to illustrate the perversity of the 'licensed evil' perspective: 'how lamentable that people who have not fully awakened from drunkenness are urged to more drunkenness and those still in the grips of poison encouraged to take yet more poison' (*CWS*, p.553).

The ice of blind passions necessarily melts

Shinran sees ethics as a spontaneous response to the arising of shinjin. Shinjin initiates a profound process of ethical transformation through which our astonishment and gratitude begin to permeate our moral sensibility. This instigates a thoroughgoing reformation of our conduct in the light of Amida's compassion. We could understand such a model of ethics in terms of sudden awakening/gradual cultivation or, perhaps better, sudden awakening/spontaneous cultivation. Our existential reorientation is sudden, since we immediately come to realize that we are destined for the Pure Land and so for final awakening, but this insight then permeates gradually through our lives and transforms every aspect of it as we become more fully aligned with Amida's mind. In an evocative metaphor Shinran writes:

Through the benefit of the unhindered light,
We realize shinjin of vast, majestic virtues,
And the ice of our blind passions necessarily melts,
Immediately becoming water of enlightenment.

Obstructions of karmic evil turn into virtues;
It is like the relation of ice and water:
The more the ice, the more the water;
The more the obstructions, the more the virtues. (*CWS*, p.371)

This process can be characterized as 'evil transforming into good' (*ten'aku jōzen*), which is listed as one of ten benefits that arise from shinjin (*CWS*, p.112).[7] In awakening to shinjin, we see that we are inevitably compromised by blind passions and wonder how it could be possible that, in spite of our persistent karmic delinquency, we are nevertheless grasped by Amida's compassionate embrace and so are destined for birth in the Pure Land. The working of Amida within us causes us to move away from selfish ends and to orient ourselves towards the spiritual welfare of others and the well-being of the world as a whole. In awakening to our endemic blind passions, we come to understand the human condition and so, instead of arrogantly condemning the karmic errors of others, we are drawn towards them in humble empathy. This in turn stimulates us to help them bring about their own liberation through saying the nembutsu and in other practical ways. Ethical practice reveals itself as a kind of graceful overflow, the joyful expression of shinjin within our daily lives. No longer is our ethical decision-making tainted by the frantic, self-referential concern to liberate ourselves: instead it consists in a serene abundance and responsiveness to the cries of the world.

Chapter Twelve

The Darkness of Ignorance
Has Already Cleared

How joyous I am, my heart and mind being rooted in the
Buddha-ground of the universal Vow, and my thoughts and
feelings flowing within the dharma-ocean, which is beyond
comprehension! I am deeply aware of the Tathāgata's immense
compassion, and I sincerely revere the benevolent care behind
the masters' teaching activity. My joy grows even fuller, my
gratitude and indebtedness ever more compelling. (*CWS*, p.291)

Attuning to a sacred excess

This passage forms part of Shinran's postscript to *True Teaching*,
and highlights how joy and gratitude are primary religious
emotions for someone living within Other Power. Imagine your joy
at realizing that you have been gifted your deepest desire without
any obligation to do anything in return, and knowing that you
have done nothing in particular to deserve it. We are not talking
about the fulfilment of some mundane desire, such as to meet your
favourite film star or visit Buckingham Palace, but rather the gift
of connection with the enlightened mind, an unbreakable bond
with your ultimate concern. Besides, this gift does not happen at a
particular moment but rather is something that has been bestowed
primordially. It is not that at some future moment we will receive
it, or have the possibility of doing so, but rather that, in a sense,
we have already received it but not at any particular instant of
time. Rather, we are always in the precise moment of waking up
to having received it, of attuning to a sacred excess that begins to
saturate our perception. In this chapter, I open out the implications
of living within this context of *adhiṣṭhāna* or blessing.

We have received the most supreme gift that we could ever hope for: an intimate connection with the enlightened mind. As we reflect on this staggering, priceless, and unearned gift, it begins to work on us. Instead of feeling hard done by, outraged by all the injustices we have suffered, we may begin to course in a state of blessedness, of completeness rather than brokenness, or even of completeness in spite of being broken. Instead of anxiously seeking wholeness, freedom, and even inner peace, we can relax into the awareness that our mind and heart are somehow wedded to Amida's wisdom and compassion. It has never been otherwise. We are *always* in the moment of being gifted something of supreme value, and we are *always* in the process of waking up to this. This spectacular gift never becomes a past event, but is *always* unfolding in the drama of the present moment, perpetually revealing itself as soon as awareness attends to it.

Practice ceases to be a means to an end, a utilitarian raft towards awakening, and instead transforms into living within this attentiveness. Practice does not make us worthy or deserving, but instead expresses a joyful, superabundant gratitude. Practice becomes a kind of eternal remembrance, constantly returning to an awareness of being blessed that our awakening is assured thanks to the dynamic working of Other Power, the compassionate action of Amida. Moreover, awakening can never become 'ours' in the sense of something we can look back on as an achievement of the egocentric mind. Rather, we awaken constantly to the undeserved nature of this gift, and this calls forth again and again our gratitude.

This situation is almost the exact opposite of the one evoked in Kafka's nightmarish, existential tale *The Trial*. In that story, the protagonist, Josef K, is arrested, but he doesn't know by whom or even for what crime. It is assumed that he is guilty, and he himself even supposes this although he does not know what he is guilty of. Acquittal is regarded as practically impossible. According to the Amida myth, in contrast, we are released from our self-created prison; Amida liberates us, not because we have deserved or somehow earned it, but rather because Amida's compassion is so complete, so generous, and beyond the tyranny of reciprocity that it invites us to share in their infinite merit. This then draws us towards the Pure Land. Instead of discovering that we are guilty of some unspecified crime, we discover that we have been gifted a connection with the awakened mind, with liberation itself, even though our own tainted actions could never merit such supreme good fortune.

Sangharakshita has said that gratitude ought to be an ever-present characteristic of our existence. While we can all point to examples of where others have been unfair with us, even violent, it takes only a moment to notice how all the privileges and opportunities that we enjoy depend upon others. We are the inheritors of the entire cultural history of human beings. While some of this legacy is dark and heavy to carry, such as the traumas of invasions, wars, and so on, much of it is uplifting, humanizing, and precious. Take the gift of being able to read. What an amazing, mysterious human accomplishment. Owing to the efforts of my teachers at a modest primary school in rural south Gloucestershire, I have coursed in the thoughts of Shakespeare, Dostoyevsky, and Rilke, to name but a few writers who have lit the touchpaper of my imagination. I recall the first time I witnessed a live performance of Shakespeare. It was *Macbeth* at the Royal Shakespeare Theatre in Stratford-upon-Avon and I was sixteen. Nothing could have prepared me for the catharsis that I experienced. I was lifted out of myself and, at least momentarily, grasped by a world of saturated value. We so easily take such gifts for granted. To be grateful, then, requires a sensitivity to the principle of conditionality, an awareness of the ways in which we benefit from all the many things that others have done that permit us to flourish.

To be grateful does not at all imply that we should ignore the violence meted out by others and so turn a blind eye to injustice. But it can help us put grievances into an enlarged perspective, one that is balanced by the startling legacy of human cultural life that we are heirs to. Imagine what it would be like to live in a state of constant gratitude, consistently attentive to all of the wonderful gifts that you have received. Sometimes I fall into a pit of self-pity, even martyrdom, in which I am driven to think that people don't value me (after all I have done for them!), that I have few genuine blessings, and that others are seldom generous with me. When this happens I pay attention to small things: the fact that someone gave me a free Portuguese lesson, someone bought me lunch, or simply that someone reached out to ask me how I am. When we start to notice, we can see that we are in the midst of a constant flow of generosity. This can activate our gratitude and so provide an antidote to feeling hard done by.

Sometimes I am tempted to identify as a victim, zeroing in on all of the bad things that have happened to me, collapsing in on myself, becoming the 'bitter animal' of which the poet Jaime Sabines writes.[1] Yet resentment is corrosive, self-destructive, and small-minded. It is rooted in lack, in ego-clinging, in blaming rather than overcoming. It is a self-made prison in which we make ourselves suffer, and it goads us to mete out suffering upon others. Resentment is a leg iron constantly pulling us back, pulling us down. Gratitude, by contrast, consists in awakening the imagination, an expansion beyond inward-looking awareness, and a recognition of our interdependence. Its nature is to decentre the self and so see it as more like a node in a web of abundant connections. Gratitude dissolves away self-pity and lack, and helps us to see how we are constant receivers.

How does our sense that life has a sacred dimension arise? My first hints of what I might now name the sacred came via Sunday school. I was nine or ten. Each Sunday, I went to the Baptist chapel in the village near where I lived. The place had a musty smell, pregnant with furniture polish – a smell not of the home but of a different kind of realm. I didn't want to be at home. It was a violent, unhappy place. A member of the church, I want to call him Martin, came to pick me up. This routine gesture strikes me today as an unwarranted blessing. I wasn't used to such kindness.

The fusty pews were cold and hard. We learned parables like the Good Samaritan and the story of seeds being scattered on stony ground. The wise man who built his house upon the rock. I was bewildered and felt that I didn't belong. There was something different here, something extra-ordinary, but at the same time it felt distant. The teachers were parents of my school friends, and their attitude was benevolent, nurturing, in contrast to what I returned to at home. Even back then, something in my impulse to participate revealed a resonance with the sacred dimension.

I now find myself within the horizon of the Dharma. But it was never a decision that I made. Now Buddhist images and ideas are

The Promise of a Sacred World

my cardinal points. The Dharma has opened something within me. It is usual to characterize this in terms of personal will or motivation. But we might think instead of something communicating to us and through us. Other Power has seeped into me. Awakening to Other Power is living within a context of blessedness, of wonder, that we can always return to. To approach the Pure Land is to find oneself oriented to a new horizon of meaning. The myth of Amida and their forty-eight vows confirms that, in spite of the painful and sometimes tragic events that may mark our lives, there is an affirming, existential current that flows towards and through us.

The story of Suppabuddha the leper, found in the early Buddhist scriptures, reflects this.[2] In search of a square meal, he arrives when the Buddha is about to give a talk. There is no food, but he stays to listen anyway. Very soon the Buddha notices that Suppabuddha is unusually receptive, and he begins to tailor his message towards him. Suppabuddha's Dharma Eye opens. He glimpses the truth. And his response is really wonderful: '*Abhikkantaṁ, bhante! Abhikkantaṁ, bhante!* How marvellous venerable sir, how amazing!' A series of similes then follows: it is as though something that had been knocked over has been set upright, as though what was hidden has been revealed, as though someone has pointed out the way to a person lost, as though someone has brought a lamp to illuminate the darkness so that all may see. These are stock phrases, but they communicate something of the excitement of glimpsing the Dharma.

According to the text, Suppabuddha sees decisively into the nature of reality and so will not fall back from this understanding. On the basis of his transformative insight, the urge to go for refuge to the Three Jewels wells up from within. So going for refuge is not the means to liberation but its articulation. Going for refuge overflows as a grateful, humble response to having seen the Dharma.

The hidden jewel

Awakening is awareness, awareness is awakening. The givenness of awareness is itself an unearned gift. It is sacramental, it is full, unemptiable, it is a sacred excess. The lighting up of the moment.

We circle and circle around this reality as we absorb its staggering implications. We will never be closer to awakening than we are right now, nor will we ever be further away. Amida's myth reveals an existential fact, or perhaps an additional existential dimension, that we are constantly losing sight of and so need to remember again and again. Not exactly discover again but receive back into awareness, allowing it to infuse our experience right now so that it becomes perfumed by this existential depth.

This existential condition of always already being in possession of what we seek, but losing sight of the fact, is expressed through a number of myths. The *Lotus Sutra*, for instance, recounts the 'Parable of the hidden jewel'.

> [I]t was like the case of a man who went to the house of a close friend and, having become drunk on wine, lay down to sleep. At that time the friend had to go out on official business. He took a priceless jewel, sewed it in the lining of the man's robe, and left it with him when he went out. The man was asleep drunk and knew nothing about it. When he got up, he set out on a journey to other countries. In order to provide himself with food and clothing he had to search with all his energy and diligence, encountering very great hardship and making do with what little he could come by.
>
> Later, the close friend happened to meet him by chance. The friend said, 'How absurd, old fellow! Why should you have to do all this for the sake of food and clothing? In the past I wanted to make certain you would be able to live in ease and satisfy the five desires, and so on such-and-such a day and month and year I took a priceless jewel and sewed it in the lining of your robe. It must still be there now. But you did not know about it, and fretted and wore yourself out trying to provide a living for yourself.'[3]

Imagine your joy at realizing that your deepest desire is always-already within your grasp. There was never any need to look afar for it. The awakening mind is not apart from us, but is constantly revealing itself to us and through us. We need only be attentive to this perpetual blessing.

This model of our relationship with the awakened mind could be likened to Plato's notion of *anamnesis*, or knowledge as remembrance, which is articulated in his dialogues *Meno* and *Phaedo*. In *Meno*, what comes to be known as 'Meno's Paradox' is introduced, which proposes that it would seem impossible for us to seek either what we already know or what we do *not* know. As for what we already know, well, there is clearly no need to seek it; equally, since we do not know what to look for, neither can we seek what we do not already know.

Plato's solution to this paradox is a theory of knowledge as remembrance. In the dialogue, the character of Socrates declares 'for all enquiry and all learning is but recollection'.[4] In Plato's case, he is interested to examine whether virtue can be taught or is somehow 'remembered'; for Shinran, the question is 'how is awakening realized?' Following Meno's Paradox, it would seem impossible for an ignorant being to become awakened, since their apparatus for understanding will only serve to further confirm their ignorance, like a horse stuck in quicksand trying to pull itself out. Shinran's answer is that the awakening mind is a gift from *outside*, or at least from beyond the egocentric mind, and that, moreover, it is a gift that has *primordially* been given. According to Shinran:

> The compassionate light of the Buddha of unhindered light [Amida] always illumines and protects the person who has realized shinjin; hence the darkness of ignorance has *already cleared*, and the long night of birth-and-death is *already dispelled* and become dawn [...] Know that when one realizes shinjin, it is as though dawn has broken. (*CWS*, p.519, emphasis added)

Even to our bones becoming dust

A common objection to Shinran's religious vision is that it seems to offer no motivation for practice. Rather than lift us into a state of joyous gratitude, it is more likely to invite passivity, indolence, and even arrogance. If my mind is already connected to the Buddha mind, why should I make an effort? Moreover, since I am basically a Buddha, no one knows better than me and so others should follow my guidance. Such a way of thinking could readily become an obstacle but, properly speaking, expresses a lack of appreciation of the priceless gift that is the awakening mind. After all, if you were sincerely aware of being gifted a wise, compassionate mind, why would you choose to act selfishly? Such action only becomes possible when we lose sight of the compassionate grace within which our lives are unfolding, when we lose sight of how Amida's compassionate light rays are constantly pouring down upon us, blessing us, purifying us, and renewing us.

If we have been gifted something that is supremely valuable, which we have done nothing to merit, not only are we likely to be filled with gratitude but we may also feel a sense of indebtedness. We may feel that we must try to make ourselves worthy of the precious gift that we have received. Shinran expressed this sentiment in a celebrated hymn:

> Such is the benevolence of Amida's great compassion,
> That we must strive to return it, even to the breaking of our
> bodies;
> Such is the benevolence of the masters and true teachers,
> That we must endeavour to repay it, even to our bones
> becoming dust. (*CWS*, p.412)

According to the logic of Other Power, the impulse to respond to our ultimate concern is itself a gift. The impulse to go for refuge is *given*. In Shantideva's guide to living like a bodhisattva, he exclaims: 'As a blind man might find a jewel in heaps of rubbish, so too this Awakening Mind [bodhichitta] has somehow appeared in me.'[5] It is a kind of miracle that the urge towards a more awakened consciousness wants to make itself known through us. Yet instead of receiving this gift with gratitude, we are more likely to appropriate it into our ego-self. In this way, we lose sight of amazement, and fall back into habitual awareness and our nagging sense of lack. Shinran was alive to wonder. He constantly returned to his amazement at the generosity, abundance, and compassion symbolized by Amida's vow. The present moment is amazing because of what it promises right now. At the same time, Shinran constantly circles back to his own fragility and vulnerability. In this way, the nembutsu and Amida become ever more precious and sacred as he deepens his insight into his own limitations.

Having received such a priceless gift, we are called upon to honour and cherish it. The German theologian Bonhoeffer made a distinction between what he called 'cheap grace' and 'costly grace'.[6] Cheap grace is like a lazy response to Other Power: Amida has gifted me his merits so I can put my feet up. I don't need to do anything, just bask in my own glory. Everything can stay as it is. The nembutsu is easy but not cheap. Costly grace is like the true working of Amida within us. We are called upon to participate in the activity of a compassionate impulse. As Kenneth K. Tanaka puts it: 'When a person realises *shinjin* in this life, one "joins" in the dynamic compassionate workings called "Amida."'[7]

To return to Caputo's conception of the event, it 'stirs restlessly, endlessly, like an invitation or a call, an invocation ("come") or a provocation, a solicitation or a promise, a praise or benediction.'[8] In coming alive to astonishment at the gift that is this moment, something is required of us. We are called into question and called upon, even as we are reassured.

How can we repay Amida's infinite generosity and compassion? In short, we can't. But, at the very least, we can cease to act in ways that are harmful to others. A sense of indebtedness may serve to counteract arrogance, pride, and entitlement and inspire us to become more humble and attentive to our persistent shortcomings. Our gratitude and indebtedness may begin to overflow as an aspiration to serve others, to call them towards the Dharma. The early Buddhist text known as the *Dhammapada* says: 'The gift of the Dharma conquers all gifts.'[9] My own teacher has said:

[T]he greater the gift, the greater the gratitude that we should feel. We should not only feel that gratitude, not only feel it in our hearts, we should give expression to it in words and deeds. And how do we do this? We give expression to it in three ways. By singing the praises of our spiritual friends, by practising the Dharma they have given us and by passing on that Dharma to others to the best of our ability.[10]

It strikes space and resonates

In the state of blessedness, of gratitude, practice becomes, in the style of Whitman's live-oak, 'uttering joyous leaves of dark green'.[11] As Rilke puts it: 'Superabundant being wells up in my heart.'[12] Instead of postponing enlightenment until an indefinite future, practice becomes an affirmation of its perpetual disclosure. Moreover, instead of a means to make ourselves worthy, practice becomes a gift, an expression of solidarity and affirmation. Our meditation, our devotion, our friendship, our study, become affirmations and revelations of our intimate connection with Amida's compassionate mind, with the nature of awakening, and so reveal themselves as disclosures of our true nature before others. Our practice becomes sacramental, an exuberant offering to the world around us. It becomes an upwelling of gratitude, the incarnation of Amida's vow within our daily lives.

This state of affairs can be likened to the imaginative vision outlined by Dōgen when he writes:

> Zazen, even if it is only one human being sitting for one moment, thus enters into mystical cooperation with all dharmas, and completely penetrates all times; and it therefore performs, within the limitless universe, the eternal work of the Buddha's guiding influence in the past, future, and present [...] The practice is not confined to the sitting itself; it strikes space and resonates, [like] ringing that continues before and after a bell. How could [the practice] be limited to this place?[13]

According to this dazzling vision, practice becomes a joyous revelation of the awakening mind for all beings and so contributes to *their* process of awakening, resonating throughout the entire universe, blessing the entire universe. If sincerely engaged with, Dharma practice can never be selfish because its implications outstrip individual purposes.

What suppresses the heart

This all sounds great and lovely, doesn't it? But what if we *don't* feel blessed, as I am sure is all too common? So often, I feel trapped within my mundane self, submerged by my daily cares, fettered by my sense of lack, by my craving for more. We don't always feel grateful, even when we have every reason to do so, and Shinran was acutely aware of this. Far from living in constant joy, owing to being destined for birth in the Pure Land, Shinran admitted that he was still subject to 'blind passions' and even indifference. In *Tannishō*, for instance, his disciple Yuien-bo confesses that, despite his faithful recitation of the nembutsu, he is not filled with joy at Amida's compassionate gift and he lacks the urgency to aspire towards the Pure Land. He records that Shinran responded to this confession in the following way:

> When I reflect deeply on it, by the very fact that I do not rejoice at what should fill me with such joy that I dance in the air and dance on the earth, I realize all the more that my birth is completely settled. What suppresses the heart that should rejoice and keeps one from rejoicing is the action of blind passions [...] If we had the feeling of dancing with joy and wishing to go to the Pure Land quickly, we might wonder if we weren't free of blind passions.
> (*CWS*, pp.665–6)

In other words, our very awareness of our own lack of gratitude and joy is a reminder both that we have not fully overcome our unskilful habits and that Amida Buddha, in their wisdom and compassion, aware of our lack of determination and contaminated aspiration, nevertheless gifts us their infinite merit. More precisely, they gift us merit *because* we lack the capacity to transcend our own unskilful impulses. To put this another way, the bodhisattva reaches out compassionately to others not because they are 'deserving' but because they are suffering.

Shinran never denies our day-to-day worries, or even the inner emptiness or despair that may sometimes catch us unawares in pauses and silences. He affirms that we remain ordinary, foolish beings. In spite of this, shinjin continues to bless us, like the sun behind the clouds. It is always inviting us to redirect our gaze towards the bigger picture. When gratitude irrupts within us, we are able to reach outside the self-cherishing mind and see that our lives unfold within a much bigger context that gives meaning and purpose to them. In spite of the burdensome cares, we are blessed by something transcendent, and we can always be opening out into this, like remembering to open our eyes to see that the sun is still shining. Our practice affirms this before others and invites them to share in this awakening context.

The basic Buddhist message, especially as framed by the Four Noble Truths, is that we experience suffering, our suffering is caused by our craving and grasping, awakening is release from this, and there is a path that leads to that awakening. Shinjin points towards an existential reality beyond this psychological dynamic – not by rubbing out suffering but by calling us towards a context in which our lives have ultimate meaning, in which we are woven into the tapestry of universal awakening, in which we ourselves are a revelation of awakening both for ourselves and for others. Rather than being simply insufficient, we are already intimately connected with what we thought we were looking for and it could never be otherwise. But this does not absolve us from mundane sufferings. This is the paradox of shinjin. Yes, we have been grasped never to be abandoned by Amida. Yes, we are irrevocably connected to the mind of awakening. Yet we still have feet of clay, we must still confront the burden of existence, we must still live with the frustrations of our ordinary mind and its habits.

This may seem like an uncomfortable, unresolved condition. It may appear as though we are living according to a paradox: we are connected with the enlightened mind and yet we are still ignorant beings. Yet the paradox is only truly uncomfortable if we remain committed to the idea of dominion of reality, the idea of fully grasping it in some forever-and-always grip. Dōgen reminds us that awareness is never complete:

When the Dharma fills body and mind, one thinks something is [still] lacking [...] Within the dusty world and beyond, there are innumerable aspects and characteristics;

we only see or grasp as far as the power of our eye of study and practice can see. When we listen to the reality of myriad things, we must know that there are inexhaustible characteristics in both ocean and mountains, and there are many other worlds in the four directions. This is true not only in the external world, but also right under our feet or within a single drop of water.[14]

The fact that Dharma practice reveals 'something is [still] lacking' need not be a source of frustration, but can instead invite greater openness, curiosity, and wonder. Understanding is never finished, enlightenment is never achieved, rather both are always in the process of unfolding themselves before us. Gratitude never appropriates: it is only the grasping mind that is not grateful. Consequently, the expression of gratitude reflects a condition of constant attentiveness to having received something that is undeserved and always will be, even a gift that we don't properly understand but are in the process of waking up to. One of Shinran's main disciples put it like this:

How joyful and how grateful I feel [...] Nevertheless, distracted by the business of everyday life, I tend to be negligent for hours at a time. Still, whether day or night it never slips from my mind, and there is only the act of rejoicing in Amida's compassion; there is solely the diamondlike shinjin whether walking, standing, sitting, or reclining, without any thought of the propriety of time or place; there is only the saying of the Name out of gratitude for the Buddha's profound benevolence and for the joy imparted by the benevolence of the masters. (CWS, p.542)

Chapter Thirteen

Free of Any Form of Calculation

Have no scruples in your minds thinking how to curry favour
with Amida or whether you are really embraced by them. These
scruples come from not having fully abandoned the thought of
selfhood. Resign yourselves to the grace of Amida and let them
do what they choose with you; whether you are to be saved after
or before all your sins are wiped clean, is the business of Amida
and not yours.[1]

Sounds easy, doesn't it? My teacher, Sangharakshita, tells the story
of an old woman who visits her local temple every day to pray
to the Buddha. 'Merciful Buddha. Come and take me away from
this suffering world.' Every day the same. One day the temple
priest decides to teach her a lesson. So he hides himself behind the
Buddha statue while the old lady is praying in front of it and, as
once again she pleads for her deliverance, the priest booms out,
'Your prayers have been answered! I am coming for you now.'
Terrified at this unearthly voice, she rushes towards the door and
cries out: 'But won't the Buddha get my little joke?'[2]

It would seem easy enough to place our confidence in Amida
Buddha, in Other Power. After all, it is 'the true teaching easy to
practise for small, foolish beings; it is the straight way easy to traverse
for the dull and ignorant' (CWS, p.3). And yet Shinran also points out
that '[i]t is the quick path difficult for people to accept' (CWS, p.79).
This seems like a contradiction. The 'genuine difficulty', he points out,
is not the attainment of complete enlightenment but rather the arising
of shinjin. Why should this be? It is difficult, he explains, because 'this
realization takes place through the Tathāgata's supportive power;

because it comes about through the power of great compassion and all-embracing wisdom' (*CWS*, pp.79–80). So we have a paradox: the easy path is in fact difficult!

It is common to disparage the path of Other Power as an accommodation to 'popular' forms of religiosity, as a consolation, if you will, for the less spiritually adept. Such people are not capable of fulfilling more demanding practices like ethics, renunciation, meditation, Dharma study, and so on. Their only option is to trust in 'faith'. For the more psychologically sophisticated, it is therefore not to be taken seriously as a path to liberation. Instead, seemingly more advanced ritual and meditation practices have tended to catch the imagination of new converts, including practices that demand rigorous discipline and effort. Richard Payne has suggested that Zen and Tibetan Buddhism, for instance, have attracted considerable attention because they have been 'successfully commodified as offering solutions to personal problems, specifically those that can be constructed as psychological in nature'.[3] Through aligning with the language of personal growth and fulfilment, they have shared in some of the cultural capital afforded to therapeutic models, which generally focus on *internal* solutions. In other words, they are framed in terms of self-power. Shinran's seemingly naive reliance upon a supra-personal force does not align with this vision.

Yet Sangharakshita has suggested that, instead of being a 'nirvana-lite' option, the Other Power perspective embodies an advanced path. In commenting on the Pure Land approach, he once wrote: 'The path of dependence on self-power is for the spiritually *less* advanced, and the path of dependence on other-power for the spiritually *more* advanced.'[4] Why might this be? At first glance, making efforts to liberate oneself seems harder than relying upon the help of some external factor or influence. But if we look closely into ourselves, we may notice that it is difficult to let go of the idea that we are in control of our own destiny. We cling to a sense of our own power, and so believe ourselves capable of liberating ourselves through our own efforts. This vision of the world can, however, become a trap that impedes our path towards more authentic freedom.

To abandon self-power and to embrace Other Power requires us 'to abandon the conviction that one is good, to cease relying on the self; to stop reflecting knowingly on one's evil heart, and further to abandon the judging of people as good and bad' (*CWS*, p.459). But we cling so tightly to our own sense of goodness and of capacity that it is difficult for us to give it up.

To make yourself worthy

Self-power (*jiriki*) expresses our habitual relationship with the world. We see ourselves as the agents of our own lives, as capable of making decisions, and of shaping our course through the challenges and opportunities that we meet. Assuming responsibility for our actions in this way is integral to becoming a mature human being. Moreover, self-power seems to be the orientation recommended in the early Buddhist teachings. In the chapter on the 'self', for instance, the *Dhammapada* affirms:

> Self is protector of self:
> What other protector could there be?
> With your self well tamed
> You find a protector who's hard to find.[5]

The text goes on to say, 'Purity and impurity are individual matters: No one can purify another.'[6] The message here is clear: we are in charge of our destiny and, more specifically, we are responsible for our own process of purification. No one can do it for us. This seems like common sense and even empowering. We are not at the mercy of fate, or others, or even some transcendental force. Our will is sovereign and our future is in our hands.

Yet Shinran came to a radically different view – at least on the surface. Instead of the self-directed will being a means towards liberation, it is the cause of our entrapment in saṃsāra. Consequently, while we rely on self-power we entrench our boundedness. Shinran defines self-power in the following terms:

> Self-power is the effort to attain birth, whether by invoking
> the names of Buddhas other than Amida and practising
> good acts other than the nembutsu, in accordance with
> your particular circumstances and opportunities; or by

endeavouring to make yourself worthy through mending
the confusion in your acts, words, and thoughts, confident
of your own powers and guided by your own calculation.
(*CWS*, p.525)

It is notable that Shinran repudiates the invocation of *all* Buddhas
besides Amida, as well as *all* other forms of religious practice. He
also rejects ethical purification as a means to rebirth in the Pure
Land. In his writings, Shinran makes repeated use of the term
'calculation' (*hakarai*) and refers to the 'calculating mind'. This
calculating mind sees liberation as a trophy that it can win through
its own efforts. It seeks to *earn* liberation. But, as he makes clear:

> Birth into the Pure Land has nothing at all to do with
> the calculation of foolish beings. Since it is completely
> entrusted to the Primal Vow of the Buddha, it is indeed
> Other Power. It is ridiculous to try to calculate it in various
> ways. (*CWS*, p.548)

Our assurance of birth depends neither on karmic purity nor on the
accumulation of good acts, as these bases are embedded in the logic
of calculation, and so, ultimately, become obstacles to liberation.
In this regard, the Tibetan teacher Trungpa Rimpoche once said:
'decency is the absence of strategy [...] you having nothing up
your sleeve; therefore a sense of genuineness comes through.'[7]
Liberation is not a question of manipulating circumstances in our
favour, of building up credits, but indicates a deepening sincerity,
honesty, and letting go.

While apparently committed to a self-power model, Shinran's
contemporary Dōgen nevertheless wrote: 'Do not think of good
or bad, right or wrong. Do not interfere with the workings of the
mind, nor try to control the movements of your thoughts. Give
up the idea of becoming a buddha.'[8] *Give up the idea of becoming
a Buddha*. Shinran might have written that line. What is this if
not an injunction to abandon calculating effort? While Dōgen's
perspective seems to lack the moral complexity that Shinran
constantly makes plain, he is, just the same, signalling the need
to go beyond the self-serving efforts of the habitual mind.

Intrigued by the quotation from Sangharakshita cited above concerning advanced practice, I wrote to him asking for clarification. This is how he answered:

> In the ordinary activities of life we are accustomed to making an effort. There are all sorts of things that we want, and we work hard to get them. In all this we rely upon our own efforts, i.e. on self-power. When we take up the spiritual life we naturally tend to adopt a similar approach. We seek to 'gain' wisdom or 'attain' Enlightenment. The path of self-power therefore makes fewer demands of us, inasmuch as it is in accordance with our natural human tendency and does not require a fundamental shift in this respect. For this reason I say that the path of dependence on self-power is for the spiritually less advanced. As for the path of dependence on other-power being for the spiritually more advanced, this is because in order to follow this path one has to surrender to the other-power, which means giving up one's self-power. *Such surrender, or complete letting go of self-power, is extremely difficult, directly opposed as it is to our natural human tendency.* Hence I say that the path of dependence on other-power is for the spiritually more advanced.[9]

The prospect of self-liberation is more amenable, safer, more in keeping with our basic vision of the universe. It enables us to continue to believe that we are in charge. To give this up in order to entrust ourselves to something that seems unknown, that is beyond our dominion, appears to us as menacing, as a big risk. We fear losing control, although our idea of being in control is itself a delusion. Shinran's teaching of Other Power overturns the logic of our habitual way of functioning. It seems alien, even a threat to our delusion of autonomy and capacity.

No working is true working

The term Other Power (Ch. *tali*, Jp. *tariki*) was incorporated into Pure Land discourse by Tanluan (c.488–554) and stands in clear contraposition to self-power. In the most obvious sense, Other Power refers to Amida Buddha and, more specifically, the power of their vows. But what does this mean? What can Amida's vows mean to us at an existential level? Among other things, the vows communicate that we have the potential to relate and act in ways that go beyond the logic of the petty, reactive mind, obsessed as it is with its own wish fulfilment, with reciprocity, and what it believes is due to it. There is a potential for the irruption of generosity and compassion through us that can never be 'ours' or, better, that we can never appropriate through egocentric clinging. Moreover, this is not just a passive potentiality but an urging that wants to reveal itself. It wants to make itself known.

Other Power indicates that we should rely not upon our distorted notion of the self and its supposed capacities, but rather on the generosity and blessing of Amida Buddha. Other Power is to be free of any calculation or contriving: 'In Other Power, no working is true working.' In other words, we cannot bargain our way to the Pure Land. In fact, our rebirth in the Pure Land has nothing to do with our mundane goodness or our ego-driven efforts. According to Shinran, Tanluan 'criticizes self-power endeavour in the myriad good practices, and encourages us solely to say the fulfilled Name embodying true virtue' (*CWS*, p.72). Besides this: 'He shows that the cause and attainment of birth in the fulfilled land lie in the Vow. Our going and returning, directed to us by Amida, come about through Other Power; the truly decisive cause is shinjin' (*CWS*, p.72). Other Power seems to contradict our habitual understanding of the world. Of greater concern, perhaps, is that it would seem to remove any responsibility from us to transform ourselves since all our efforts are dismissed as no more than calculation (*hakarai*). However, as Sangharakshita writes:

> This teaching is not the antinomianism for which it might
> at first sight be mistaken. It is merely intended to assert
> the absolute discontinuity of the Transcendental and the
> mundane. The Real is not to be attained by means of a series
> of increments of the unreal. In the last resort emancipation
> depends upon the irruption into the universe of a factor
> that confronts our ego-consciousness as the Other Power.[10]

The Promise of a Sacred World

The notion of Other Power is itself a metaphor. A new factor enters into our lives *as though* it came from outside. However, Other Power is not literally outside us in the way a table or lamp is outside us, and it does not enter into us either like a spirit or a quesadilla:

> ' The compassion of all the Buddhas, though transcending all the categories of thought, including those of subject and object, appears to our ego-distorted perception as a force which acts upon us externally – as the Other Power [...] To surrender to the Other Power means to transcend the distinction between subject and object. As we identify ourselves with Amida, so Amida identifies himself [*sic*] with us.[11]

Other Power is not so much in tension with self-power but rather symbolizes its transcendence in a higher understanding of oneself and of reality itself. Thus Other Power is really beyond self and other, beyond the dualistic mind.

The Buddha becoming me

Our usual way of thinking and structuring experience is dualistic: the other is outside, the self inside. For this reason, we think in terms of self-power or self-effort and Other Power or help from outside or beyond us. The surface structure of Pure Land thought is also dualistic: we abandon self-power, we adopt Other Power. But is Other Power really *other*?

Soga Ryōjin (1875–1971), an important Pure Land thinker of the twentieth century, highlighted the significance of Dharmākara in understanding the Amida myth and how we might apply it at the existential level. He rejected the idea that the Buddha should be conceived as a force or influence from outside that acts upon us, and instead asserted that Dharmākara Bodhisattva is the Buddha 'deigning to become me'. He argues that the idea of a transcendent, distant Buddha is of no real help:

> An eternal Tathāgata of timeless truth can never be our saviour as we stand face to face with life's realities. To

mediate the gap between the human and Buddha world, *a real world saviour has to be one who too merges with this world of reality.*[12]

He goes on to assert that:

> That voice beckoning to living beings everywhere does not come to us from on high, from the lofty reaches of the world of pure light, nor are we being beckoned to by some objectively distinct personality who exists as an individual separate from us. The voice of Dharmākara Bodhisattva issues forth from within the breast of each person trapped in the darkness of suffering and despair.[13]

Instead of seeing liberation as a passive acceptance of the Buddha's gift, we hear Dharmākara calling to us from the depths of our own being, calling us to wake up to who we truly are and how we might better order our lives. According to Soga, it is when we discover Dharmākara within ourselves that shinjin arises. Dharmākara *becomes* us. Dharmākara is never presented as a historical figure since he 'is born directly in the hearts and minds of human beings'.[14] We could term this an existentialist reading of Other Power. Dharmākara is 'Amida Tathāgata who attained timeless Buddhahood; at the same time, he is the person who truly seeks salvation [...] "The Tathāgata is perfectly identical to myself."'[15] This unification of oneself and the Buddha signifies the birth of Dharmākara Bodhisattva within us.

This reminds me once again of Dōgen, who writes: 'Conveying oneself toward all things to carry out practice-enlightenment is delusion. All things coming and carrying out practice-enlightenment through the self is realisation.'[16] We *are* reality, reality manifests through us. We are connected to everything and don't exist apart from it. Our present experience is a manifestation of the *dharmadhatu*, the realm of reality. We don't 'attain' awakening, but instead awakening reveals itself *through* us. In Soga's words: 'The Buddha becomes me.'[17]

Other Power challenges the fiction of our independence and self-sufficiency. It invites us to recognize that we are not ultimately

The Promise of a Sacred World

islands unto ourselves but rather part of a greater web, part of reality itself, not separate from it. We are interconnected with Other and others through a vast network of conditions, and these conditions are constantly impinging upon us, informing and reforming our subjectivity, our sense of being *us*, which can never mean anything independently of them. Our lives depend upon others, historically, materially, emotionally, economically, and so on. Recognizing this can enable us to expand our vision of what it means to be human and dissolve our deeply rooted egocentric stories. This in turn can open us up to gratitude and humility as we recognize how much our capacity to be ourselves depends upon so many others.

Other Power indicates that transcendence is not personal but *interpersonal*. It expresses a kind of intersubjectivity in which we participate. We are not trapped on our own karmic ghost train; rather, we share in the cumulative merits of all other beings. The practice of others manifests to us as the blessing of Other Power and, at the same time, our own practice reveals itself before them as Other Power. Such an idea seems to harmonize with the following mystical affirmation from Dōgen:

> If a human being, even for a single moment, manifests the Buddha's posture in the three forms of conduct, while [that person] sits up straight in samādhi, the entire world of Dharma assumes the Buddha's posture and the whole of space becomes the state of realisation.[18]

To put this another way, all practice is inherently a transference of merit, bidirectionally, from others towards us and from us towards them so that all beings are 'reciprocally endowed with the limitless buddha-virtue'.[19] Moreover, through their constant and dedicated practice, beings 'permeate the inside and the outside of the entire universe with the limitless, unceasing, unthinkable, and incalculable Buddha-Dharma'.[20] This also means that where we abandon the path we are depriving others of the benefits that they would otherwise receive. Practice thus unfolds within a fundamentally altruistic context.

Chapter Fourteen

A Newness that Renews Us Ceaselessly

> When one realizes true and real shinjin, one is immediately grasped and held within the heart of the Buddha of unhindered light, never to be abandoned.
>
> 'To grasp' (*sesshu*) means to take in (*setsu*) and to receive and hold (*shu*). When we are grasped by Amida, immediately – without a moment or a day elapsing – we ascend to and become established in the stage of the truly settled; this is the meaning of *attain birth*. (*CWS*, p.475, original emphasis)

In standard approaches to the Buddhist path, enlightenment is a future possibility that we aspire towards, strive for, even long for. It is therefore both deferred and uncertain. It may – or may not – happen in the future, perhaps even in some distant future long after our current life has ended. Its uncertainty underlines that inherent within it is a degree of jeopardy. If we don't practise in a sufficiently disciplined way, or if we do the wrong practice, or fail to apply a specific practice at the right juncture, we may fail in our aspiration to gain awakening and so continue to circle around the wheel of becoming. This seems to have been the view of early Pure Land Buddhism, especially in its focus on deathbed rituals as instrumental in reaching Sukhāvatī. Such a way of thinking posits the Pure Land, and so enlightenment, as possible future lifeworlds rather than as present horizons of meaning.

Shinran was alive to the shortcomings inherent in such a future-oriented approach to awakening. First, if awakening belongs to the future, then the entire flow of our present should be oriented towards preparing for that future, rather than on fulfilling the promise of the present by realizing its sacred agency. At best, this would seem to lead to a kind of half-life in which we have at least one eye (if not both) fixed on the future. Staring into the distance, we are barely aware of what is around us and even less able to fulfil its potential. Consequently, the present has value only insofar as it is a stepping stone towards the future, which will surely be better. The present is sacrificed for the future. Second, such a view may lead to a kind of anxiety of attainment. We fret about when enlightenment might happen, how it might happen, and we may fall into doubt. Am I carrying out the appropriate practices and efforts to ensure that awakening *will* happen? Given that, in a sense, enlightenment constitutes a rupture with our non-enlightened experience, this anxiety would seem entirely understandable since the 'trigger' or the entrance way to the realm of nirvana remains unknown and seemingly out of reach.

A frequent response to these circumstances that we have already noticed is a kind of *technicism*. This is common to many Buddhist schools: if you follow the prescribed sequence of ritual actions, or a certain programme of meditative exercises, or a precise series of purification practices, then you will have the best chance of somehow mysteriously activating some higher factor that will then carry you towards enlightenment. Deathbed nembutsu seemed to function in this way. But we have also seen that, if the commensurate actions were not properly carried out, or were not carried out at the right time, or with the right attitude, the dying person, despite a lifetime of striving, might miss out on *raigō* – Amida's compassionate welcome at death. This all seems rather stressful and precarious.

To have attained what one shall attain

The quotation that begins this chapter comes from a commentarial work by Shinran in which he analyzes a short text by Ryūkan (1148–1227), a fellow disciple of Hōnen.[1] In his close analysis, Shinran offers extended reflections on the nature of time and, more specifically, its relationship to attainment or enlightenment. While I have already touched on some of these reflections above, dwelling on them in more detail will show more fully how Shinran's religious imagination gets to work on us.

An obvious and persistent question is: when does enlightenment happen? There is a range of possible answers: in the future, as already mentioned, right now, that is to say in this very moment, or in the past. If enlightenment is in the future, then it has not yet happened and so we orient ourselves towards it as a possibility. If it is right now, then it is disclosing itself to us in this very moment; it is not finished but in process of unfoldment. If enlightenment is in the past, then it has already happened, it is already part of the structure of what and who we are. Each model has its problems and, for that reason, it seems to me that Shinran makes use of all of them at different times. However, he also adds additional possibilities, one of which we might term: *already but not yet*. In this way, Shinran transgresses day-to-day notions of the temporal and causal order.

Shinran wants to get away from the idea that enlightenment is something uncertain but, at the same time, he wants to avoid declaring that we are already enlightened just as we are now. So shinjin is not so much enlightenment itself but rather the guarantee that we will become enlightened in the future. The whole structure of Amida's vows is like this: guaranteeing a future event based on actions that took place in the primordial past. This indicates that we are evoking something that transcends our everyday notions of time. When talking of attainment, for instance, Shinran writes: '*Attain* means to have attained what one shall attain' (*CWS*, p.474). This is a paradox. How can you have attained what you will attain? This collapsing of the future into the present (and even the past) draws on the literary technique of prolepsis, which is to speak of a future event as though it had already occurred. This emphasizes not only that it is *certain* to occur but also that it defies our habitual relationship to time.

We might also understand this in terms of what Jean-Louis Chrétien has named the 'unforgettable'. To be grasped never to be abandoned by Amida means never to forsake the mind that seeks awakening, the bodhichitta. Chrétien puts it like this: 'The unforgettable is not what we perpetually grasp and what cannot withdraw from memory, but *what does not cease to grasp us* and from which we cannot withdraw.'[2] The unforgettable is not just a matter for the past, a question of nostalgia, but promises the future. It determines our horizon. It 'shines from the very brilliance of the future'.[3] In this way, what is unforgettable collapses our imagined trajectory of time. The primordial promise of awakening is unforgettable because it 'destines us'.

This can also be related to notions of irreversibility towards enlightenment that are found in various Buddhist teachings, such as Stream Entry, which is a kind of precursor or anticipation of enlightenment and guarantees its future unfoldment. Once we enter the stream, it is certain that the current will carry us forward to the sea that is enlightenment. Shinjin is a similar kind of concept, and Shinran regularly emphasizes both its irreversibility and its existential agency. In particular, he makes use of the idea of definite assurance or being 'truly settled' (shōjōju), which he contrasts with the notion of being falsely settled and not settled (CWS, p.481). Someone who is 'not settled' practises the nembutsu in the spirit of self-power or in doubt, and so is not yet assured of rebirth in the Pure Land. Someone who is 'falsely settled' fulfils a range of spiritual practices and disciplines in the spirit of self-power. As a consequence, they become deluded and even inflated about their own spiritual progress. This means that they live precariously since they believe themselves to be destined for the Pure Land when, according to Shinran, they are just floundering in confusion.

Shinran's notion of the 'truly settled' arises from his interpretation of Amida's eleventh vow and related fulfilment passages found in the Larger Scripture. He describes the condition of the truly settled as 'to have become one who will unfailingly attain Buddhahood' (CWS, p.475). Shinran refers to this vow as 'the Vow of necessary attainment of nirvana', and glosses it in the following way: 'If, when I attain Buddhahood, the human beings and devas in my land do not dwell among the settled there also, necessarily attaining nirvana, may I not attain perfect enlightenment.'[4] He then draws on an additional translation of the same scripture in which the vow reads as follows: 'If, when I become Buddha, the sentient beings in my land do not decidedly attain the equal of perfect enlightenment, so that they realize great nirvana, may I not attain enlightenment' (CWS, p.475). In his own footnotes, Shinran glosses 'the equal of perfect enlightenment' as 'to have become one who will definitely become the true Buddha' (*CWS*, p.475). So far it is clear that the assurance of awakening, or the necessary attainment of nirvana, or the condition of being 'truly settled', only applies *after* someone has been born in Sukhāvatī and not before. However, Shinran carries out what might seem like a sleight of hand through employing a quotation from Tanluan's commentary. This enables him to extend the range of the 'truly settled' to include those within whom shinjin has arisen in the current life. He cites Tanluan as writing:

> The sutra declares, 'Those who, simply hearing of the purity and happiness of that land, earnestly desire to be born there, and those who attain birth, immediately enter the stage of the truly settled.' This shows that the land's very name performs the Buddha's work [of saving others]. How can this be conceived?[5]

In his analysis of this passage, which is actually a paraphrase of the fulfilment passage of the Eighteenth Vow as found in the *Larger Scripture*,[6] Shinran clarifies that not only does the person who is reborn in Sukhāvatī immediately enter the stage of the truly settled, but so does 'the person who realizes shinjin and aspires to be born there' (*CWS*, p.477). Consequently, he extends the scope of the eleventh vow from the future, when we might hope to be reborn in the Pure Land after death, to embrace the present. In doing this, Shinran removes any doubt or anxiety in relation to the future attainment of enlightenment. Those who place their confidence in Other Power need no longer worry about preparing for their future rebirth or have any concern about its certainty, and can instead rejoice in the present, since their attainment of enlightenment is assured. The present is not sacrificed to the future because it prefigures it. It is as though persons of shinjin have already been reborn in the Pure Land.

A film of bamboo

After having repositioned the realization of shinjin as equivalent to perfect enlightenment, Shinran goes on to cite the Chinese master Wang Rixiu (d.1173):[7] 'The being of the nembutsu, as such, is the same as Maitreya' (*CWS*, p.477). Shinran glosses 'the being of nembutsu' as someone who has realized shinjin. Moreover, he interprets the phrase 'as such' to mean 'immediately'. He understands 'same' to mean that those who are dedicated to the nembutsu and, more precisely, those who have realized shinjin are the same as Maitreya in the sense that they are destined to attain complete nirvana. There is no room for doubt.

Elsewhere he writes of persons of shinjin:

> Such people have become established in the stage of the truly settled and are declared, therefore, to be the equal of Maitreya Buddha. This means that since they have realized true shinjin, they will necessarily be born in the true and real fulfilled land. (*CWS*, p.527)

Persons of shinjin thus come to live in a kind of 'doubled-time'. In accepting their karmic boundedness they dwell fully within the present. At the same time, their assurance of eventual enlightenment comes to pervade and transform that present. Thus Amida Buddha and their cosmic vows reveal a dynamic, transformative relationship to time.

In one of his pastoral letters, Shinran establishes a chain of correspondences between various key terms that not only underlines the elevated status of persons of shinjin but also confirms his proleptic reading of the relationship between awakening and time. After equating the arising of shinjin with the stage of the truly settled, he then equates this state as being the equal to enlightenment (since it assures future enlightenment). He then equates this with the rank of Maitreya:

> Since Maitreya is already close to Buddhahood, it is the custom in various schools to speak of him as Maitreya *Buddha*. Since those counted among the truly settled are of the same stage as Maitreya, they are also said to be equal to the Tathāgatas. Know that *persons of true shinjin can be called the equal of Tathāgatas* because, even though they themselves are always impure and creating karmic evil, their hearts

and minds are already equal to Tathāgatas. (*CWS*, p.528, emphasis added)

Even though persons of shinjin are still assailed by unskilful habits, they are essentially equal to a Buddha or, as Shinran puts it, 'equal to Buddhas' (*CWS*, p.549). Moreover, Shinran paraphrases Shandao as saying that 'the heart of the person of shinjin *already and always* resides in the Pure Land. "Resides" means that the heart of the person of shinjin constantly dwells there' (*CWS*, p.528, emphasis added). Such a person, to all intents and purposes, is then *already* reborn in the Pure Land. This hints at how the Pure Land itself may be understood as much existentially as cosmologically, that is as an expansion of consciousness.

Shinran goes still further and points out that Maitreya's path is the path of self-power but that the path of shinjin is Other Power, which brings with it significant advantages:

> Maitreya's attainment of the perfect enlightenment will be long in coming, but we shall reach nirvana quickly. He awaits the dawn 5,670,000,000 years hence, but we are as though separated by only a film of bamboo. Among gradual and sudden teachings, his is the sudden and ours is the sudden within the sudden. (*CWS*, p.544)

Shinran affirms the liberative power of the present moment and so reinstates its sacred dignity. His perspective promotes not hope but rather assurance. Now is not a step on the way towards then, but is the transformative instant. In Bachelard's words: 'it is the present instant that bears the full weight of temporality. The past is as empty as the future. The future is as dead as the past.'[8]

Time at its ultimate limit

A further idea that informs Shinran's conception of when the assurance of liberation arises is *ichinen* or 'one thought-moment'. In this regard, he cites the passage declaring the fulfilment of the Primal Vow from the *Larger Scripture*:

All sentient beings, as they hear the Name, realize even one thought-moment [*naishi ichinen*] of shinjin and joy, which is directed to them from Amida's sincere mind, and aspiring to be born in that land, they then attain birth and dwell in the stage of nonretrogression.[9]

In analyzing this passage, Shinran identifies the 'Name' (the nembutsu) with the content of the Primal Vow. The potency of the vow is latent *within* the name such that, in voicing the name, the vow's transformative power is called forth. Moreover, hearing the name indicates the arising of shinjin. In his explanation of *ichinen*, Shinran writes: '*One thought-moment* [*ichinen*] is time at its ultimate limit, where the realization of shinjin takes place' (*CWS*, p.474, original emphasis). 'Time at its ultimate limit' indicates both the briefest instant of time and the disruption of the conventional, temporal sequence. Given that there is no process that we can initiate within time that might trigger entry into the life of shinjin, its arising must necessarily emerge not gradually but abruptly, in an instant. To borrow from Bachelard, 'when it strikes, the instant imposes itself all in one blow, completely'.[10] Elsewhere, Shinran refers to the 'ultimate brevity of the instant in which the true cause of one's birth in the fulfilled land becomes definitely settled through one's hearing the power of the Vow' (*CWS*, p.38) and the 'ultimate brevity of the instant of the realization of shinjin' (*CWS*, pp.110–11).

Shinjin entails the fusing of past and future within a 'present that is more present than any particular present'.[11] It is in this instant that sentient beings attain birth 'immediately, without any time elapsing, without a day passing' (*CWS*, p.474). This instant that makes time stand still and transcends our everyday notions of sequential order is beautifully captured in Chrétien's analysis of the 'joyously unhoped for' (*anelpistôi eutukhiai*), which he derives from classical sources. He writes: 'When it emerges, the unhoped for necessarily has a sudden and discontinuous character. It surprises, since it has not been foreseen, anticipated, contained in advance by our thoughts. It strikes like lightning, all at once.'[12] He goes on to say that 'by its interruption it opens a new time, a newness that does not pass and renews us ceaselessly'.[13] The unhoped for, he says, lies outside all progress. That is to say, it is not a moment in time, where time is considered as a sequence of moments, but rather 'lays hold of us'.[14] For this reason, it is not something that can become the past but is always disclosing itself as if for the first time.

The one thought-moment in which shinjin arises also describes a certain quality of attention. Shinran writes: '[*Ichinen*] indicates single-heartedly practising the nembutsu. Single-heartedly practising the nembutsu is a single voicing. A single voicing is saying the Name. Saying the Name is constant mindfulness. Constant mindfulness is right-mindedness. Right-mindedness is the true act' (*CWS*, p.298). This idea of 'constant mindfulness' seems to incorporate both a radical dwelling in the present, since it is the exclusive locus of liberation, and an enduring watchfulness that underlines how the one thought-moment is not just a moment within a sequence of moments but rather the always present, which never passes away into the past. So the time when the Primal Vow becomes fulfilled is also the present, as is the time when our future enlightenment is assured. It is being perpetually reconfirmed and revealed in each instant.

Past, present, and future fuse into an absolute present, which provokes a kind of doubled self-awareness. Thus shinjin irrupts into present awareness as an existential fact and, as such, remains a constant that perfumes every instant of consciousness. But given our distracted nature we lose sight of it – like the sun obscured behind clouds. When awareness opens out again, shinjin irrupts anew, the sun shines again, as a perpetual blessing and assurance and, at the same time, a reminder of our limitedness.

In whatever moment we encounter ourselves, the Pure Land is always a future possibility or destination. It is like the horizon: it is always present before us, guiding us, leading us forward, but we never reach it or surpass it. For this reason, the Pure Land is *promised*. As Nishitani puts it: 'The Pure Land of Amida is one which is, for sentient beings at any point in time, always the future [...] The Pure Land is the future farther future than any future.'[15]

At the same time, in the arising of shinjin, the Pure Land impinges on the present, sacralizing it, but without ever ceasing to be the future. The future *informs* our actions in the present.

Consequently, we can 'rejoice beforehand at being assured of attaining what one shall attain' (*CWS*, p.474). Shinran is, properly speaking, concerned not with the afterlife but with closing the existential distance between ourselves and the Three Jewels.

Chapter Fifteen

Coming About of Itself: Jinen

We are made to acquire the Tathāgata's virtues through entrusting ourselves to the Vow-power; hence the expression, 'made to become so'. Since there is no contriving in any way to gain such virtues, it is called *jinen* [naturalness] [...] it is written that supreme shinjin is made to awaken in us through the compassionate guidance of Śākyamuni, the kind father, and Amida, the mother of loving care. Know that this is the benefit of the working of *jinen*. (*CWS*, pp.453–4)

Naturalness

One of the most mysterious terms found in Shinran's writings is 'jinen' (自然), which is often translated as 'naturalness' or even 'spontaneity'. It can mean 'naturally, of course, certainly' and as an adjective it can be translated as 'spontaneous, self-existent'. As with shinjin, I will leave it untranslated as we gradually build up its field of significance. Shinran refers to jinen in a number of places. Most notably, he wrote a short text when he was eighty-six entitled 'Jinen Honi': 'that which is made to become so of itself' (*CWS*, p.427).

Before elaborating further, I should sound a note of caution since, according to Shinran, saying too much about jinen has its own dangers:

> Amida Buddha fulfils the purpose of making us know
> the significance of *jinen*. After we have realized this,
> we should not be forever talking about *jinen*. If we
> continuously discuss *jinen*, that no working is true working

will again become a problem of working. It is a matter of inconceivable Buddha-wisdom. (*CWS*, p.428)

I take this to mean that we need to beware of over-theorizing the concepts Shinran uses since their primary purpose is practical and transformative rather than abstract and theoretical. Jinen is not an idea to be grasped intellectually but a living reality that may open itself out through us. Moreover, it hints at a reality that ultimately cannot be captured in words.

We have already seen how Shinran has a tendency to equate a whole string of concepts as being in some sense equal. Jinen is no different. He sees jinen as a synonym for Other Power, which in turn means that it is the same as Amida Buddha, Buddha-nature, Dharmicness, and the supreme Buddha. He also defines jinen as 'being made so from the very beginning', 'to be made to become so', 'without the practicer's calculating in any way whatsoever', and 'no contriving'. We might see some parallels between jinen and the notion of spontaneity as found in the Tibetan Dzogchen tradition.[1] Jinen calls into question our ordinary notions of effort and self-directed purposes. It points towards a source of direction that doesn't depend on striving but naturally seeks to make itself known through and within us.

Jinen was a key theme in classical Chinese thought, especially Daoism. Pronounced *ziran* in Mandarin, it defined the ideal way of living. It is often translated as 'the natural' or 'naturalness', but more literally rendered it means 'self-so' or that which is 'so-of-itself'. As a quality ascribed to something, it may mean 'true' or 'primal', and signifies transcendence. In the *Daodejing*, for instance, it is proposed that peace, harmony, and happiness can be achieved if individuals simply 'unlearn' social norms and return to their natural way of functioning. In this sense, we could even think of it as a kind of Rousseauian ideal: the problem is what human society overlays on our basic nature. Thus *ziran* is linked to a positive vision of human potentiality.

Ziran indicates a condition in which we act in a way that is uncontrived. To live in the spirit of *ziran* is to be ourselves, even our 'foolish selves', to be authentic, without artifice or contrivance. It is to live without masks, without smoke and mirrors. It is to drop the idea of playing a part or role in order to impress or appease. It is to allow one's unique nature to reveal itself without calculation or design. To be *ziran* is to be natural in the fullest sense, to honour one's own true nature. We could say that it is to live with integrity. In respecting *ziran*, we let life act and speak through us without ego-directed intention and so permit the natural force that is within everything to work itself out freely.

Ziran defines the way the world plays out by itself without anyone making it do so. It also indicates mystery: we do not know what produces life, but can only gaze in amazement as it reveals itself before us. *Ziran* then underlines human ignorance with respect to the ineffable nature of life. Under Buddhist influence, *ziran* also came to mean 'non-substantial', 'having no nature of its own', as opposed to that which is governed by cause and effect. In this sense, it is a synonym for 'emptiness'.

Shinran derives his notion of jinen directly from the Pure Land scriptures. He makes several references to the *Larger Scripture* in his elaboration of it. He cites, for instance, the following:

> The power of the Buddha's Primal Vow is such
> That those who, hearing the Name, aspire for birth,
> All reach that land –
> Their attainment of nonretrogression *coming about of itself.*
> (*CWS*, p.494, emphasis added)[2]

In his commentary on this passage, Shinran notes that 'of itself' indicates jinen and this means without any calculation on our part. In other words, jinen transcends the egocentric will. It transcends self-clinging since it belongs to a different mode of functioning. Shinran also writes:

> Through the karmic power of the great Vow, the person
> who has realized true and real shinjin naturally is in accord
> with the cause of birth in the Pure Land and is drawn by
> the Buddha's karmic power; hence the going is easy, and
> ascending to and attaining the supreme great nirvana is
> without limit. Thus the words, *one is drawn there by its*
> *spontaneous working* (*jinen*). One is drawn there naturally by

the cause of birth, the entrusting with sincere mind that is
Other Power; this is the meaning of *drawn*. *Jinen* means that
there is no calculating on the part of the practicer. (*CWS*,
pp.496–7, original emphasis)

Made so from the very beginning

In some contexts, jinen seems to signify a force or influence that
transforms our life but that is somehow beyond time, even without
beginning. So Shinran writes:

Jinen signifies being made so from the very beginning.
Amida's Vow is, from the very beginning, designed to bring
each of us to entrust ourselves to it – saying *namu Amida
butsu* – and to receive us into the Pure Land; none of this
is through our calculation. Thus, there is no room for the
practicer to be concerned about being good or bad. This is
the meaning of *jinen* as I have been taught. (*CWS*, pp.427–8)

When Shinran speaks of 'from the very beginning', he is referring
not to a temporal sequence but rather to primordial time, a past that
in whichever moment is always past. Here we have some familiar
refrains: jinen signifies to be without calculation and so, in this
sense, it is a simile for Other Power. It also indicates something that
goes beyond ordinary notions of good and bad; in other words, it
transcends the dynamics of karma. Shinran underlines the active
character of the vow: it is 'designed to bring each of us to entrust
ourselves to it'. This suggests that the vow is not a phrase, not
a declaration made in the primordial past, but rather an active
force reaching out to claim us in the present. The vow is always
dynamically revealing itself.

Shinran goes on to comment on the term *honi*:

Honi signifies being made so through the working of the
Tathāgata's Vow. It is the working of the Vow where there
is no room for calculation on the part of the practicer.
Know, therefore, that in Other Power, no working is true
working. (*CWS*, p.427)

Jinen thus indicates a mode of functioning that is not impeded or appropriated by our self-referential tendencies. It implies a kind of receptivity, a letting go, in order to permit a new kind of will to flourish.

The notion of jinen resonates with what Sangharakshita termed the 'gestalt', a German word that means something like 'pattern' or 'configuration'.[3] He suggests that we should not restrict ourselves exclusively to a linear model of awakening in which we proceed stage by stage until we reach the goal, but we can also think in terms of a blueprint or pattern that is trying to work itself out through us. Our flourishing is multi-dimensional and cannot be pinned down to a narrative sequence. He says:

> [I]t is as though our gestalt is us, already completed, in a manner of speaking, outside time, and our life consists in the living out of that in time. That's not just a metaphysical abstraction. It's something you actually feel, a power motivating you through life.[4]

He draws on the notion of *dharmakāya*, or 'body of reality', to make sense of this relation. He describes the gestalt as 'the effect of the *dharmakāya* acting upon your best, most positive, most creative part'.[5] At the same time, he warns that we should not take such ideas too literally. The gestalt is just one among a number of metaphors and images that seek to evoke the mysterious interaction that happens between our ordinary selves and the principle of awakening, or Other Power.

Reality as Buddha

In a mysterious and tantalizing passage, Shinran writes:

> As the essential purport of the Vow, [Amida] vowed to bring us all to become supreme Buddha. Supreme Buddha is formless, and because of being formless is called *jinen*. Buddha, when appearing with form, is not called supreme nirvana. In order to make it known that supreme Buddha is formless, the name Amida Buddha is expressly used; so

I have been taught. Amida Buddha fulfils the purpose of
making us know the significance of jinen. (*CWS*, p.428)

Here Shinran brings together a cluster of correspondences. First,
we have mention of the Primal Vow itself, the vow to create a
Pure Land in which all can be reborn. Next we have the idea of
the 'supreme Buddha'. This Buddha is apparently without form
and so, for this reason, the term 'jinen' is used instead of 'supreme
Buddha'. Moreover, Shinran seems to equate supreme Buddha
with supreme nirvana. The purpose of Amida, in particular, is
to make known something that is ultimately beyond even their
exalted status.

This introduces what we might term 'reality as Buddha'. Shinran
borrows from Tanluan in conceiving of the Buddha Amida on
two levels:

[T]here are two kinds of dharma-body with regard to
the Buddha. The first is called dharma-body as suchness
and the second, dharma-body as compassionate means.
Dharma-body as suchness has neither color nor form;
thus, the mind cannot grasp it nor words describe it. From
this oneness was manifested form, called dharma-body as
compassionate means [*hōben hosshin*].[6]

The Dharma-body as 'compassionate means' references the key
Mahāyāna teaching of skilful means (*upaya*) and takes the form of
Amida. 'Supreme nirvana is uncreated dharma-body. Uncreated
dharma-body is true reality. True reality is dharma-nature.
Dharma-nature is suchness. Suchness is oneness. Amida Tathāgata
comes forth from suchness and manifests various bodies – fulfilled,
accommodated, and transformed' (*CWS*, p.153). If we follow
through the implications of this series of equations, we can see that
true reality, or suchness, is identical with the Buddha. What can this
even mean? It is not some kind of pantheism, nor is it proposing
that the Buddha is literally the essence of all phenomena. Rather,
it emphasizes how all experience directly discloses the nature of
reality. Everything manifests reality. 'Suchness' translates the
Chinese term *zhēnrú*, which in turn is a translation of the Sanskrit

term *tathatā*, which means something like 'as-it-is-ness'. It is not some ultimate reality apart from manifest things, but rather refers to the world of things in their particularity as revealing their true nature, which is ultimately ungraspable and unsayable.

'Suchness' also translates the term *hosshō*, more specifically in the term *hosshō hosshin*, 'Dharma-body as suchness'. *Hosshō* translates the Sanskrit term *dharmatā*, which is something like 'thing as it is'. It indicates how each individual thing is itself, just 'as it is'. When seen from the perspective of *dharmatā*, all things are empty of any nature that may be pinned down; ultimately, no concepts or judgements can be superimposed upon them. Reality is inconceivable.

Dōgen also included a chapter on the topic of *hosshō* in the *Shōbōgenzō*. He writes:

> This universe of things and phenomena, and the Dharma-
> nature, have far transcended discussion of sameness and
> difference and have transcended talk of disjunction or
> union. Because they are beyond past, present, and future;
> beyond separation and constancy; and beyond matter,
> perception, thought, action, and consciousness, they are the
> Dharma-nature.[7]

This underlines how the true nature of things is ultimately inexpressible and yet something that we can nevertheless witness, since it reveals itself before us in and through everything. *Everything* reveals enlightenment since everything expresses how reality ultimately is. Dōgen used the term 'Buddha-nature' (*busshō*) as a synonym for *tathatā, dharmatā, śūnyatā,* and even impermanence (*mujō*).

Dōgen concluded that even Buddha-nature cannot be exempt from impermanence or, more accurately, he concluded that Buddha-nature is in fact nothing other than the impermanence of all things. It is inseparable from dependent arising. Consequently, it is not some metaphysical principle that stands behind or apart from the flow of life. 'The very impermanence of grass and tree, thicket and forest is the Buddha-nature. The very impermanence of people and things, body and mind is the Buddha-nature. Lands and nations, mountains and rivers are impermanent because they are Buddha-nature.'[8] Since Buddha-nature is nothing apart from impermanence, we should not seek it anywhere else than in our everyday experience: 'This being so, to look at mountains and rivers is to look at the buddha-nature. And to look at the buddha-nature is to look at a donkey's jaw or a horse's nose.'[9] The way in which all reality reveals the Buddha is expressed even more explicitly in one of Dōgen's poems:

> Mountain colours,
> Valley echoes,
> Everything as it is –
> The voice and body
> Of my beloved Śākyamuni.[10]

Shinran further personalizes the manifestation of reality through the image of Amida Buddha although, at the same time, it is clear that Amida's body is non-different from suchness. Shinran is mindful of the Mahāyāna teaching of *śūnyatā* and recognizes that Amida, like all things, is ultimately empty of any fixed and permanent nature. Amida, just like everything else, reveals the underlying nature of reality.

Jinen and reverse theodicy

While Christianity has faced the perennial challenge of how to affirm the existence of a good and omnipotent God who, it would therefore seem, allows evil to flourish, Buddhism is beset by the opposing problem. If we are ignorant beings, where does the impulse towards enlightenment come from? How can an ignorant being, all of whose actions must necessarily express and confirm that ignorance, ever be freed from the endless cycle of saṃsāra? Shinran's entire religious vision could be understood as an attempt to answer this question and to offer sure grounds for the possibility of a connection with transcendent awareness and wisdom in spite of our inveterate shortcomings.

Early Buddhism emphasizes the primacy of human ignorance, that we are trapped in a cycle of greed, hatred, and delusion, graphically illustrated in the widely known symbol of the Tibetan wheel of life. It tends to emphasize that what is natural is ignorance, selfishness, and aversion. In order to reach enlightenment, we must transcend our basic nature, breaking out of what we are in order to become something new, something beyond ordinary human reality. Our nature is basically corrupt since we are profoundly contaminated by self-interest. So how can we ever get out of this?

While affirming human boundedness, Shinran allows the possibility of a new factor into our existence that, as it were, already underlies all possible experience. Moreover, this is not only a potential but rather an active force that is revealing itself, calling out to us. Everything is made of reality, reality is all around us, and it is disclosing itself to us in every moment, through every mote of dust, through every blade of grass. Reality is not to be found in some far-off future, but is dynamically revealed. This recalls the celebrated metaphor for suchness found in *The Awakening of Faith*:

> By virtue of the permeation (*vāsanā*, perfuming) of the influence of Dharma [i.e. the essence of Mind or original enlightenment], a person comes to truly discipline himself and fulfils all expedient means [of unfolding enlightenment]; as a result, he [...] puts an end to the manifestation of the stream of [deluded] mind, and manifests the dharmakāya (i.e., the essence of Mind).[11]

In the case of Shinran, rather than the true nature of reality perfuming our lived experience it breaks in on us in the spectacular form of Amida Buddha and through their compassionate calling out to us through the nembutsu: 'From this treasure ocean of oneness [i.e. suchness, formless reality], form was manifested, taking the name Bodhisattva Dharmākara, who, through establishing the unhindered Vow as the cause, became Amida Buddha' (*CWS*, p.486). Suchness materializes in the form of the Buddha to communicate to us the true nature of reality and so draw us towards enlightenment. This process is even described as a returning to oneself, or a returning to our true nature. In commenting on *raigō*, that is to say, Amida's compassionate welcome at the point of death, Shinran comments that 'Come also means to return' (*CWS*, p.454).

Elsewhere he writes:

> To return is to attain the supreme nirvana without fail because one has already entered the ocean of the Vow; this is called 'returning to the city of dharma-nature'. The city of dharma-nature is none other than the enlightenment of Tathāgata, called dharma-body, unfolded naturally. (*CWS*, p.454)

Of course this return is not a return to somewhere where we once were but a return to where, in a sense, we always already are. It underlines that there is something intimate about the process of awakening, that it is not foreign or alien but rather something near. It implies that awakening is somehow the completion of a potential inherent within the universe; its potential to become aware of itself. Rilke's poem 'Buddha in glory' seems to gesture towards this:

> Center of all centers, core of cores,
> almond, that closes in and sweetens, –
> this entire world out to all the stars
> is your fruit-flesh: we greet you.
>
> Look, you feel how nothing any longer
> clings to you; your husk is in infinity,
> and there the strong juice stands and presses.
> And from outside a radiance assists it,
>
> for high above, your suns in full splendor
> have wheeled blazingly around.
> Yet already there's begun inside you
> what lasts beyond the suns.[12]

Chapter Sixteen

The Promise of a Sacred World

> Thus, when one has boarded the ship of the Vow of great
> compassion and sailed out on the vast ocean of light, the
> winds of perfect virtue blow softly and the waves of evil are
> transformed. The darkness of ignorance is immediately broken
> through, and quickly reaching the land of immeasurable light,
> one realizes great nirvana. (*CWS*, p.56)

This passage evokes some spectacular images. While clearly a
series of metaphors, it promises a transformed reality, a sacred
world, even nirvana itself. Amida is light, immeasurable light,
compassionate light, light that is wisdom, light that is awareness,
infinite light, light that saturates with joy, light that shines on us
no matter what. According to the *Larger Scripture*, Amida's light
is grasping us right now, blessing us, gifting us transformative
awareness. Shinran affirms that 'Amida pervades the lands
countless as particles throughout the ten quarters' (*CWS*, p.501).
Amida is the Buddha of 'unhindered light' as their light 'is
unhindered by sentient beings' minds of blind passions and karmic
evil' (*CWS*, p.655). This all sounds spectacular, but what can it even
mean? To put it another way, in what sense, if any, is the myth of
Amida *true*? What transformative value can it have?

Myths and ultimate concern

The Pure Land of Sukhāvatī and its presiding Buddha Amida
are symbols, and the narrative of Dharmākara/Amida that we
encounter in the scriptures is a myth. This means that they ought

not to be interpreted literally. How can this myth be meaningfully understood? According to Tillich, 'Humankind's ultimate concern must be expressed symbolically, because symbolic language alone is able to express the ultimate.'[1] Symbols and myths, he argues, are the authentic language of religious life and the only way in which the sacred can reveal itself directly. A symbol in this sense discloses a truth or reality that cannot be expressed through any other means. A symbol cannot be fully 'translated' into other terms, but must be approached *through* the symbol itself. Since a symbol has multiple levels of significance and depth, its meaning can never be fully exhausted. It invites an endless hermeneutics.

When symbols are structured into narrative, they form myths. The story of Amida and the creation of the Pure Land offer a myth of deliverance or liberation. They offer the promise of reconciliation with ourselves by means of a dynamic state of transformative awareness that embraces both our undoubted impulse towards self-transcendence and our inescapable fallibility. Through entering into the drama of this mythic narrative, we go deeper into the significance of our own existence. To take a myth literally is idolatry; to interpret it, by contrast, unleashes its transformative potential.

Bultmann developed a bold hermeneutic approach that he termed 'demythologizing'. This consists in interpreting myths not as accounts of the nature of the universe but as revealing something vital about the meaning of our existence. It means, in other words, to recognize their symbolic character. Rather than offering a description or explanation of the visible, outer world, myth is concerned with *interiority*. Myths enable us to evoke what is of highest value and so make sense of our existence.

Through interpreting myths, we enable for ourselves a more authentic mode of existence. Myths draw on images and themes that are familiar to us and that belong to the visible world, albeit their intention is to evoke realities that are not visible and that call to us from beyond the horizon. Demythologizing does not aim to get rid of myths, nor does it simply translate them into other terms (which would then make them redundant): it consists in a never-finished exercise of interpretation. Through the practice of demythologizing, the existential riches latent within myth may be harvested.

So what might it mean for us to demythologize, or deliteralize, the myth of Amida and the Pure Land? It would mean to understand it not as a narration of historical events that happened a long time ago but as revealing something about the nature and purpose of human existence and about the possibilities that may unfold within it. The Pure Land is life understood as a field of going for refuge. From our side, from the inside, the world manifests to us as infused with sacred meaning. The world unfolds before us as a dimension that enables and invites liberation. The Pure Land is the present moment sacralized.

Bultmann proposes that myths embody the intuition that we are not fully masters of our own being and that we depend on 'forces which hold sway beyond the confines of the known'.[2] We are not in control of all that happens. We are fallible, contingent, and prone to error. Inevitably so. This insufficiency is revealed in Shinran's critique of self-power and calculation. Mercifully, however, there are benevolent forces beyond the fragile will that also inform our lives and that can be invoked in the service of liberation. These forces are personified in the compassionate work of Amida Buddha.

Amida transcends the forces within the visible world, more specifically, the bonds of karma and cyclic existence. Amida opens a path to the other world, which need not be thought of as a world apart from this one but is rather an additional dimension. We could say then that myth offers out the promise of a sacred world that intersects with the known and so reveals its deeper significance. It is by means of this sacred intersection that Amida's vows are fulfilled. Amida symbolizes the sacred world breaking in on us or irrupting within us. In Shinran's refrain, we are 'grasped never to be abandoned'.

Sacralizing awareness

In April 2019, I was on retreat in Spain at a place called Guhyaloka, in the mountains overlooking Alicante. It wasn't just any old retreat but an ordination course. More than a dozen men were about to enter into the Triratna Buddhist Order, as I had done in the very same place back in 1992. I was now there as preceptor to two of those men, one from Venezuela and another from Mexico, now Achalamati and Ruchiramati. I was only due to participate in the ordination phase, which lasted two weeks, and so the retreat was already in full swing when I got there. To establish the context for the ordinations, the retreat leader, Maitreyabandhu, imparted a series of inspired meanderings or homilies, one each evening. I almost wrote 'sermons' since he spoke with such reverence, faith, and love that I felt blessed just listening to the words pour out of him.

One of Maitreyabandhu's regular refrains was: 'We don't know what we are doing with ritual.' This might easily have sounded disconcerting given that we were firmly in a ritual context – ordination is all about that. But I took him to mean that ritual has profound consequences for us and the world, consequences that we cannot readily observe or articulate. I felt that Maitreyabandhu was opening up spiritual pathways towards my inner depths that had long been overgrown. This made me feel both elated and sad at once – elated to remember that those pathways and depths still existed, but sad that I had not been fully honouring them.

I don't remember everything that Maitreyabandhu mused about in the homilies, but one topic stood out because it moved me to tears. He was talking about ordination as something *sacred*; even just this word reverberated through me – like I was remembering that I speak some ancient language. Our Buddhist names are sacred. We are living sacred lives. He went on to talk about what our relatively small Buddhist order and community offer the world. 'We offer the possibility of a life with meaning; our order offers a context in which our life has meaning.' This remark touched something deep within me, something that cannot speak or think in words. It seemed as though the sacred dimension was being invoked, remembered, and even restored. The symbolic world was bursting through into life.

I cried both in shame and in relief. I felt shame for all the times when I had failed to honour the promise implicit in my own ordination, when I had even hidden who I really was, and when I had taken for granted the sacred gifts entrusted to me. And I felt immense relief that I was actually there, in that moment, in more or less acceptable condition to witness the going for refuge

The Promise of a Sacred World

of two cherished friends. Despite all my ups and downs, all my doubts, all my backsliding, there was still a thread of connection with my own ordination that had taken place some twenty-seven years before. I had not wandered so far from the path that I could not find my way back.

A poem by Gwendolyn MacEwen called 'Dark pines under water' seems to resonate with this experience:

This land like a mirror turns you inward
And you become a forest in a furtive lake;
The dark pines of your mind reach downward,
You dream in the green of your time,
Your memory is a row of sinking pines.

Explorer, you tell yourself, this is not what you came for
Although it is good here, and green;
You had meant to move with a kind of largeness,
You had planned a heavy grace, an anguished dream.

But the dark pines of your mind dip deeper
And you are sinking, sinking, sleeper
In an elementary world;
There is something down there and you want it told.[3]

'There is something down there and you want it told.' Even though we ignore it, the urging continues. I suddenly realized that, at least in some respects, I had become subtly distanced from my own religious calling and even from my conviction or *śraddha*. Through embarrassment, or just not wanting to draw attention to myself, I had fallen into downplaying or even hiding the sacred context of my life, making it invisible to others and so in part to myself. I had secularized my social face, even deconsecrated myself in order to fit in, to avoid rejection or judgement, to avoid seeming to appear like some awkward orientalist. I had fallen into an inadvertent secularism. I realized that I had tended to present Buddhism in terms more palatable to a secular vision than to a religious one, and this had made me reticent about carrying out even basic acts of reverence such as the salutation of the five points (*panchang pranam*) or chanting the *Tiratanavandana* to honour the Three Jewels. I had fallen into a kind of subtle, yet insidious, devaluing of the sacred dimension of my life. And I was now recovering it.

If this was a film, perhaps around about this time we might hear some soothing piano music, *Gymnopédie No. 1* by Eric Satie or something of that sort. The camera would pan slowly away, Tarkovsky-like, from the rapt expression on my face, as though I had just discovered the true meaning of life and reached ultimate peace. But it wasn't quite like that. Yes, I felt connected once again with deeper significance, with my ultimate concern, but equally I was still *me*, still the mundane being who, even while connecting with the profound, was obsessing about whether the names I had chosen sounded odd and when I could get back to regular showers.

Along these same lines, Subhuti wrote the following:

> I have become more vividly aware, from time to time, of
> the highly personal, not to say egocentric, manifesting
> in parallel with what transcends the personal – the two
> appearing side by side, absolutely simultaneously [...] I
> can only say that it is as if it is the nature of that something
> infinite, having been invoked, to burst through and express
> itself, but the nature of our petty personalities is to resist
> what we ourselves have invited.[4]

We 'resist what we ourselves have invited'. This underlines the double-awareness that Shinran talks about in the arising of shinjin: we are awakening at the same time to the light of Amida's compassion *and* to our own limitations. As we glimpse the infinite, we confirm our finitude. Shinran puts it like this:

> I know truly how grievous it is that I, Gutoku Shinran, am
> sinking in an immense ocean of desires and attachments
> and am lost in vast mountains of fame and advantage
> so that I rejoice not at all at entering the stage of the
> truly settled, and feel no happiness at coming nearer the
> realization of true enlightenment. How ugly it is! How
> wretched! (*CWS*, p.125)

Sacred awareness is living with an orientation towards our ultimate concern. In Buddhist terms, it is living as going for refuge. The sacred world or sacralized awareness that I am trying to open out here is also gestured at in Dōgen's notion of 'existence-time' (*uji*). This indicates a kind of absolute presence, a sacred present in which we are fully attentive to how reality reveals itself inexhaustibly:

> When we arrive in the field of the ineffable, there is just one [concrete] thing and one [concrete] phenomenon, here and now, [beyond] understanding of phenomena and non-understanding of phenomena, and [beyond] understanding of things and non-understanding of things. Because [real existence] is only this exact moment, all moments of existence-time are the whole of time, and all existent things and all existent phenomena are time.[5]

The present becomes completely *full*. Dōgen points at a realization that is unfolding before and within us, a kind of saturated awareness, one that is teeming with sensibility towards the disclosure of reality in this instant. This sense of hierophanic presence is also suggested by the Austrian poet Georg Trakl. In 'Winter evening' he writes:

> When snow falls against the window,
> Long sounds the evening bell...
> For so many has the table
> Been prepared, the house set in order.
>
> From their wandering, many
> Come on dark paths to this gateway.
> The tree of grace is flowering in gold
> Out of the cool sap of the earth.
>
> In stillness, wanderer, step in:
> Grief has worn the threshold into stone.
> But see: in pure light, glowing
> There on the table: bread and wine.[6]

In his dense analysis of this poem, Heidegger remarks on the line: 'The tree of grace is flowering in gold', and recalls an ode by the Greek poet Pindar (c.518–438 BCE): 'the poet calls gold *periosion panton*, that which above all shines through everything, *panta*, shines through each thing present all around. The splendour of gold keeps and holds everything present in the unconcealedness of its appearing.'[7] 'That which above all shines through everything': to see this means to be responsive to the sacred disclosure that takes place when we pay attention. It indicates a kind of blessedness, a heightened level of being and perception. I have read this poem many times, and I am constantly thrilled by the words 'in pure light, glowing there'.[8] The objects on the table are *gleaming* (*erglänzt*). The verb *erglänzen* can be translated as 'to begin to sparkle'. This recalls a comment by Shinran when expounding the phrase 'constantly illumined'. He writes: '*Constantly* means that Amida's light illuminates the person of true shinjin always, without interruption, at all times and places. *Illumined* means that one is taken into the Buddha's heart' (*CWS*, p.507). 'Constantly' here means *eternally*, beyond or outside of time as we usually conceive it. To me this indicates a condition of grace or blessedness. But it doesn't mean that everything is suddenly wonderful. It is easy to marvel at a hummingbird taking nectar from a flower and feel blessed, but not so much when, on returning to our car, we find that someone has smashed in the window and stolen our cell phone. Saṃsāra and nirvana are present in our experience right now. Realization and delusion continue to coexist in us. In their distinctive ways, both Shinran and Dōgen point towards what we could call the 'transcendent moment', a kind of absolute present that is the ground of all blessing and all suffering. As Shinran puts it:

> When the one thought-moment of joy arises,
> Nirvana is attained without severing blind passions;
> When ignorant and wise, even grave offenders and slanderers
>   of the Dharma, all alike turn and enter shinjin,
> They are like waters that, on entering the ocean, become one in
>   taste with it.
> The light of compassion that grasps us illumines and protects us
>   always;

The darkness of our ignorance is already broken through;
Still the clouds and mists of greed and desire, anger and hatred,
Cover as always the sky of true and real shinjin. (*CWS*, pp.70, 517)

The promise of a sacred world

Amida Buddha's vows, and especially the Eighteenth Vow, may be understood as a sacred and eternal promise. Amida promised to follow the path towards enlightenment and, in doing so, to create a world into which we can all be reborn. Amida's mythic narrative offers out the promise of a sacred world. This sacred world is not in some far-off place or in some hoped-for future life, but opens out before us in this instant. Shinran discourages future orientation and instead insists that the present is the moment of transformation, the moment in which the dawn of awakening begins to break, in which it is always breaking. Thus Shinran offers a vision not of hope but of reassurance. Equally, he suggests a path not of heroic triumph but of grateful humility. While we are constantly reminded of our finitude and erring, we are nevertheless assured of a liberation that our ego-directed actions could never merit.

In this sacred world, practice overflows in grateful, joyous surplus since it is not contaminated by anxious self-justification. Practice is not calculated to make us worthy because we have always been worthy; we are constantly receiving the gift of Amida's merits transferred to us *unconditionally*, independently of any mundane accomplishments or qualities that we may have garnered. If we live within this awareness, there can be no question of exploiting our favourable circumstances and so of neglecting ethics, since to transcend our egocentric willing means to surrender ourselves to the bodhichitta, the compassionate willing of Amida. Our practice thus becomes an offering, a turning over of merits to others that may inspire them to open themselves to embrace and be embraced by their ultimate concern.

Shinran's religious vision arises from profound psychological insights about the nature of human particularity, aspiration, and constraint. It overturns all self-centred motives and objectives that may taint Dharma practice since it points to the limits of the ego-directed will. But this does not mean that we should abandon practice altogether. Rather, practice irrupts within us as a joyful response to a solicitation. Practice enacts our sacred connection with the infinite, with awakening. Practice enacts the Buddha.

Somehow, a connection with the Dharma has arisen through me. Something has been set in train. And it seems like a kind of miracle. Shinran's teaching of absolute Other Power reassures me that my ethical fragility is not an insurmountable obstacle to awakening. In recognizing my bounded, erring nature, I may open the way for something that transcends – but does not erase – that nature. Shinran's affirmation that he, I, and all of us are inevitably prone to error consoles me. If we pay close attention to our limits, a letting go or a letting through may happen. We may see that we are encompassed by the measureless light that Amida Buddha epitomizes.

Amida is revealed through a kind of sacramental perception, both in its capacity to notice unique particulars and to bless with the light of compassion. As Merleau-Ponty puts it, 'I am, as a sensing subject, full of natural powers of which I am the first to be filled with wonder.'[9] Living within Other Power means to be enfolded within a context of sacramental awareness, a context that is always present.

Shinran interprets going for refuge (kimyō) as 'the command of the Primal Vow calling to us and summoning us' (CWS, p.38). Through their vows, Amida Buddha calls out to us. Amida is constantly calling, calling us to come fully alive in the unfolding moment so that we may open out its most exalted possibilities.

Amida Buddha breaks in on me. Amida shatters my conceit and restores my pride. Amida burns me with the searing light of wisdom and compassion, and releases me. In the words of Shantideva: 'Today my birth is fruitful. My human life is justified. Today I am born into the family of the Buddha.'[10]

Appendix:

A Guide to Shinran's Writings and Sources

Shinran's collected writings run to more than 600 pages in English translation. As already noted, he made use of a number of genres.[1] On first reading, his principal works may appear to be little more than a sea of quotations. So where to start?[2]

In approaching Shinran, one needs to determine not just what to read, but also how. In order to benefit from his writings we need above all to exercise the principle of hermeneutic charity. This means to put aside, at least for a while, some of the expectations that we normally bring to a text. We need to be willing, at least insofar as is possible, to enter into Shinran's textual and religious world.

In writing about how to approach poetry, Heidegger remarks:

> Every great poet creates his poetry out of one single poetic statement only [...] The poet's statement remains unspoken. None of his individual poems, nor their totality, says it all. Nonetheless, every poem speaks from the whole of the one single statement, and in each instance says that statement.[3]

We could also apply this hermeneutic intuition to reading Shinran's works. As Heidegger remarks, 'the statement emerges from a hidden source'. We don't have direct access to this source, but the words we read are sort of echoes or reverberations coming from it. Heidegger goes on to say that to read a great poet is to locate or intuit the 'poet's statement'. In doing so, we allow the poem to become our own voice, so that it speaks through us. This implies a receptive and reverential approach to interpretation, a sacramental attunement.

All of Shinran's known works belong to the latter decades of his life, when he returned to Kyoto after a long period of living in the Kantō region. His collected works have been translated into English, and all of the writings discussed below are found there: *The Collected Works of Shinran*, trans. Hongwanji International Center Translation Committee, 2 vols., Jodo Shinshu Hongwanji-ha, Kyoto 1997.

The second volume of this publication contains useful notes, introductions, a glossary, and other supporting materials. The *Collected Works* is available free by writing to the following email: kokusai@hongwanji.or.jp. The *Collected Works* can also be accessed at http://shinranworks.com, accessed on 7 December 2021.

Shinran's writings

Kyōgyōshinshō (*True Teaching*)

Shinran's most elaborate and also most extensive work, *True Teaching*, doesn't make for easy reading. While esteemed as his magnum opus, its detailed examination is generally reserved for the specialist.[4] Completed around 1247 (when Shinran was already well into his seventies) and running to almost 300 pages in English translation, *True Teaching* is a kind of patchwork of scriptural and commentarial quotations arranged to reflect Shinran's vision of the 'true essence of the Pure Land way'. These citations are stitched together with sparse explanatory comments and occasional epiphanies.[5]

The work has been criticized for its seemingly cavalier attitude to textual sources whereby Shinran 'interprets' – or basically *rewrites* – scriptural passages so that they read as saying what he intends them to say. While in modern-day textual analysis this move is not generally considered legitimate, Shinran was following an established hermeneutic tradition known as *kanjindoku* (mind-contemplation reading). This was widely practised within his 'mother school' of Tendai, and was put at the service of his spiritual intentions.

According to one scholar, the impact of *kanjin*-style textual interpretations rests on the fact that 'they undercut or reverse conventional understandings'.[6] Such an approach relies on a mastery of the textual sources at hand, and seeks to reveal hidden meanings within texts and so open up deep religious insights. By the strategic application of Japanese-reading notations (*kunten*) to the Chinese ideograms, Shinran modifies key scriptural passages such that they sometimes read as the exact opposite of what his source texts said. He makes use of various techniques including 'breakdown reading' (*yomikudashi*), which, while preserving the original characters, permits a radically different interpretation of their meaning.[7] This process of creative rereading, or even rewriting, of traditional texts is also known as *eisegesis*. To lend support to his hermeneutic approach, Shinran draws on the well-worn image of the finger pointing to the moon – the finger being the words and the moon being their meaning.[8]

Another notable feature of the work is that it contains almost no recognizable argument. Instead, it reveals a cyclical pattern of scriptural quotations followed by interpretive remarks by Pure Land masters, and occasional comments by Shinran himself. A noteworthy device is Shinran's use of two distinct translations of the *Larger Scripture* in order to more readily support his particular reading. Quotations from these texts signal the introduction of a new topic and also function as textual anchors.

It has been suggested that *True Teaching* was never written for general consumption, but rather constitutes a record of Shinran's personal, spiritual practice that enabled him to actively construct and participate in his Pure Land lineage.[9] The words of the text become 'mediated by the inner transformation Shinran has gone through'.[10] Other theories propose that it was intended as a systematic defence of Hōnen's teachings, and its proposed readership was the learned monks of the established traditions.

An additional translation of the first four chapters of this work that offers some variant readings of key terms is: *Shinran's Kyōgyōshinshō: The Collection of Passages Expounding the True Teaching, Living, Faith, and Realizing of the Pure Land*, trans. D.T. Suzuki, Oxford University Press, Oxford 2012.

Passages on the Pure Land Way

A good place to start when reading Shinran's own works is *Passages on the Pure Land Way*,[11] which, according to Dennis Hirota, 'shines forth like a polished gem' and is unsurpassed as a relatively brief exposition of Shinran's teachings.[12] It is a relatively short work, around twenty-two pages in English translation, which in content and form closely models *True Teaching*. Traditionally, *Passages* has been classified as a condensed version of that text. It can be divided into three main sections: exposition, hymn, and questions and answers (*mondō*). In its exposition, it makes use of the three pillars of teaching, practice, and realization, but also refers to the two aspects of transference of merit (*ekō*), which is the working of Amida Buddha. The transference of merit is analyzed in terms of Amida's gift to us in order that, first, we may go to the Pure Land (*ōsō ekō*) and, second, we may return to this world in order to benefit others (*gensō ekō*). In other words, what we may think of as 'our practice' is, properly speaking, Amida's practice gifted to us. The hymn is similar in structure and content to the *Shōshinge* (see below).

Shōshinge (*Hymn of True Faith*)

The *Hymn of True Faith* forms the final part of chapter 2 of *True Teaching*, and runs to around five pages (*CWS*, pp.69–74). It comprises 120 lines organized into sixty verses. After offering a brief summary of Shinran's theological vision, the *Hymn* is notable for the way in which it lays out Shinran's conception of the Pure Land lineage. It outlines his view of the distinctive contributions of Nāgārjuna, Vasubandhu, Tanluan, Daochuo, Shandao, Genshin, and finally Hōnen to the development of Pure Land thought. The *Hymn* is widely chanted in Shin Buddhist Dharma meetings.[13]

Commentarial works

Shinran wrote several commentaries on other texts, notably *Notes on the Essentials of Faith Alone* (*CWS*, pp.451–69), *Notes on Once-Calling and Many-Calling* (*CWS*, pp.473–90), and *Notes on the*

Inscriptions of Sacred Scrolls (*CWS*, pp.493–520). These three texts collectively form a genre of extended notes and, given that they were written between the ages of seventy-eight and eighty-six, express Shinran's most mature thought. The first two are Shinran's explanations of passages in Chinese quoted by fellow disciples of Hōnen: *The Essentials of Faith Alone* (*CWS*, pp.685–97) by Seikaku (1166–1235) and *The Clarification of Once-Calling and Many-Calling* (*CWS*, pp.701–4) by Ryūkan (1148–1227). *Sacred Scrolls* comprises Shinran's commentaries on the scriptural texts included on hanging scrolls inscribed with the nembutsu or on portraits of teachers from the Pure Land tradition.

Letters

Shinran's pastoral letters offer invaluable insights into his relationship with his followers. Particularly in the collection known as *Lamp for the Latter Ages* (*Mattoshō*),[14] he communicates both doctrinal and practical advice to confused or struggling disciples. Moreover, he admonishes, reassures, and clarifies as the situation demands, writing in a direct and personal style that contrasts with the formal structure of, for instance, *True Teaching*. Through his letters, we witness Shinran dealing with various controversies and challenges, notably the apparent rejection of ethical norms on the part of some who claimed to be his supporters and doubts about shinjin.

Tannishō

Tannishō, or *Record in Lament of Divergences*,[15] while not directly written by Shinran, has become a revered text and offers an accessible summary of many of his key teachings. Possibly compiled by his disciple Yuien-bo around 1280, the work is organized into eighteen sections divided into two parts, with each part introduced by a foreword. It closes with a postscript.

The first part of the text, from the opening to the tenth passage, consists of Yuien-bo's personal recollections of the teachings that he directly received from Shinran himself. The second part, from the eleventh to the eighteenth passage, consists in Yuien-bo's own refutation of divergences from the true teaching that had arisen after Shinran's death.[16] In support of his arguments, he cites further sayings from the master.

There are many translations of *Tannishō* available in English and other Western languages, as well as numerous commentaries.

An accessible way into reading Shinran is through *The Essential Shinran: A Buddhist Path of True Entrusting*, ed. Alfred Bloom, World Wisdom, Bloomington, IN, 2007. This book contains selections from Shinran's writings organized thematically.

Shinran's sources and the Pure Land masters

The Pure Land scriptures

Shinran's principal sources of authority were what are now known as the three Pure Land scriptures, especially the *Larger Scripture*, although he made use of dozens of other eminent texts in his writings. A translation of all three scriptures is the following: *The Three Pure Land Sutras*, trans. Hisao Inagaki, Numata Center for Buddhist Translation and Research, Berkeley, CA, 2010. This can also be downloaded for free from https://bdkamerica.org/product/the-three-pure-land-sutras/, accessed on 7 December 2021.

Ratnaguna's *Great Faith, Great Wisdom: Practice and Awakening in the Pure Land Sutras of Mahayana Buddhism*, Windhorse Publications, Cambridge 2016, offers a contemporary and stimulating commentary on the three Pure Land scriptures. It has the added bonus of including fresh translations of these texts by Sraddhapa.

Luis Gomez's *The Land of Bliss: The Paradise of the Buddha of Measureless Light*, University of Hawai'i Press, Honolulu, HI, 1996, comprises multiple translations of the two Amida scriptures, first from Sanskrit versions and then from Chinese in order to highlight differences between recensions of the texts. He also incorporates a good deal of explanatory material.

Works by the Pure Land masters

Following Hōnen's example, and general East Asian practices, Shinran constructed a Pure Land lineage of seven masters (see

Chapters 7 and 8). These figures do not constitute a direct line of transmission, but rather are included because they are attributed texts and teachings that became central to Shinran's presentation of Pure Land doctrine and practice. Shinran celebrates the contributions of these masters in the *Hymn of True Faith* and also in his *Hymns of the Pure Land Masters* (*CWS*, pp.359ff.).

First master: Nāgārjuna (c.150–250)

The great Indian master Nāgārjuna, best known for his Madhyamaka teaching, is credited by the Pure Land tradition as the author of the *Discourse on the Ten Bodhisattva Stages*.[17] More specifically, the ninth chapter of this work, on 'easy practice', is revered as the source text for the distinction between the easy path (the path of Other Power) and the traditional, difficult path of self-effort. Shinran cites this work in several places.[18]

A translation of this chapter has been published as: *Nāgārjuna's Discourse on the Ten Stages (Dasabhumika-vibhasa): A Study and Translation from Chinese of Verses and Chapter 9*, trans. Hisao Inagaki, Ryukoku University, Kyoto 1998. A translation of this chapter can be found online at https://jodoshinshu.faith/nagarjunas-commentary-on-the-ten-bodhisattva-stages-chapter-on-easy-practice/, accessed on 7 December 2021.

Second master: Vasubandhu (fl. fourth–fifth century CE)

Renowned for his Abhidharma and Yogācāra writings, Vasubandhu is also traditionally credited with the short work *Discourse on the Pure Land*.[19] Running to about twenty pages, the text consists in a verse section followed by an auto-commentary in prose and introduces meditative practices that facilitate birth in the Pure Land. In particular, it introduces a model of Five Gates of Practice, which was taken up by Tanluan and then by later Pure Land thinkers.[20] It is revered as a primary source for Pure Land teaching and practice.

For a translation, see '*Jōdoron* 淨土論: *Discourse on the Pure Land*', trans. David Matsumoto, *Pacific World* 17 (2015), pp.23–42. This translation can be downloaded at http://www.shin-ibs.edu/documents/pwj3-17/03Matsumoto.pdf, accessed on 7 December 2021.

Another translation can be found at https://jodoshinshu.faith/vasubandhus-treatise-on-the-sutra-of-the-buddha-of-immeasurable-life-with-the-verses-of-aspiration-for-birth-in-the-pure-land/, accessed on 7 December 2021.

Third master: Tanluan (c.488–554)

Tanluan wrote an extensive commentary on Vasubandhu's *Discourse on the Pure Land* known as the *Commentary on the Treatise on Birth*.[21] Amongst other things, this was Shinran's source for the notion of Other Power and also for the two kinds of dharma-body (see Chapter 15).

See *A Commentary on The Upadeśa on the Sutras of Limitless Life with Gāthās on the Resolution to Be Born Composed by the Bodhisattva Vasubandhu*, trans. Roger Corless, Takahiko Kameyama, and Richard K. Payne, *Pacific World* 17 (2015), pp.69–234. This translation can be downloaded at: http://www.shin-ibs.edu/documents/pwj3–17/05Tanluan.pdf, accessed on 7 December 2021.

A complete translation of the text can also be found at https://jodoshinshu.faith/wp-content/uploads/2020/11/Complete-Master-Tanluans-Commentary-on-the-Treatise-on-the-Sutra-of-the-Buddha-of-Immeasurable-Life-with-the-Verses-of-Aspiration-for-Birth-in-the-Pure-Land.pdf, accessed on 7 December 2021.

Fourth master: Daochuo (562–645)

Daochuo's *Collection of Passages on the Land of Peace and Bliss* is a commentary on the *Contemplation Scripture*.[22] In it he divides all Dharma teachings into just two categories: the Gateway of the Holy Path and the Gateway of the Pure Land. Making use of Nāgārjuna's distinction between the easy and difficult practices, he identifies easy practice with Pure Land. He asserts that people living at the time of *mappō* (*mofa*) should embrace only Pure Land teachings and so rely exclusively on Amida Buddha in order to be reborn in Sukhāvatī. The *Collection* was widely cited by Hōnen, who begins the first chapter of his *Selection* (*Senchakushū*) with an extensive quotation from it.

See Hisao Inagaki, *Collection of Passages on the Land of Peace and Bliss, An Le Chi, by Tao-ch'o*, Horai Association International, Osaka 2014.

Fifth master: Shandao (613–681)

Daochuo's *Collection* inspired Shandao's *Commentary on the Contemplation Sutra*.[23] This commentary deeply influenced Hōnen and he cited it widely, as did Shinran. Hōnen came to regard Shandao as a direct manifestation of Amida, and wrote that Shandao's commentary 'is the [very] guide to the Western Land and is essential to practitioners [...] it can be said that the commentary is the direct exposition of Amida himself' (*Sen*, p.152). The extent to which Shandao's writings influenced Shinran can be found in one of the *Hymns of the Pure Land Masters* (*kōsō wasan* 高僧和讃), where Shinran states that Shandao's teachings 'fulfilled the Buddha's fundamental intent'.[24]

For a translation of the *Commentary*, see *The Land of Pure Bliss: Sukhāvatī*, trans. Peter Johnson, An Lac Publications, n.p. 2020.

See also Julian Pas, *Visions of Sukhāvatī: Shan-tao's Commentary on the Kuan Wu-Liang-Shou-Fo-Ling*, SUNY Press, Albany, NY, 1995. See pp.116–35 for an overview of the *Commentary*.

Sixth master: Genshin (942–1017)

Genshin, whom Shinran later named the first Japanese Pure Land master, was writing more than 300 years after Shandao. His *Essentials of Birth in the Pure Land* (*Ōjōyōshū*) became a Pure Land classic as well as a notable work of Japanese literature (see Chapter 8).[25] Like many other commentarial works, the bulk of *Essentials* consists of carefully selected quotations from scriptural and commentarial sources, as well as some questions and answers. In all, Genshin draws on some 160 different texts in assembling his work. It is recognized as a seminal contribution to the emergence of Japanese Pure Land Buddhism since it assembled a fund of Dharma resources that subsequent teachers could draw from. More specifically, *Essentials* shines a light on the works of Daochuo and Shandao.[26]

Essentials is noted for its graphic depictions of the hell realms and for its exquisite evocations of the Pure Land. For this reason it has been compared to Dante's *Divine Comedy*. *Essentials* explores in detail the Five Gates of Practice, as introduced in the *Jōdoron* (see above), although Genshin's exposition of these topics is significantly influenced by the interpretations of Daochuo and Shandao as well as by Tendai commentaries. In later chapters, Genshin goes on to provide detailed instructions for various forms of nembutsu practice as well as describing their benefits. He also confirms that even the most destitute may be reborn in the Pure Land, and for the least capable recommends nembutsu recitation as the most adequate practice.

Hōnen went on to make liberal citations from this work. While there is no complete translation of this text available in English, the first two chapters can be found in A.K. Reischauer, 'Genshin's *Ojo Yoshu: Collected Essays on Birth into Paradise'*, *The Transactions of the Asiatic Society of Japan*, 2nd series, vol.7 (1930), pp.16–97. The first chapter focuses on the hell realms while the second evokes the alluring qualities of the Pure Land.

The following studies offer helpful overviews:

Allan A. Andrews, 'The essentials of salvation: a study of Genshin's *Ōjōyōshū*', *The Eastern Buddhist* 4:2 (1971), pp. 50–88.

Robert F. Rhodes, *Genshin's Ōjōyōshū and the Construction of Pure Land Discourse in Heian Japan*, University of Hawai'i Press, Honolulu, HI, 2017.

Seventh master: Hōnen (1133–1212)

Hōnen's most noted work is the *Selection* (*Senchukushū*). Completed in 1198, it runs to just under one hundred pages in English translation and comprises sixteen chapters, which combine quotations from scriptural and commentarial sources interspersed with Hōnen's careful analysis and commentary. Above all, the purpose of the *Selection* is to legitimize the Pure Land approach and, more specifically, to argue for the efficacy and priority of the sole practice of nembutsu recitation. The notion of 'selection' (*senchaku*) is central to this work and is explored from many different perspectives. From the point of view of the practitioner, there are three kinds of selections to be made: to select the Pure Land gate instead of the gate of the holy path; to select the 'five right practices' instead of other sundry practices; and to select the nembutsu over the other four 'right practices'. The latter selection is 'the most fundamental notion of all' (*Sen*, p.145). The nembutsu is interpreted as having been selected in Amida's Eighteenth Vow (the Primal Vow) on the grounds that it is the most effective means to attain birth in the Pure Land and can be readily practised by anyone, regardless of spiritual aptitude.

Shinran was granted permission to copy this text, underlining his status as a close disciple.

See *Hōnen's Senchakushū: Passages on the Selection of the Nembutsu in the Original Vow*, trans. English Translation Project, Kuroda Institute, University of Hawai'i Press, Honolulu, HI, 1998. This publication includes a very useful introduction and several helpful appendices.

A variant edition of this translation can be downloaded from https://bdkamerica.org/product/senchaku-hongan-nembutsu-shu-a-collection-of-passages-on-the-nembutsu/, accessed on 7 December 2021.

Contemporary readings

Expositions of Shinran's teaching in English are scant, and those that do exist are generally directed towards academic specialists and often out of print. Here are some options:

Alfred Bloom, *Shinran's Gospel of Pure Grace*, University of Arizona Press, Tucson, AZ, 1973.

Hee-Sung Keel, *Understanding Shinran: A Dialogical Approach*, Asian Humanities Press, Freemont, CA, 1995.

A Soga Ryōjin Reader, trans. Jan Van Bragt, CreateSpace Independent Publishing Platform, Nagoya 2017.

Yoshifumi Ueda and Dennis Hirota, *Shinran: An Introduction to His Thought*, Hongwanji International Center, Kyoto 1989.

For accessible introductions to the Pure Land perspective see:

Charles B. Jones, *Pure Land: History, Tradition, and Practice (Buddhist Foundations)*, Shambhala, Boulder, CO, 2021.

John Paraskevopoulos, *Call of the Infinite: The Way of Shin Buddhism*, Angelico Press, Brooklyn, NY, 2016.

Takamaro Shigaraki, *Heart of the Shin Buddhist Path: A Life of Awakening*, trans. David Matsumoto, Wisdom Publications, Boston, MA, 2013.

Kenneth K. Tanaka, *Ocean: An Introduction to Jodo-Shinshu Buddhism in America*, WisdomOcean Publications, Berkeley, CA, 1997.

Kaspalita Thompson and Satya Robyn, *Just As You Are: Buddhism for Foolish Beings*, Woodsmoke Press, Malvern 2015.

Taitetsu Unno, *Shin Buddhism: Bits of Rubble Turn into Gold*, Doubleday, New York 2002.

Taitetsu Unno, *River of Fire, River of Water: An Introduction to the Pure Land Tradition of Shin Buddhism*, Doubleday, New York 1998.

Jeff Wilson, *Buddhism of the Heart: Reflections on Shin Buddhism and Inner Togetherness*, Wisdom Publications, Boston, MA, 2009.

The Shin Buddhist Classical Tradition: A Reader in Pure Land Teaching, ed. Alfred Bloom, vol.1, World Wisdom, Bloomington, IN, 2013.

The Shin Buddhist Classical Tradition: A Reader in Pure Land Teaching, ed. Alfred Bloom, vol.2, World Wisdom, Bloomington, IN, 2014.

Notes

Foreword

1 Hans Küng *et al.*, *Christianity and the World Religions*, Orbis Books, Maryknoll, NY, 1986, pp.371, 373 (emphasis added).
2 *Ibid.*, p.373 (emphasis added).
3 *Hymns of the Dharma-Ages*, verse 34, *CWS*, p.407.

The Primal Vow

1 *The Land of Bliss: The Paradise of the Buddha of Measureless Light*, trans. Luis Gomez, University of Hawai'i Press, Honolulu, HI, 1996, p.167. I have abridged the vow slightly. An alternative translation by Inagaki reads: 'If, when I attain buddhahood, sentient beings in the lands of the ten directions who sincerely and joyfully entrust themselves to me, desire to be born in my land, and think of me even ten times should not be born there, may I not attain perfect enlightenment.' See *The Three Pure Land Sutras*, trans. Hisao Inagaki, Numata Center for Buddhist Translation and Research, Berkeley, CA, 2010, p.14.

Chapter 1

1 From 'Childhood friends', in *Rumi's Little Book of Love and Laughter: Teaching Stories and Fables*, trans. Coleman Barks, Hampton Roads Publishing, Newburyport 2016, p.149.
2 See Kulananda, *Teachers of Enlightenment: The Refuge Tree of the Western Buddhist Order*, Windhorse Publications, Cambridge 2004. Shinran sits alongside Kukai (also known as Kōbō Daishi, 774–835 CE), Dōgen Zenji (1200–1253), and Hakuin Ekaku (1686–1769) as one of just four Japanese teachers.
3 For a translation, see *A Primer of Soto Zen: A Translation of Dōgen's Shōbōgenzō Zuimonki*, trans. Reiho Masunaga, University of Hawai'i Press, Honolulu, HI, 1979.

4 Kōshō Uchiyama, *Deepest Practice, Deepest Wisdom: Three Fascicles from Shōbōgenzō with Commentaries*, trans. Daitsū Tom Wright, Wisdom Publications, Somerville, MA, 2018, p.xvii.

5 D.H. Lawrence, *Mornings in Mexico*, Tauris Parke Paperbacks, New York 2009, p.9; first published in 1927.

6 *Ibid.*, p.9.

Part 1

1 Marcel Proust, *Time Regained*, trans. Stephen Hudson, available at https://uberty.org/wp-content/uploads/2015/12/proust-7.pdf, accessed on 7 December 2021, p.136.

Chapter 2

1 From *Feeling the Shoulder of the Lion: Poetry and Teaching Stories of Rumi*, versions by Coleman Barks, Shambhala, Boston, MA, 2000, p.48. The full text of the poem reads:

A lover doesn't figure the odds.

He figures he came clean from God
as a gift without a reason,
so he gives without cause
or calculation or limit.

A conventionally religious person
behaves a certain way
to achieve salvation.

A lover gambles everything, the self,
the circle around the zero!
He or she cuts and throws it all away.

This is beyond any religion.

Lovers do not require from God any proof,
or any text, nor do they knock on a door
to make sure this is the right street.

They run,
and they run.

2 Ratnaguna (with Sraddhapa) went on to write *Great Faith, Great Wisdom: Practice and Awakening in the Pure Land Sutras of Mahayana Buddhism*, Windhorse Publications, Cambridge 2016. This is a must-read.

3　Being a Buddha, Amida is often referred to as male. However, in Japan it is common to refer to Amida as *oyasama*, a gender-neutral word for 'parent'. Shinran also sometimes refers to Amida as 'mother'. There is a history of representing Amida in androgynous form that evokes Amida's non-gendered nature. The human manifestation of Amida is a skilful means and not the 'true Buddha', which, according to Shinran, is 'formless' and altogether beyond gender representation. Throughout this book some translations and citations have been modified to reflect this.

4　There are various forms of the nembutsu: *namo'mitābhāya buddhāya* might be how a Sanskrit version would read.

5　Pierre Bühler, 'Ricoeur's concept of distanciation as a challenge for theological hermeneutics', *Zurich Open Repository and Archive* (2011), p.164.

6　A number of academics have explored the resonances between Shinran and Luther. See, for instance: Paul Ingram, 'Faith as knowledge in the teaching of Shinran Shōnin and Martin Luther', *Buddhist-Christian Studies* 8 (1988), pp.23–35.

7　Miguel de Unamuno (1864–1936). From his poem *Sombra de Humo*, '¿Es acaso una palanca para hundirse en lo infinito?' My translation.

8　Pierre Hadot, *Philosophy as a Way of Life*, Blackwell, Oxford 1995, p.91.

9　Paul Ricoeur in *Hermeneutics and the Human Sciences: Essays on Language, Action and Interpretation*, ed. J. Thompson, Cambridge University Press, Cambridge 2016, p.140.

10　In an analysis of references in the *New York Times* since 1910, Richard Payne found a total of fifteen references to 'Shin Buddhism' or 'Pure Land Buddhism'. In contrast, 'Zen Buddhism' generated 675 results and 'Tibetan Buddhism' 784. See his 'Pure Land or pure mind? Locus of awakening and American popular religious culture', *Journal of Global Buddhism* 16 (2015), pp.16–32 (p.21).

11　*Ibid.*, p.21. Payne goes on to say, 'Shin has no technology to commodify, no product to put on sale. In some ways this may indeed be a strength in that it can make the easily accepted products with their offers of internal transformation more problematic' (*ibid.*, note 6, pp.21–2).

12　*Ibid.*, p.22. Payne also notes how conflation with Christianity does not encourage greater interest in Pure Land Buddhism (*ibid.*, pp.23ff.).

13　Payne notes: 'Shin has an external locus of awakening, while Zen and Tibetan forms generally share an internal locus. Having an internal locus of awakening allows for those traditions to be more easily integrated into the religio-therapeutic culture of the United States that is itself internally oriented. With its external locus, Shin is less easily integrated into that culture and more easily conflated with Christianity. Consequently, Shin does not have the same consumer appeal, it is not a "compelling religious product"' (*ibid.*, p.28).

14 David Brazier offers an engaging approach to this topic in his book *Buddhism Is a Religion: You Can Believe It*, Woodsmoke Press, Malvern 2014.

15 As Kenneth K. Tanaka writes: 'Some may raise their eyebrows and question the use of the term theology since no "God" is affirmed in Buddhism. However, there exists a broader meaning to this term, namely "to discourse (*logia*) about the divine (*theo*)". And I believe that *divine* can refer to what, in Shin Buddhism, is considered "true and real", i.e. Amida Buddha, the Pure Land, shinjin etc.' *IASBS Newsletter* 21:1 (May 2010), available at http://www.iasbs.org/wp-content/uploads/2016/10/2010-05-IASBS-Newsletter-21-1.pdf, accessed on 7 December 2021. Payne, by contrast, offers a strong critique of the use of the term 'theology' to talk about Buddhism since, he argues, it involves framing Buddhist concerns in relation to Christian assumptions and points of reference. Instead, he tentatively proposes 'Buddhist praxis', which means 'thinking about things in terms of some or any of the key ideas that give structure to Buddhist practices'. See 'Why "Buddhist theology" is not a good idea: keynote address for the fifteenth biennial conference of the International Association of Shin Buddhist Studies, Kyoto, August 2011', *The Pure Land* 27 (2012–13), pp.37–72 (p.69).

16 It is intriguing, and perhaps a little ironic, that one of few notable Europeans to take an interest in Pure Land theology was the Jesuit Cardinal Henri de Lubac (1896–1991). De Lubac believed that, far from being a secular teaching, Shin Buddhism could actually help to awaken a renewed sense of the sacred within Christianity. See David Grumett and Thomas Plant, 'De Lubac, Pure Land Buddhism, and Roman Catholicism', *The Journal of Religion* 92:1 (2012), pp.58–83.

17 Rudolf Bultmann, *Jesus Christ and Mythology*, Scribner's Sons, New York 1958, p.19.

18 *Ibid.*, p.50.

19 Paul Ricoeur, *The Symbolism of Evil*, Harper & Row, New York 1967, p.355.

20 *Ibid.*, p.356.

Chapter 3

1 Directed by Franco Zeffirelli, 1972.

2 George Orwell, 'Reflections on Gandhi' (1949), available at https://www.orwellfoundation.com/the-orwell-foundation/orwell/essays-and-other-works/reflections-on-gandhi/, accessed on 7 December 2021.

3 *Ibid.*

4 Michel de Certeau, as cited by Hayden White in 'The practical past', *Historein* 10 (2010), pp.10–19 (p.10).

5 White, 'The practical past', pp.10–19. This concept is derived from the philosopher Michael Oakeshott.

6 *Ibid.*, p.16.

7 On Shinran's life, see Alfred Bloom, 'The life of Shinran Shonin: the journey to self acceptance', *Numen* 15:1 (1968), pp.1–62; revised ed., *IBS Monograph Series 1*, Institute of Buddhist Studies, Berkeley, CA, 1994.

8 As with the Jōdo Shu, the Jōdo Shinshū has a number of branches, although these reflect administrative differences more than theological ones.

9 Richard Slotkin, 'Fiction for the purposes of history', *Rethinking History* 9:2–3 (2005), pp.221–36.

10 Burton Watson, *Saigyō: Poems of a Mountain Home*, Columbia University Press, New York 1991, p.81.

11 Owing to their lifestyles and resistance to official control, we don't know how many there were. Such monks commonly declined to write or engage in scholarship, which makes it hard to trace their stories. Some who did write chose to burn their writings before death as a gesture of non-attachment. It has been estimated that some of the *bessho* (別所, lit. 'separate place') where these itinerant practitioners gathered may have housed hundreds of monks at peak times.

12 For a more detailed account of these practices, see Daniel B. Stevenson, 'The four kinds of samadhi in early T'ien T'ai Buddhism', in *Traditions of Meditation in Chinese Buddhism*, ed. Peter N. Gregory, Kuroda Institute, University of Hawai'i Press, Honolulu, HI, 2021, pp.45–98.

13 This derives from the *Pratyutpanna Samādhi Sūtra*. Translated into Chinese, this is the *banzhou sanmei*; *Banzhou sanmei jing* (T.418). T stands for Taishō Shinshū Daizokyō, a collection of East Asian Buddhist scriptures and other canonical writings. Citations from works included in this collection generally give the document number and/or volume number, with the prefix 'T'.

14 This is a complex matter about which there is much debate.

15 It is not certain whether Shinran married in Kyoto before his exile (in which case it may have been a contributory cause) or afterwards in Echigo. He may also have married more than once. Bloom, 'The life of Shinran Shonin', pp.13–16.

16 Shinran makes use of many technical terms (expressed in Chinese characters) and these are often complex. In order to read his works, except perhaps the letters, considerable knowledge of kanji and a sound grounding in Buddhist scripture are required. Many of the people with whom Shinran corresponded were ordained (self-ordained in some cases) people who had some familiarity with Buddhist scholarship.

Chapter 4

1 Paul Ricoeur, *Fallible Man*, trans. Charles A Kelbley, Fordham University Press, New York 1986, p.25.

2 *Ibid.*, pp.24–5.

3 See *Pascal's Pensées*, E.P. Dutton and Co., New York 1958, p.19, no.72.

4 From the *First Duino Elegy*, in *The Selected Poetry of Rainer Maria Rilke*, trans. Stephen Mitchell, Picador Classics, London 1982, p.151.

5 Subhuti, 'Three myths of the spiritual life', *Madhyamavani* 10 (July 2004), available at http://madhyamavani.fwbo.org/10/threemyths.html, accessed on 7 December 2021.

6 Some other ways to classify approaches to awakening include: sudden versus gradual and whether awakening has an internal or external locus.

7 For a fascinating discussion of this, see James L. Ford, 'Jōkei and the rhetoric of "Other-Power" and "easy practice" in medieval Japanese Buddhism', in *Critical Readings on Pure Land Buddhism in Japan*, ed. Galen Amstutz, vol.2, Brill, Leiden 2020, pp.561–99.

8 Jean-Luc Marion, 'They recognized him; and he became invisible to them', *Modern Theology* 18:2 (April 2002), pp.145–52 (p.150).

9 Paul Tillich, *Dynamics of Faith*, Harper & Bros, New York 1957, p.1.

10 Cited in Subhuti, *Sangharakshita: A New Voice in the Buddhist Tradition*, Windhorse Publications, Birmingham 1994, p.212.

11 See Sangharakshita, *Know Your Mind*, Windhorse Publications, Birmingham 1998, pp.119ff.

12 Sangharakshita, *The Bodhisattva Ideal* (*The Complete Works of Sangharakshita*, vol.4), Windhorse Publications, Cambridge 2019, p.241.

13 Jean-Luc Marion, *Being Given: Toward a Phenomenology of Givenness*, Stanford University Press, Stanford, CA, 2002, p.124.

14 Jean-Louis Chrétien, *The Unforgettable and the Unhoped For*, Fordham University Press, New York 2002, p.99, emphasis added.

15 Gaston Bachelard, *The Poetics of Reverie: Childhood, Language, and the Cosmos*, Beacon Press, Boston, MA, 1971, p.13.

16 Dōgen, *Shōbōgenzō: The True Dharma-Eye Treasury*, trans. Gudu Wafu, 4 vols., BDK America, Moraga, CA, 2007–2008, vol.1, p.6, emphasis added.

17 Wendell Berry, *Standing by Words*, Catapult, San Diego, CA, 2011, p.97.

18 See Julian Pas, *Visions of Sukhāvatī: Shan-tao's Commentary on the Kuan Wu-Liang-Shou-Fo-Ling*, SUNY Press, Albany, NY, 1995, pp.147–9. The parable is quoted by both Hōnen (*Sen*, pp.107–10) and Shinran (*CWS*, pp.89–91).

19 John Caputo, *The Weakness of God: A Theology of the Event*, Indiana University Press, Bloomington, IN, 2006, p.105.

20 *Ibid.*, p.103.

Chapter 5

1 Richard Kearney, *Anatheism: Returning to God after God*, Columbia University Press, New York 2010, p.86.

2 Denise Levertov, 'Bearing the light', in *Sands of the Well*, New Directions, New York 1998, p.37.

3 Sangharakshita, *A Survey of Buddhism / The Buddha's Noble Eightfold Path* (*The Complete Works of Sangharakshita*, vol.1), Windhorse Publications, Cambridge 2018, p.325.

4 *Ibid.*, p.325.

5 *The Land of Bliss: The Paradise of the Buddha of Measureless Light*, trans. Luis Gomez, University of Hawai'i Press, Honolulu, HI, 1996, pp.61ff. See also Ratnaguna and Sraddhapa, *Great Faith, Great Wisdom: Practice and Awakening in the Pure Land Sutras of Mahayana Buddhism*, Windhorse Publications, Cambridge 2016, p.249ff.

6 See Gomez, *The Land of Bliss*, pp.64ff. and 162ff.

7 The Sanskrit text has only forty-seven vows, but given the authority that the Chinese text has gained it has become the standard.

8 Gomez, *The Land of Bliss*, p.167. Note: I have abridged the vow slightly.

9 *Ibid.*, p.168.

10 For translations of both the sutras from Sanskrit and Chinese see Gomez, *The Land of Bliss*.

11 For a translation see Ratnaguna and Sraddhapa, *Great Faith, Great Wisdom*, pp.301ff.

12 *Lotus Sutra*, trans. Burton Watson, available at https://nichiren.info/buddhism/lotussutra/text/chap16.html, accessed on 7 December 2021.

13 *Ibid.* One estimate says that a *nayuta* is ten million. *Asamkhya* refers to a number beyond calculation.

14 Yoshifumi Ueda and Dennis Hirota, *Shinran: An Introduction to His Thought*, Hongwanji International Center, Kyoto 1989, p.121.

15 This is a model that Shinran adopted from Tanluan.

16 *CWS*, pp.161, 461; see also pp.165, 486–7.

17 *Samyutta Nikāya* iii.120. For this passage see, for instance, *The Connected Discourses of the Buddha: A Translation of the Samyutta Nikāya*, trans. Bhikkhu Bodhi, Wisdom Publications, Somerville, MA, 2000, p.939.

18 Norman Waddell and Maso Abe, *The Heart of Dōgen's Shōbōgenzō*, SUNY Press, New York 2002, p.13.

19 *A Soga Ryōjin Reader*, trans. Jan Van Bragt, CreateSpace Independent Publishing Platform, Nagoya 2017, vol.1, 'The doctrinal lineage of the seven patriarchs', emphasis added.

20 Paul Tillich, 'The religious symbol', *Daedalus* 87:3 (1957), pp.4–5.

21 Jean-Luc Marion, *In Excess: Studies of Saturated Phenomena*, Fordham University Press, New York 2002, p.159.

22 Rudolf Bultmann, *Jesus Christ and Mythology*, Scribner's Sons, New York 1958, p.19.

23 Subhuti and Sangharakshita, *Seven Papers*, Triratna InHouse Publications, n.p. 2013, pp.97–8.

Chapter 6

1 Shahab al-Din Yahya ibn Habash Suhrawardi (1154–1191); cited in Henry Corbin, *Spiritual Body and Celestial Earth: From Mazdean Iran to Shi'ite Iran*, Princeton University Press, Princeton, NJ, 1997, p.123.

2 Sangharakshita, *Through Buddhist Eyes: Travel Letters*, Windhorse Publications, Birmingham 2000, p.287.

3 A notable example is the Archimedes Palimpsest, a parchment codex palimpsest. This contains two works by Archimedes that were thought to have been lost (the *Ostomachion* and the *Method of Mechanical Theorems*) and the only surviving original Greek edition of his work *On Floating Bodies*.

4 Paul Harrison, 'Mediums and messages: reflections on the production of Mahāyāna sutras', *Eastern Buddhist* 35:1–2 (2003), pp.115–51.

5 *Ibid.*, p.122.

6 Ratnaguna and Sraddhapa's excellent *Great Faith, Great Wisdom* offers a contemporary commentary on all three Pure Land scriptures: *Great Faith, Great Wisdom: Practice and Awakening in the Pure Land Sutras of Mahayana Buddhism*, Windhorse Publications, Cambridge 2016.

7 Besides the translations of this text by Gomez and by Sraddhapa, an online version of Inagaki's translation can be found at http://web.mit.edu/stclair/www/larger.html, accessed on 7 December 2021.

8 Various recensions of the *Larger Scripture* were translated from Sanskrit into Chinese (five survive), and it was these translations that came to inform Pure Land devotion in East Asia. While the first Chinese translation may have been completed as early as the latter part of the second century ce, the most well-known version was probably translated around 400 ce. These matters are difficult to determine, and debate continues. See Jan Nattier, *A Guide to the Earliest Chinese Translations: Texts from the Eastern Han and Three Kingdoms Periods*, The International Research Institute of Advanced Buddhology, Soka University, Tokyo 2008, especially pp.86–7.

9 Another possible translation of this Buddha's Chinese name (世自在王) is the 'king who freely abides in the world'.

10 *The Land of Bliss: The Paradise of the Buddha of Measureless Light*, trans. Luis Gomez, University of Hawai'i Press, Honolulu, HI, 1996, p.177.

11 This section, traditionally called 'The five evils', seems to be a Chinese addition to the translation of the Sanskrit text. It is not found in the Sanskrit version of the texts and reads very differently. See Gomez, *The Land of Bliss*, p.253, note 80.

12 This analysis is different from the three scopes already summarized, and indicates that the text does not express a fully coherent message.

13 *Foshuo Amituo Jing*, T.366. See Ratnaguna and Sraddhapa, *Great Faith, Great Wisdom*, pp.241ff.

14 While several Chinese translations are extant, Kumārajīva's version is used almost universally for liturgical purposes owing to its musicality.

15 In the Sanskrit version, the Buddhas praise their own Buddha-lands; see Gomez, *The Land of Bliss*, pp.19–20.

16 *Ibid.*, p.151.

17 *Guan Wuliangshoufo Jing*, T.365.

18 Shinran cites in detail the *Nirvāṇa Sūtra*, which recounts Ajātaśatru's story after having killed his father, *CWS*, pp.125ff.

19 Ratnaguna and Sraddhapa, *Great Faith, Great Wisdom*, p.310.

20 Paul Ricoeur and Richard Kearney, 'Myth as the bearer of possible worlds', *The Crane Bag* 2:1–2 (1978), pp.112–18 (p.116).

21 Paul Ricoeur, *The Symbolism of Evil*, Harper & Row, New York 1967, p.5.

22 Ricoeur and Kearney, 'Myth as the bearer of possible worlds', pp.117–18.

23 James Hollis, *Tracking the Gods: The Place of Myth in Modern Life*, Inner City Books, Scarborough, ON, 1995, p.8.

24 Sangharakshita, *The Inconceivable Emancipation*, Windhorse Publications, Birmingham 1995, p.25.

25 Sangharakshita, *A Survey of Buddhism / The Buddha's Noble Eightfold Path* (*The Complete Works of Sangharakshita*, vol.1), Windhorse Publications, Cambridge 2018, p.340, emphasis added.

26 *The Vimalakirti Sutra*, trans. Burton Watson, Columbia University Press, New York 1997, chapter 1.

Chapter 7

1 These words are uttered as part of the ceremony.

2 This theme is explored in Allan A. Andrews, 'The "Senchakushu" in Japanese religious history: the founding of a Pure Land school', *Journal of the American Academy of Religion* 55:3 (autumn 1987), pp.473–99. Hōnen's list comprised: Tanluan, Daochuo, Shandao, Huaigan (n.d.), and Shaokang (d.805). For more about Hōnen's lineage chart, see Michael Conway, 'The creation of tradition as an exercise in doctrinal classification: Shinran's forging of the seven Shin patriarchs', *The Eastern Buddhist* 45:1–2 (2014), pp.113–50 (pp.124ff.).

3 This term is often translated as 'patriarch'. Another term that Shinran frequently uses is *kōsō* (高僧), literally 'high monks', which doesn't translate so well into English.

4 Cited in Minor Rogers and Ann Rogers, *Rennyo: Second Founder of Shin Buddhism*, Asian Humanities Press, Berkeley, CA, 1991, p.142.

5 The treatise is known as the *Commentary on the Ten Bodhisattva Stages* (*Shizhupiposhalun* T.1521 十住毘婆沙論, Jp. *Jūjū bibasha ron*). Shinran cites a series of passages from this work in *True Teaching*: see *CWS*, pp.18–24. Chapter 9 of the work focuses on 'easy practice'.

6 Available at https://jodoshinshu.faith/nagarjunas-commentary-on-the-ten-bodhisattva-stages-chapter-on-easy-practice/, accessed on 8 December 2021 (emphasis added).

7 This is Conway's translation: see 'The creation of tradition as an exercise in doctrinal classification', p.131. See also *CWS*, pp.485–6.

8 *Jingtu lun* (T.1524). For a translation see '*Jōdoron* 淨土論: *Discourse on the Pure Land*', trans. David Matsumoto, *Pacific World* 17 (2015), pp.23–42.

9 *CWS*, p.71. The translation used here is taken from Conway, 'The creation of tradition as an exercise in doctrinal classification', p.137.

10 Matsumoto, '*Jōdoron* 淨土論: *Discourse on the Pure Land*', pp.35–6.

11 *Jingtu lun zhu* (T.1819). For a translation, see *A Commentary on The Upadeśa on the Sutras of Limitless Life with Gāthās on the Resolution to Be Born Composed by the Bodhisattva Vasubandhu*, trans. Roger Corless, Takahiko Kameyama, and Richard K. Payne, *Pacific World* 17 (2015), pp.69–234. Accessible resources on Tanluan can be found in a special issue of the journal *Pacific World* (2000), available at https://pwj.shin-ibs.edu/third-series-number-2-fall-2000, accessed on 8 December 2021.

12 To give just one example, in *True Teaching*, chapter 4 ('Realization'), Shinran cites a fifteen-page extract from it, which amounts to around 20 per cent of the entire work. (*CWS*, pp.159–74). The reverence that Shinran accorded Tanluan (or Donran in Japanese) can be seen in the fact that Shinran incorporated the second half of Donran's name (*ran* 鸞) into his own (Shinran 親鸞). The other part of the name (*shin* 親), comes from the Japanese name for Vasubandhu (Tenshin).

13 For more on Tanluan's influence on Shinran, see Bandō Shōjun, 'Shinran's indebtedness to T'an-luan', *The Eastern Buddhist*, new series, 4:1 (1971), pp.72–87. This essay is reprinted in *Pacific World*, 3rd series, no.2 (autumn 2000), pp.17–30.

14 Cited in *True Teaching*, *CWS*, p.25.

15 This passage is cited in *True Teaching*, *CWS*, p.26 (emphasis added). Here I have used a slightly modified translation as the original doesn't scan well.

16 Cited in *Hōnen's Senchakushū: Passages on the Selection of the Nembutsu in the Original Vow*, trans. English Translation Project, Kuroda Institute, University of Hawai'i Press, Honolulu, HI, 1998, p.56.

17 For a study of Shandao and his teachings see Julian Pas, *Visions of Sukhāvatī: Shan-tao's Commentary on the Kuan Wu-Liang-Shou-Fo-Ling*, SUNY Press, Albany, NY, 1995.

18 *Ibid.*, pp.143–6.

19 As Pas documents, Shandao also gave considerable attention to Buddha contemplation (*guanfo*), but its application was likely to be more at the elite level; *ibid.*, pp.163–206.

20 *Guan wuliangshoufo jing zhu* (T.1753).

21 See Pas, *Visions of Sukhāvatī*, pp.216–19. The 'threefold mind' (*sanzhong xin*) comprises: (1) *zhicheng xin*; (2) *shenxin*; and (3) *huxiang fayuan xin*. Shinran cites a seven-page extract from Shandao's *Commentary* in *True Teaching* (*CWS*, pp.84–91) that explores the three minds. This culminates in the 'Parable of the white path'.

22 *CWS*, pp.93–114 and 212–27.

Chapter 8

1 For a useful overview of earlier developments in Pure Land thought and practice in Japan, see Allan A. Andrews, 'Genshin's "Essentials of Pure Land rebirth" and the transmission of Pure Land Buddhism to Japan, Part I: the first and second phases of transmission of Pure Land Buddhism to Japan: the Nara period and the early Heian period', *Pacific World* 5 (1989), pp.20–32.

2 Sarah Horton, 'The influence of the *Ōjōyōshū* in late tenth- and early eleventh-century Japan', *Japanese Journal of Religious Studies* 31:1 (2004), pp.29–54.

3 Cited in D.T. Suzuki, *Manual of Zen Buddhism*, Rider and Co., London 1950, p.14.

4 Cited in Allan A. Andrews, 'The essentials of salvation: a study of Genshin's *Ōjōyōshū*', *The Eastern Buddhist* 4:2 (1971), pp.50–88 (p.65).

5 *Ibid.*, p.69.

6 *Ibid.*, p.73.

7 Cited in Ratnaguna and Sraddhapa, *Great Faith, Great Wisdom: Practice and Awakening in the Pure Land Sutras of Mahayana Buddhism*, Windhorse Publications, Cambridge 2016, p.317.

8 Sarah Horton, '*Mukaekō* practice for the deathbed', in *Death and the Afterlife in Japanese Buddhism*, ed. Jacqueline I. Stone and Mariko Namba Walter, University of Hawai'i Press, Honolulu, HI, 2017, pp.27–60.

9 Cited in Ratnaguna and Sraddhapa, *Great Faith, Great Wisdom*, p.322.

10 Jaqueline I. Stone, 'Shinran's rejection of deathbed rites', in *Chūsei bunka to Jōdo Shinshū* [*Shin Buddhism and Medieval Culture in Japan*], Shibunkaku Shuppan, Kyoto 2012, pp.614–596 (reverse pagination, p.611).

11 Jaqueline I. Stone, 'By the power of one's last nenbutsu: deathbed practices in early medieval Japan', in *Approaching the Land of Bliss: Religious Praxis in the Cult of Amitābha*, ed. Richard Karl Payne and Kenneth Ken'ichi Tanaka, University of Hawai'i Press, Honolulu, HI, 2004, pp.77–119 (pp.101–2).

12 Hōnen is also known as Genkū, which was part of his Tendai ordination name of Hōnen-bo Genkū. For an overview of Hōnen's life and teaching, see James C. Dobbins, *Jōdo Shinshū: Shin Buddhism in Medieval Japan*, University of Hawai'i Press, Honolulu, HI, 2002, pp.11–20. For a detailed study see Sōhō Machida, *Renegade Monk: Hōnen and Japanese Pure Land Buddhism*, University of California Press, Berkeley, CA, 1999.

13 Allan A. Andrews, 'Hōnen on attaining Pure Land rebirth: the selected nembutsu of the original vow', *Pacific World* 6 (2004), pp.89–107 (pp.91ff.).

14 *Ibid.*, p.99.

15 Mark L. Blum, *The Origins and Development of Pure Land Buddhism: A Study and Translation of Gyōnen's Jōdo Hōmon Genrushō*, Oxford University Press, Oxford 2002, p.13.

16 Recent scholarship indicates that it oversimplifies Shandao's approach to suggest that he stressed the exclusive practice of recitation. Nevertheless, he did promote it for those of low spiritual capacity. This is a complex issue treated in Julian Pas, *Visions of Sukhāvatī: Shantao's Commentary on the Kuan Wu-Liang-Shou-Fo-Ling*, SUNY Press, Albany, NY, 1995, pp.266–75.

17 Blum suggests he observed as many as 84,000 recitations per day (*The Origins and Development of Pure Land Buddhism*, p.31).

18 *Senchakushū*. Its full title is *Senchaku hongan nembutsu shū* (*Collection of Passages on the Selection of Nembutsu of the Original Vow*), T.2608. This has been translated into English as *Hōnen's Senchakushū: Passages on the Selection of the Nembutsu in the Original Vow*, trans. English Translation Project, Kuroda Institute, University of Hawai'i Press, Honolulu, HI, 1998.

19 These are basically the same five categories first outlined in the *Jodōron* and expounded by various Pure Land teachers.

20 Cited in Hōnen, *Senchaku hongan nembutsu shū: A Collection of Passages on the Nembutsu Chosen in the Original Vow*, trans. Morris J. Augustine and Kondō Tesshō, Numata Center for Buddhist Translation and Research, Berkeley, CA, 1997, p.24. This work is a different edition of *Hōnen's Senchakushū*, and has some variant, and at times preferable, readings. This passage was also cited by Shinran at *CWS*, p.37.

21 *Anantarika-karma*: killing one's father, killing one's mother, killing an arhat, injuring a Buddha, and causing schism in the sangha.

22 *Scripture of the Lotus Blossom of the Fine Dharma*, trans. Leon Hurvitz, Columbia University Press, New York 1976, pp.130ff.

23 Stone, 'By the power of one's last nenbutsu', p.105.

24 'What is the Western Buddhist Order?', in Subhuti and Sangharakshita, *Seven Papers*, Triratna InHouse Publications, n.p. 2013, pp.11–12.

Chapter 9

1 *The Rhinoceros Horn and Other Early Buddhist Poems* (*Sutta Nipāta*), trans. K.R. Norman, Pali Text Society, Oxford 1984, p.184.

2 Bhadantacariya Buddhaghosa, *Visuddhimagga*, trans. Bhikkhu Ñānamoli, Buddhist Publications Society, Colombo 2010, p.188. The recollection of the Buddha is analyzed on pp.188–209.

3 *The Pratyutpanna Samādhi Sūtra and the Śūraṅgama Samādhi Sūtra*, Numata Center for Buddhist Translation and Research, Berkeley, CA, 1998, pp.17–18.

4 *Ibid.*, p.19.

5 *Ibid.*, p.20.

6 This depends on how we read the kanji 念 (*nian*, *nen*), which can mean both vocalization and thought. As a consequence, within Pure Land tradition it is often interpreted to indicate recitative practice.

7 Julian Pas, *Visions of Sukhāvatī: Shan-tao's Commentary on the Kuan Wu-Liang-Shou-Fo-Ling*, SUNY Press, Albany, NY, 1995, p.264.

8 Item 3 incorporates item 2, since one will hear the name as one recites it. When Hōnen was asked how loud we should recite the nembutsu, his answer was 'loud enough that it reaches your ear'.

9 Cited in Pas, *Visions of Sukhāvatī*, p.271. Hōnen renders this passage as 'to recite single-mindedly and wholeheartedly the name of Amituo Fo [Amida Buddha] whether walking or standing still, whether seated or lying down, without considering whether the time involved is long or short and without ceasing for an instant' (*Sen*, p.63).

10 Pas argues that 'The oral invocation is not the most recommended form of *nianfo*. It is [...] merely the "back door" to Sukhāvatī' (Pas, *Visions of Sukhāvatī*, p.275).

11 As I began to reflect more on these affinities, I came across the following article, which addresses some of the thoughts that were also arising within my own mind: Lisa Grumbach, 'Nembutsu and meditation: problems with the categories of contemplation, devotion, meditation, and faith', *Pacific World*, 3rd series, no.7 (2005), pp.91–105.

12 From *Bendōwa*, translated in Norman Waddell and Maso Abe, *The Heart of Dōgen's Shōbōgenzō*, SUNY Press, New York 2002, p.19.

13 By playing on the Japanese word for Adam's apple (*nodo hotoke* 喉仏, lit. 'throat Buddha') some Shinshu teachers talk about the throat being a little Buddha that lives in our body, as it is with the throat that we embody Amida in saying the nembutsu.

Chapter 10

1 'Extending the hand of fellowship', in Sangharakshita, *The Three Jewels 1 (The Complete Works of Sangharakshita*, vol.2), Windhorse Publications, Cambridge 2019, p.567, emphasis added.

2 'Initiation into a new life', in Subhuti and Sangharakshita, *Seven Papers*, Triratna InHouse Publications, n.p. 2013, p.130.

3 See, for example, Sangharakshita, *The Meaning of Conversion in Buddhism*, Windhorse Publications, Birmingham 1994.

4 Śāntideva, *The Bodhicaryāvatāra*, trans. Kate Crosby and Andrew Skilton, Oxford University Press, Oxford 1995, chapter 1, verses 18–19, pp.6–7.

5 Sangharakshita, *The Bodhisattva Ideal: Wisdom and Compassion in Buddhism*, Windhorse Publications, Birmingham 1999, pp.38–9.

6 Cited from the *Nirvāṇa Sūtra, CWS*, p.99, emphasis added.

7 John Caputo, 'Spectral hermeneutics: on the weakness of God and the theology of the event', in John Caputo and Gianni Vattimo, *After the Death of God*, ed. Jeffrey W. Robbins, Columbia University Press, New York 2007, pp.47–85 (p.47).

8 *Ibid.*, p.47.

9 *Ibid.*, p.48.

10 *Ibid.*, p.183, note 4.

11 Alain Badiou, *Ethics: An Essay on the Understanding of Evil*, Verso, London 2013, p.123.

12 Caputo, 'Spectral hermeneutics', p.52.

13 Martin Heidegger, *Country Path Conversations*, trans. Bret W. Davis, Indiana University Press, Bloomington, IN, 2016, p.70.

14 *Ibid.*, p.70.

15 *Ibid.*, p.76.

16 Dennis Hirota, 'The holistic apprehension of religious life in Shinran and Heidegger: an experiment in comparative Shin Buddhist thought', *Journal of Ryukoku University [Ryukoku Daigaku Ronshu]* 474–5 (2010), pp.37–8.

17 *CWS*, p.512. This is cited from the *Senchakushū*, emphasis added.

18 *The Sutta-Nipāta*, trans. H. Saddhatissa, Curzon Press, Richmond 1985, p.72.

Chapter 11

1 *Dhammapada: The Way of Truth*, trans. Sangharakshita, Windhorse Publications, Birmingham 2001, verses 121–2, pp.48–9. Modified for gender.

2 Subhuti and Sangharakshita, *Seven Papers*, Triratna InHouse Publications, n.p. 2013, p.152.

3 *Ibid.*, p.152.

4 *Ibid.*, p.152.

5 *Ibid.*, p.152.

6 Emmanuel Levinas, *Ethics and Infinity*, Duquesne University Press, Pittsburgh, PA, 1985, p.98.

7 These ten benefits are: (1) the benefit of being protected and sustained by unseen powers, (2) the benefit of being possessed of supreme virtues, (3) the benefit of our karmic evil being transformed into good, (4) the benefit of being protected and cared for by all the Buddhas, (5) the benefit of being praised by all the Buddhas, (6) the benefit of being constantly protected by the light of the Buddha's heart, (7) the benefit of having great joy in our hearts, (8) the benefit of being aware of Amida's benevolence and of responding in gratitude to his virtue, (9) the benefit of constantly practising great compassion, and (10) the benefit of entering the stage of the truly settled (*CWS*, p.112).

Chapter 12

1 Jaime Sabines, 'Lento, amargo animal que soy' ('Slow, bitter animal that I am'), in *Recuento de poemas: 1950/1993*, Joaquín Mortiz, Mexico City 1997, p.11.

2 *Udāna*, 5.3. See, for instance, *The Udāna and the Itivuttaka: Two Classics from the Pāli Canon*, trans. John D. Ireland, Buddhist Publication Society, Kandy 1997, pp.66–9.

3 *Lotus Sutra*, trans. Burton Watson, available at https://nichiren.info/buddhism/lotussutra/text/chap08.html, accessed on 9 December 2021.

4 Plato, *Meno*, trans. Benjamin Jowett, available at https://www.gutenberg.org/files/1643/1643-h/1643-h.htm, accessed on 8 December 2021.

5 Śāntideva, *The Bodhicaryāvatāra*, trans. Kate Crosby and Andrew Skilton, Oxford University Press, Oxford 1995, chapter 3, verse 27, p.22.

6 See Dietrich Bonhoeffer, *The Cost of Discipleship*, Touchstone, New York 1995.

7 Kenneth K. Tanaka, 'Amida and Pure Land within a contemporary worldview: from Shinran's literal symbolism to figurative symbolism', in *Critical Readings on Pure Land Buddhism in Japan*, ed. Galen Amstutz, vol.3, Brill, Leiden 2020, pp.1005–32 (p.1030).

8 John Caputo, *The Weakness of God: A Theology of the Event*, Indiana University Press, Bloomington, IN, 2006, p.5.

9 *The Dhammapada*, trans. Valerie J. Roebuck, Penguin Classics, London 2010, verse 354, p.69.

10 Sangharakshita, 'Looking at the bodhi tree', available at https://
www.freebuddhistaudio.com/texts/read?num=192&at=text&p=5,
accessed on 8 December 2021

11 From the poem 'I saw in Louisiana a live-oak growing', available
at https://www.poetryfoundation.org/poems/45471/i-saw-in-
louisiana-a-live-oak-growing, accessed on 8 December 2021.

12 From the *Ninth Duino Elegy*, in *The Selected Poetry of Rainer Maria Rilke*,
trans. Stephen Mitchell, Picador Classics, London 1982, p.203.

13 Dōgen, *Shōbōgenzō: The True Dharma-Eye Treasury*, trans. Gudu Wafu, 4
vols., BDK America, Moraga, CA, 2007–2008, vol.1, p.7.

14 Dōgen, *Genjōkōan*, translated in Shoaku Okumura, *Realising Genjōkōan:
The Key to Dogen's Shōbōgenzō*, Wisdom Publications, Somerville, MA,
2010, p.3.

Chapter 13

1 Shichiri Kōjun cited in J. Fredericks, 'a hermeneutics of grace: Henri
de Lubac's reception of Hōnen and Shinran', *The Eastern Buddhist*, new
series, 48:1 (2017), pp.159–76 (pp.167–8). Quote modified for gender.

2 Sangharakshita, *Living Wisely: Further Advice from Nagarjuna's Precious
Garland*, Windhorse Publications, Cambridge 2013, p.39.

3 Richard Payne, 'Pure Land or pure mind? Locus of awakening and
American popular religious culture', *Journal of Global Buddhism* 16
(2015), pp.16–32 (p.22).

4 Sangharakshita, *Through Buddhist Eyes: Travel Letters*, Windhorse
Publications, Birmingham 2000, p.288, original emphasis.

5 *The Dhammapada*, trans. Valerie J. Roebuck, Penguin Classics, London
2010, verse 160, p.33.

6 *Ibid.*, verse 165, p.34.

7 Trungpa Rimpoche, *Cutting Through Spiritual Materialism*, Shambhala
Publications, Boulder, CO, 1973.

8 Dōgen, *Fukanzazengi*, available at http://www.brunnenhofzendo.ch/
index_htm_files/Genjokoan%20English%20Okumura%20plus%20
Fukanzazengi%20Rumme%20A5.pdf, accessed on 8 December 2021.

9 Personal correspondence with author, January 2014, emphasis added.

10 Sangharakshita, *A Survey of Buddhism / The Buddha's Noble Eightfold
Path* (*The Complete Works of Sangharakshita*, vol.1), Windhorse
Publications, Cambridge 2018, p.332.

11 *Ibid.*, pp.346–7.

12 Soga Ryōjin, 'The significance of Dharmākara Bodhisattva as earthly
saviour', in *Living in Amida's Universal Vow: Essays in Shin Buddhism*,
ed. Alfred Bloom, World Wisdom, Bloomington, IN, 2004, pp.13–18
(p.15), emphasis added.

13 *Ibid.*, pp.16–17.

14 *Ibid.*, p.16.

15 *Ibid.*, p.18.
16 Dōgen, in Shoaku Okumura, *Realising Genjōkōan: The Key to Dogen's Shōbōgenzō*, Wisdom Publications, Somerville, MA, 2010, p.1.
17 Soga, 'The significance of Dharmākara Bodhisattva as earthly saviour', p.18.
18 Dōgen, *Shōbōgenzō: The True Dharma-Eye Treasury*, trans. Gudu Wafu, 4 vols., BDK America, Moraga, CA, 2007–2008, vol.1, pp.5–6.
19 *Ibid.*, p.6.
20 *Ibid.*, p.6.

Chapter 14

1 See *CWS*, pp.701–4.
2 Jean-Louis Chrétien, *The Unforgettable and the Unhoped For*, Fordham University Press, New York 2002, p.90.
3 *Ibid.*, p.86.
4 *CWS*, p.475. Gomez translates the vow in the following way: 'May I not gain possession of perfect awakening if, once I have attained perfect buddhahood, the humans and gods in my lands are not assured of awakening, and without fail attain liberation.' *The Land of Bliss: The Paradise of the Buddha of Measureless Light*, trans. Luis Gomez, University of Hawai'i Press, Honolulu, HI, 1996, p.167.
5 *CWS*, p.477. According to one translation, the original text reads: 'The [Pure Land] sutra says that if someone merely hears of Sukhāvatī, it will be engraved on their minds and they will resolve to be born there and, having been born there, will enter the company of those who are properly settled. This name of that land is the work of Buddha. How is this conceivable?' *A Commentary on The Upadeśa on the Sutras of Limitless Life with Gāthās on the Resolution to Be Born Composed by the Bodhisattva Vasubandhu*, trans. Roger Corless, Takahiko Kameyama, and Richard K. Payne, *Pacific World* 17 (2015), pp.69–234 (p.180).
6 This passage is cited below. See Gomez, *The Land of Bliss*, p.187.
7 The author of *Lung-shu's Writings on the Pure Land* (*Longshu zengguang jingtu wen* 龍舒增廣淨土文, *Ryūjo Zōkō Jōdomon*, T.1970).
8 Gaston Bachelard, *Intuition of the Instant*, Northwestern University Press, Evanston, IL, 2013, p.28.
9 *CWS*, pp.80, 474. 'Nonretrogression' is another way of talking about being 'truly settled'. Gomez has: 'Any living beings who hear his name and vow to be reborn in his realm, with a trusting mind, rejoicing even if only for a single moment of thought, single-mindedly dedicating their thoughts with the resolution to be reborn there, immediately gain rebirth there and dwell in the condition of not falling back.' Gomez, *The Land of Bliss*, p.187.
10 Bachelard, *Intuition of the Instant*, p.15.

11 Keiji Nishitani, 'The problem of time in Shinran', *Eastern Buddhist* 11:1 (1978), pp.13–26 (p.22).
12 Chrétien, *The Unforgettable and the Unhoped For*, p.106.
13 *Ibid.*, p.106.
14 *Ibid.*, p.106.
15 Nishitani, 'The problem of time in Shinran', p.24.

Chapter 15

1 See, for instance, Namkhai Norbu, *The Crystal and the Way of Light: Sutra, Tantra, and Dzogchen*, Snow Lion Publications, Ithaca, NY, 2000.
2 See also *CWS*, pp.494–7, for further citations that clarify the notion of jinen.
3 For an extended discussion of this theme, see Sangharakshita, *Milarepa and the Art of Discipleship 1* (*The Complete Works of Sangharakshita*, vol.18), Windhorse Publications, Cambridge 2018, pp.267–87.
4 *Ibid.*, p.282.
5 *Ibid.*, p.282.
6 *CWS*, p.461. See also *A Commentary on The Upadeśa on the Sutras of Limitless Life with Gāthās on the Resolution to Be Born Composed by the Bodhisattva Vasubandhu*, trans. Roger Corless, Takahiko Kameyama, and Richard K. Payne, *Pacific World* 17 (2015), p.208: 'All buddhas and bodhisattvas have a double *dharmakāya*: first, the *dharmakāya* of dharma-nature (*faxingfashen* 法性法身); second, the *dharmakāya* of skillful means (*fangbianfashen* 方便法身). The *dharmakāya* of dharma-nature produces the *dharmakāya* of skillful means, and the *dharmakāya* of dharma-nature emerges from the *dharmakāya* of skillful means. These two *dharmakāya*s are different, but indivisible; they are one, but not the same.'
7 Dōgen, *Shōbōgenzō: The True Dharma-Eye Treasury*, trans. Gudu Wafu, 4 vols., BDK America, Moraga, CA, 2007–2008, vol.3, p.172.
8 Norman Waddell and Maso Abe, *The Heart of Dōgen's Shōbōgenzō*, SUNY Press, New York 2002, pp.76–7.
9 Dōgen, *Shōbōgenzō*, vol.2, p.8.
10 Cited in Miranda Shaw, 'Nature in Dōgen's philosophy and poetry', *The Journal of the International Association of Buddhist Studies* 8:2 (1985), pp.111–32 (p.121).
11 *The Awakening of Faith*, trans. Yoshito S. Hakeda, Numata Center for Buddhist Translation and Research, Berkeley, CA, 2005, pp.20–21.
12 From Rilke, *New Poems 1908*, trans. Edward Snow, North Point, Albany, CA, 1987.

Chapter 16

1 Paul Tillich, *Dynamics of Faith*, Harper & Bros, New York 1957, p.41.
2 'The New Testament and mythology', in Rudolf Bultmann *et al.*, *Kerygma and Myth*, Harper TorchBooks, New York 1961, p.11.
3 Gwendolyn MacEwen, 'Dark pines under water', in *Volume 1 (The Early Years)*, Exile Editions, Toronto 2001, p.156.
4 Subhuti and Sangharakshita, *Seven Papers*, Triratna InHouse Publications, n.p. 2013, p.191.
5 Dōgen, *Shōbōgenzō: The True Dharma-Eye Treasury*, trans. Gudu Wafu, 4 vols., BDK America, Moraga, CA, 2007–2008, vol.1, p.144.
6 This translation of the poem is cited in Janae Sholtz, *The Invention of a People: Heidegger and Deleuze on Art and the Political*, Edinburgh University Press, Edinburgh 2015.
7 Martin Heidegger, *Poetry, Language, Thought*, Harper Perennial, New York 2001, p.199.
8 'Da erglänzt in reiner Helle.'
9 Maurice Merleau-Ponty, *Phenomenology of Perception*, trans. Donald A. Landes, Routledge, Abingdon 2012, p.223.
10 Śāntideva, *The Bodhicaryāvatāra*, trans. Kate Crosby and Andrew Skilton, Oxford University Press, Oxford 1995, chapter 3, verses 25–6, p.22.

Appendix

1 More than 800 now that the *Saihōshinanshō* has been published. The *Saihōshinanshō* (*Guide to the Western World*) is one of Shinran's final works and consists largely of Hōnen's lectures and letters, albeit selected and briefly commented on by Shinran. Because of its focus on Hōnen, Jōdō Shinshū institutions have historically neglected it. Because it was written by Shinran, Jōdō Shū has also traditionally sidelined it. *Saihōshinanshō* is not included in *CWS* but offers a nuanced understanding of Shinran's perspective in relation to Hōnen. See *The Path to the Pure Land: A Translation of and Commentary on Shinran's Saihō-Shinan-shō*, trans. and annotated by Toshikazu Arai, American Buddhist Study Center, n.p. 2021.
2 In vol.2 of *CWS*, Dennis Hirota offers a series of very useful overviews of key works by Shinran.
3 Martin Heidegger, *On the Way to Language*, trans. Peter D. Hertz, Harper & Row, New York 1971, p.160.
4 For a complete translation see *CWS*, pp.3ff. Also available at http://shinranworks.com/the-major-expositions/chapter-on-teaching/, accessed on 8 December 2021.
5 For a fascinating analysis of the structure of chapter 3 (on shinjin), see Laeticia Söderman, 'Medieval Buddhist textuality: *Kyōgyōshinshō* as

literature', in *Rethinking 'Japanese Studies' from Practices in the Nordic Region*, International Research Center for Japanese Studies, Kyoto 2014, pp.105–18.

6 Jacqueline I. Stone, *Original Enlightenment and the Transformation of Medieval Japanese Buddhism*, University of Hawai'i Press, Honolulu, HI, 1999, p.167.

7 For some detailed examples of Shinran's approach, see Eisho Nasu, '"Rely on the meaning, not on the words": Shinran's methodology and strategy for reading scriptures and writing the *Kyōgyōshinshō*', in *Critical Readings on Pure Land Buddhism in Japan*, ed. Galen Amstutz, vol.1, Brill, Leiden 2020, pp.322–46.

8 *CWS*, p.241. The often ambiguous nature of kanji favours Shinran's creative and sometimes unconventional interpretations. Things like who dedicates merits to whom are easy to determine in a language like Sanskrit, but in Chinese, although there might be an implication (from context, previous tradition, etc.) that it is the practitioner who turns over their merits, the indeterminate language allows for the possibility that it is the Buddha who turns over merit to us. Guided by his sensibility, Shinran exploits the ambiguities of his source texts.

9 Laeticia Söderman, 'Writing as participation: textual streams and argumentative patterns in Shinran's *Kyōgyōshinshō*', in *Frontiers of Japanese Philosophy: Japanese Philosophy Abroad*, ed. James W. Heisig and Rein Raud, Nanzan Institute for Religion & Culture, Nagoya 2010, pp.190–206.

10 *Ibid.*, p.203.

11 In Japanese, *Jōdo monrui jushō*.

12 *The Collected Works of Shinran*, trans. Hongwanji International Center Translation Committee, 2 vols., Jodo Shinshu Hongwanji-ha, Kyoto 1997, vol.2, p.75. For a translation, see *CWS*, pp.293ff., available at http://shinranworks.com/the-major-expositions/passages-on-the-pure-land-way/, accessed on 8 December 2021.

13 'Hymn' translates 偈. Other translations might be 'verse', 'poem', or 'song'.

14 *CWS*, pp.521ff., available at http://shinranworks.com/letters/lamp-for-the-latter-ages/, accessed on 8 December 2021.

15 *CWS*, pp.661–80, available at http://shinranworks.com/related-works-by-other-authors/a-record-in-lament-of-divergences/, accessed on 8 December 2021.

16 The authorship of the text is uncertain. Yuien-bo may be fulfilling the same persona that Ananda and Shariputra occupy in other Buddhist scriptures. There is no certainty that this text was written so close to Shinran's own time.

17 *Shizhupiposha lun* (T.1520 十住毘婆沙論, Jp. *Jūjū bibasha ron*). The title of this text has been sanskritized as *Daśabhūmika-vibhāṣā-śāstra*. There are no extant Sanskrit originals for any of the 'Nāgārjuna texts' that

Shinran quotes. It is quite possible that these texts were written in China and attributed to Nāgārjuna, the revered teacher from the faraway land of India. Many other texts were similarly credited to him.

18 See especially *True Teaching*, chapter 2 (*CWS*, pp.18–24).

19 *Jingtu lun* (T.1524 淨土論). In Japanese this text is known as the *Jōdoron*.

20 See Richard Payne, 'The five contemplative gates of Vasubandhu's *Rebirth Treatise* as a ritualized visualization practice', *Pacific World* 17 (2015), pp.43–67.

21 *Jingtu lun zhu* (T.1819).

22 *Anleji* 安楽集; Jap. *Anrakushū* (T.1958).

23 *Guan wuliangshoufo jing zhu* (T.1753).

24 *CWS*, p.377. On the differences between Shandao's and Shinran's understanding of the Pure Land path, see Julian Pas, *Visions of Sukhāvatī: Shan-tao's Commentary on the Kuan Wu-Liang-Shou-Fo-Ling*, SUNY Press, Albany, NY, 1995, pp.318–23.

25 *Ōjōyōshū* (T.2682).

26 Allan A. Andrews, 'Genshin's "Essentials of Pure Land rebirth" and the transmission of Pure Land Buddhism to Japan, Part II: the third phase of transmission: a quantitative survey of the resources utilized by Genshin', *Pacific World* 6 (1990), pp.1–15 (p.12).

Index

MacEwen, Gwendolyn 205
Mahāsthāmaprāpta 74, 95–6,
117
Mahāyāna 40, 85, 91, 131, 136
cosmology 54
scriptures 5, 66, 76
teaching 80, 198
Maitreya 54, 69, 186–7
Maitreyabandhu 204
mappō 29, 54, 88, 99–100,
119–20
Marion, Jean-Luc 41–2, 59
masters 31–4, 66, 77, 81–2, 93,
157, 164, 169
Chinese 92, 98, 115
Indian 82, 84
Japanese 91
venerable 81–2
Mattoshō 215
meditation 73–4, 112, 118–19,
121, 123, 127, 166, 172
memories 23, 25, 183, 205
merit
infinite 158, 167
spiritual 51, 144
stock of 73, 118
transfer 53, 74, 86–7, 89, 116
transference of 87, 100, 179,
214
merits, incalculable 14, 59, 70,
102–3, 109, 116, 129
metaphors 5, 42, 56, 58, 155,
195, 199, 201
mind
aspiring 128, 130, 148
awakened 14, 111, 159, 163
Buddha 121, 163
calculating 135, 140, 143,
149, 154, 174
compassionate 158, 163–4,
166
deep 89, 128–9
deluded 35, 123
egocentric 158, 163
enlightened 39, 111, 145,
157–8, 168
entrusting 128–9
essence of 199
habitual 36, 174
ordinary 75, 134, 147, 168
reactive 20, 176
to save sentient beings
148–51
secular 139–40
sincere 42, 87, 89, 116,
128–30, 188, 194

single 129–30
threefold 89–90, 129–30
true 42, 90, 125, 130
mindfulness 103, 111, 137
constant 137, 189
miscellaneous practices
99–102
models 39–40, 44, 56–7, 72, 80,
144–6, 155, 163
self-discovery 43
mofa 88
monastic life 30, 97, 103
monks 27–8, 30, 32, 71, 77–8,
81, 95, 98
motivation 3, 123, 129, 147,
161, 163
Mount Hiei 27–9
mountains 28, 30, 169, 198,
203, 206
mundane 69, 128, 145–6, 157,
167, 176, 206
mundane goodness 141, 176
mythic time 67
myths 5, 19–21, 39–40, 57–8,
60, 64, 74–5, 201–3
of Amida 15, 17, 20, 60, 158,
161, 201, 203

Nāgārjuna 80, 82–3, 214,
217–18
Namu Amida Butsu 14, 57, 96,
109, 126, 152, 194
naturalness 6, 133, 191–4
nature
basic 29, 192, 199
Buddha 58
deepest 43, 58
true 166, 193, 197, 199
nembutsu 91–4, 100–105,
109–10, 114–18, 120–3,
126–7, 140, 150–3
deathbed 94, 103, 117, 182
practice 92, 94, 98, 114, 118,
151–2
deathbed 52, 103
recitation 33, 94, 97 8,
100–102, 114, 127, 151
vocal 31, 92, 94, 103–4,
113–14
net of doubt 138–41
newness 181–9
nian 113–14
nianfo 89, 113
nirmāṇakāya 57
nirvana 35, 56, 76, 182, 184–5,
187, 201, 208

great 125, 184, 193, 201
supreme 193, 195–6, 200
non-attachment 24
non-persons 142
nonretrogression 83, 87, 188,
193
no-practice 6, 110
norms
ethical 143–4
social 192
*Notes on Once-Calling and
Many-Calling* 33, 116
*Notes on the Essentials of Faith
Alone* 33, 214

ocean, treasure 84, 114, 199
ōcho 84
Ōjōyōshū 92, 219–20
oneness 55–6, 119, 196, 199
ordinary mind 75, 134, 147, 168
ordinary persons 24, 92, 94,
98, 130
ordination 13, 203–5
orientation 19–20, 69–70, 77,
81, 89, 129, 207, 209
compassionate 126, 143
devotional 103, 118
Pure Land 88, 91
Orwell, George 24
other power 6, 85–7, 128, 172,
175
perspective 123, 144, 172

Pali Canon 40, 56, 142
panchang pranam 205
panjiao 79–80, 99
paradoxes 46, 121, 163, 168,
172, 183
Parinirvāṇa Sūtra 88
Passages on the Pure Land Way
214
*Passages on the Types of Birth in
the Pure Land Sutras* 65
passions 28, 56, 93, 143, 154
blind 36, 143, 146–7, 149,
155–6, 167, 201, 208
past
ancestral 67
beginningless 35, 152
infinite 53, 55
practical 25–6
primordial 54, 183, 194
pastoral letters 27, 151, 153, 186
paths
bodhisattva 52, 68, 99,
102–3, 131–2
of dependence 128, 172, 175

threefold mind 89–90, 129–30
Tibetan Buddhism 17, 41, 172
Tillich, Paul 41, 58, 202
time, ultimate limit 187–90
Tiratanavandana 206
Trakl, Georg 207
transcendence 17, 19, 24–5, 38, 41, 53–4, 128–9, 177
  crosswise 84
transcendent reality 5, 19
transfer, merit 53, 74, 86–7, 89, 116
transference of merit 87, 100, 179, 214
transformation 15–16, 41–2, 46, 135, 137, 144, 152, 155
transformative awareness 67, 201–2
transformative insights 15, 50
transformative process 15, 136
translations 53, 63–4, 67, 71, 125, 184, 196
transmigration 36, 89
transmission 78, 80–1, 217
treasure ocean of virtues 84, 114–16, 199
Treatise on the Pure Land 77, 81–2, 84–5, 92, 218
tree of grace 207–8
trees 6–7, 50, 56–7, 68–9, 78, 197
  jewel 73–4, 95
  twin sala 136
true and real shinjin 97, 117, 127, 130, 142, 181, 193, 209
true enlightenment 84, 206
True Essence of the Pure Land Way 91–107

true intent 63–77, 81, 88
true mind 42, 90, 125, 130
true nature 166, 193, 197, 199
true reality 56, 84, 114, 196
true shinjin 117, 130, 186, 208
true teaching 12, 33, 63, 82–4, 86–7, 89, 98–9, 114
true working, no working as 175–7
truly settled 19, 126, 137, 184–5
trust 14, 19, 89, 122, 129, 139, 144, 146
twentieth vow 65, 71, 136–7

uji 207
understanding 4, 21, 77, 79, 81, 161, 176–7, 207
unforgettable 183
unhindered light 49, 55, 155, 163, 181, 201
  Buddha of 49, 163, 181
universal compassion 123, 151
universal vow 90, 157
universe 41, 43, 52, 54, 67–8, 72, 166, 175–6
  religious 6–7, 78, 125
unskilful impulse 36, 144, 167

Vaidehī 72
Vasubandhu 80, 82, 84–5, 92, 214, 217–18
venerable masters 81–2
Vimalakīrti Nirdeśa 76
virtues 63, 67–8, 101, 114–16, 146–7, 149–50, 155, 191
  treasure ocean of 84, 114–16, 199
vision 31, 35, 68–9, 72, 74, 110–12, 166, 172

religious 2, 7, 20, 37, 163, 198, 209
vision-world 66–7
visualization 3, 30, 41, 67, 73, 84, 93, 98
vocal nembutsu 31, 92, 94, 103–4, 113–14
voices 19, 45–6, 65, 71–2, 82, 94, 171, 178
vows 51–2, 65, 93, 121–2, 136–7, 184, 188, 194–6
  Amida 83–4, 86, 88–9, 120–2, 144, 146, 164, 166
  bodhisattva 51, 67–8, 72, 93, 99
  compassionate 29, 154
  cosmic 51, 186
  great 84, 120, 143, 193
  seventeenth 71, 113–14
  three 65, 134–8
  twentieth 65, 71, 136–7
  universal 90, 157

wager, interpretive 21
wasan 33, 81, 83, 141, 219
water 7, 43, 45, 73–4, 94, 145, 155, 169
western bank 45–6
white path parable 45–6
wisdom 37, 40, 49–51, 64, 66, 68, 107, 110–11
Wright, Daitsū Tom 3–4

yokushō 130
Yoritomo 28
Yuien-bo 215

zazen 118, 166
Zen 17–18, 43, 118, 156, 172
ziran 192–3

WINDHORSE PUBLICATIONS

Windhorse Publications is a Buddhist charitable company based in the United Kingdom. We place great emphasis on producing books of high quality that are accessible and relevant to those interested in Buddhism at whatever level. We are the main publisher of the works of Sangharakshita, the founder of the Triratna Buddhist Order and Community. Our books draw on the whole range of the Buddhist tradition, including translations of traditional texts, commentaries, books that make links with contemporary culture and ways of life, biographies of Buddhists, and works on meditation.

As a not-for-profit enterprise, we ensure that all surplus income is invested in new books and improved production methods, to better communicate Buddhism in the twenty-first century. We welcome donations to help us continue our work – to find out more, go to windhorsepublications.com.

The Windhorse is a mythical animal that flies over the earth carrying on its back three precious jewels, bringing these invaluable gifts to all humanity: the Buddha (the 'awakened one'), his teaching, and the community of all his followers.

Windhorse Publications	Consortium Book	Windhorse Books
38 Newmarket Road	Sales & Distribution	PO Box 574
Cambridge	210 American Drive	Newtown NSW 2042
CB5 8DT	Jackson TN 38301	Australia
	USA	

info@windhorsepublications.com

THE TRIRATNA BUDDHIST COMMUNITY

Windhorse Publications is a part of the Triratna Buddhist Community, an international movement with centres in Europe, India, North and South America, and Australasia. At these centres, members of the Triratna Buddhist Order offer classes in meditation and Buddhism. Activities of the Triratna Community also include retreat centres, residential spiritual communities, ethical Right Livelihood businesses, and the Karuna Trust, a United Kingdom fundraising charity that supports social welfare projects in the slums and villages of India.

Through these and other activities, Triratna is developing a unique approach to Buddhism, not simply as a philosophy and a set of techniques, but as a creatively directed way of life for all people living in the conditions of the modern world.

If you would like more information about Triratna please visit thebuddhistcentre.com or write to:

London Buddhist Centre	Aryaloka	Sydney Buddhist Centre
51 Roman Road	14 Heartwood Circle	24 Enmore Road
London E2 0HU	Newmarket NH 03857	Sydney NSW 2042
United Kingdom	USA	Australia